Pelican Books

The Family and Marriage in Britain

Born in Yorkshire, Ronald Fletcher was educated at
Ecclesfield Grammar School, Bristol University (in
philosophy and economics), and the L.S.E. (in
sociology). For many years he was a university teacher:
in the University of London (at Bedford College
and Birkbeck College), and later at the new University
of York, where he was Professor and Head of the
Department of Sociology. Disillusioned with certain
aspects of university life and administration, he then
resigned to devote himself to study and writing. He
now lives on the Suffolk coast with his wife and younger
son, and is completely free-lance. He broadcasts
occasionally on sound radio and television; edits the
new Nelson sociology series; and is the author of many
books and articles, the most recent being *The Making of
Sociology* (three volumes) – a textbook which takes issue
with current controversies and tries to give a full and
clear account of the new science of society, and *The
Parkers at Saltram* (B.B.C.) – the book of a television
series.

The Family and Marriage in Britain

An Analysis and Moral Assessment

Ronald Fletcher

Third Edition

Penguin Books

Penguin Books Ltd, Harmondsworth,
Middlesex, England
Penguin Books Inc., 7110 Ambassador Road,
Baltimore, Maryland 21207, U.S.A.
Penguin Books Australia Ltd, Ringwood,
Victoria, Australia

First published as a Penguin Special, with the title
Britain in the Sixties: Family and Marriage, 1962
Second edition published in Pelican Books 1966
Reprinted 1967, 1968, 1969, 1970, 1971
Third edition 1973
Copyright © Ronald Fletcher, 1962, 1966, 1973

Made and printed in Great Britain
by Cox & Wyman Ltd,
London, Reading and Fakenham
Set in Monotype Baskerville

Contents

This is for all ill-treated parents
– those born, those unbegot –
for them to read when they're in trouble
and I am not.

(A. E. Housman – adapted)

List of Tables and Graphs

8 LIST OF TABLES AND GRAPHS

Englishmen are always despondent about their own times, and it would be easy to quote contemporaries in every period so that their testimony would show that we had gone downhill ever since the time of the Norman Conquest.

L. C. A. Knowles

Such misunderstandings feed the hypochondria of moralists who diagnose a diseased present because they worship a past they do not understand.

O. R. McGregor

Preface to the Third Edition

THIS book was written almost exactly ten years ago. It was revised during 1965, but, even then, the firm statistics available referred only to the early 1960s. Clearly, much has happened since then, and it is necessary, now, to take into account many changes in the law, certain statistical tendencies, and the findings of new research. Retaining the historical perspective originally laid down, this consideration of the most recent facts can round off our judgement of a decade, and provide an up-to-date picture.

At the same time, the seventies open with a rapid fire of new criticisms of the family – quite different from, and much more radical than any that have gone before – and these create difficulties. Despite all the critics say, however (and, for the present, whatever the truth or falsity of their points), marriage and the family in our society continue to enjoy a tremendous popularity; benefiting from the culmination of reforms set firmly afoot during the nineteen-thirties and even earlier: improvements in the law, in the social services, and in material and social conditions.

This preface is to mention the more important of these factors; to make clear the kinds of revision to which they have led; and to explain why I have decided to write an altogether new (companion) book in an attempt to do full justice to the new criticisms. To try to do this within the present book would be to change it unduly; to obscure unnecessarily the clear argument it tries to present; and there are good reasons why this seems not the best thing to do.

Historical perspective: true and firm

First of all, the original book presented (and *demonstrated* with detail sufficient for its argument) a historical perspective which I still believe to be true and of basic importance as a context within which to form our contemporary judgements. Marriage and the family have not declined in our time, but have become improved in most respects. If we have problems – and we have, of course, many – they are properly to be understood in terms of complex social changes and deliberately attempted improvements (of social, legal, political, economic, kinds) rather than in terms of some kind of moral deterioration of the family as such. This I believe to be firm and indisputable, and everything I have subsequently studied confirms and reinforces it. I do not know of any other period of British history in which the qualities and expectations of marriage and parenthood – in personal, social, or legal terms – were of as high a standard (and for the *whole* of the population) as they now are. And the law, with increasingly detailed scrutiny and deliberate reform, is moving ever more closely towards a fabric of social provision and regulation which is (a) within itself, consistent throughout, (b) deliberately framed to approximate as closely as possible to our ethical and political principles, and (c) more closely and realistically related to social actuality. Some critics have argued that my perspective has had reference only to a rather stark Victorianism, and to changes since then, which (it is said) covers too short a term and makes a picture of 'improvements' in the family too easily proved. But if this is their criticism, what other period of British experience would they like to choose? Consider medieval marriage – in that age of Church and chivalry – and what is to be found there? G. M. Trevelyan is quite plain, and has not a shred of doubt:

... to some vaguely accustomed to think of the Middle Ages as a period of chivalry and love, with knights ever on their knees to ladies, it may come as a shock to realize that, in the knightly and gentle class, the choice of partners for marriage had normally nothing whatever to do with love; often the bride and bridegroom were small children when they were pledged for life, and, even if adults, they were sold by their parents to the highest bidder.

The Pastons and other county families regarded the marriages of their children as counters in the game of family aggrandisement, useful to buy money and estates, or to secure the support of powerful patrons. If the victim destined for the altar resisted, rebellion was crushed – at least in the case of a female ward – with physical brutality almost incredible. Elizabeth Paston, when she hesitated to marry a battered and ugly widower of fifty, was for nearly three months on end 'beaten once in the week or twice, sometimes twice in one day, and her head broken in two or three places'. Such were the methods of her mother Agnes, a highly religious, respectable, and successful controller of the large Paston household. Many parents seem to have cared very little who married their children, provided they themselves got the money . . .

These old-established medieval customs, still vigorous in the fifteenth century, may at first seem inconsistent with the tone of medieval literature . . . But this poetry of love, from its most heavenly flight in Dante's chaste worship of another man's wife, to the more usual idealization of courtly adultery had seldom anything to do with marriage . . .*

And what of the eighteenth century, the period of the Enlightenment? We know of the harsh and depressed conditions of the peasantry, but what of the noble families who owned and governed the land? Here is the attitude towards marriage of the Duke of Kingston – who spent something like £40,000 extending his Grand Tour over ten years – a young aristocrat whose profligacy was typical of the time. He told his guardians – who had urged him to marry and settle down, anxious over his enormous gambling debts:

. . . in plain terms . . . that if he ever marries it shall be to have a woman to breed out of and not for a companion, and that neither the consideration of continuing his family or clearing his estate shall ever determine him to do it before 30, if he ever does it at all.†

In times past, then, love and marriage cannot be said to have been closely linked. But here is Trevelyan again commenting on the question as to whether the ideal of love

* G. M. Trevelyan, *Illustrated English Social History*, Vol. 1, p. 132 (Longmans, 1949–52; Penguin Books, 1964).

† G. E. Mingay, *English Landed Society in the Eighteenth Century*, p. 140 (Routledge, 1963).

(in the medieval conception) could possibly become a part
of marriage:

> ... Could this precious concept of the medieval poets be allied, by a
> further revolution, to the state of marriage? Could the lovers
> themselves become husband and wife? Could the bond of young
> love be prolonged till age and death?
>
> This change has actually taken place in England in the gradual
> evolution of the idea and practice of marriage ... the arranged
> marriage has given place to the love-match; the parents have
> yielded to the children the choice of their own destiny.*

It seems difficult, then, to find among the records of any
earlier period, as high an ethical conception – or legal and
social reality – of marriage and family relationships as those
we now enjoy. This seems to me to deserve the very greatest
emphasis as an absolutely bedrock point. Whatever problems we face in the family today – they rest upon moral,
social, legal, material foundations that are better than at any
other time.

The basic form of the book left unchanged

Because of this quite fundamental fact; because the subsequent analysis of relationships in the contemporary family
(couched within this context) still seems firm; and also
because the book has come to be widely used as a text in
various courses; it seemed right not to change its basic
nature and form. But this decision was reinforced by the fact
that – though the 1960s witnessed a rising incidence of
divorce, and many changes in the law – none of these factors
were such as to lead to any basic change in the book's
argument. It is not enough, however, just to assert this. These
are debatable issues, and it is necessary to look briefly at
some of the more important of them now – though they are
dealt with in detail later.

The increase in divorce

The most conspicuous (though not necessarily the most
significant) development which became apparent as the

* Trevelyan, op. cit., p. 136.

records of the 1960s became clearly known, was the continuous increase in the number of divorces. The facts and figures of this, the difficulties of interpreting all aspects and significances of it, are dealt with on pp. 144–68, and in the accompanying notes. All the tables, diagrams and graphs have been brought up to date from the Registrar General's Annual Statistical Reviews (up to 1967) and, occasionally and where possible, from the Annual Abstract of Statistics (up to 1970), so that the picture now given is as accurate, and as close to the end of the decade, as possible. The account of a decade is thus more or less completed.

This fact of the increase in the number of divorces is one of the most *marked* facts that has to be taken into account for several reasons. Naturally enough, it is the facts relating to the evident *breakdowns* of marriages which are taken to indicate the quality of marriage and family life in society generally. As soon as one stops to reflect on this, it is clear that this may well be a basically mistaken assumption; but it is very commonly held, and is understandable. Closely related to this, the continual increase during the 1960s was, on the face of it, a reversal of the tendencies which had been in evidence between the end of the Second World War and the end of the 1950s. *Then* – after the post-war peak – the annual number of divorces was consistently *decreasing*. There was speculation then about whether the lower pre-war rate of the 1930s might be reached; and this was the picture when this book was written. The subsequent *increase* therefore seems a turnabout, and must be scrutinized very closely.

I say that it was a reversal *on the face of it*, however, because, in fact, the interpretation of the statistics is far from easy. One important consideration is that the incidence of divorce seems always sensitive to new legislation (such as new terms of legal aid, the enactment of new grounds for divorce, etc.) and such new legislation did, in fact, occur in 1960 (the Legal Aid Act), and the *immediate* increase seemed, at least, explicable in these terms. A second fact is that of the very large accompanying increase in the number of marriages. The marriage rate has increased as consistently as has that of divorce; and the gross number of marriages each year has increased very substantially indeed. Far larger numbers are therefore 'at risk'. A third fact is that this larger number of marriages has been predominantly among men and women in the younger age-groups, in relation to which there is always a larger rate of divorce; and there is no doubt that a predominant proportion of the increased number of divorces comes from these age-groups. This tendency to early marriage, however, is related to a great many facts – educational, economic, the political change made in the age of maturity, and perhaps even to an earlier physiological maturation. And a fourth fact is that the increase in divorce following any particular piece of legislation can often be no more than evidence of an overdue *legal recognition* of a *social actuality* that has long existed. For example, the increase in divorce which has followed, and must follow, the new Divorce Reform Act (1969), will in large part be no more than a *legal* termination of marriages long ago broken *in fact* (which, indeed, will not effectively have existed for a long time), and will be followed by a regularization (by marriage) of the many stable alternative families which have, in fact, long existed. So that the increase resting on these grounds will not indicate a *new tendency* at all (excepting that for which the Act was created); it will merely be a recognition of an *old fact*.

There is, however, a final and quite basic point which perhaps few of us have considered and accepted fully. When faced by high divorce rates, our impulse, still, is immediately to look for some kind of legal or statistical 'excuse' for them – as though, in itself, a higher divorce rate is necessarily a bad thing. Now, no one can advocate divorce. A divorce, after all, is an acknowledgement of failure, sometimes a tragic one. Even so, we must consider the possibility that if the conceptions, status and expectations of marriage and family life in our society are high (and if our law is made increasingly accessible, to provide for the least harmful termination of those relationships which are found to be 'irretrievably' unworkable and unhappy) then it may be that *we must expect* a greater degree of resort to divorce. May it not be that high standards and expectations of marriage and family life actually *entail* a high rate of resort to divorce? This is something which, at present, we are reluctant to concede. And we may be right to be reluctant; but it is at least possible that a higher rate of divorce might well be indicative of a higher conception, a healthier condition, of marriage in society, rather than of a worsening of it. These are difficult problems; the face of social facts may be stranger than we think.

These facts and considerations are discussed in detail later, however (pp. 149–75). The most central concern is perhaps that of the very high divorce rate of young people during the early years of their marriage. Despite this, though, there seem to be no grounds for changing the original and basic argument of the book – that these figures do not indicate a growing instability, or qualitative worsening of the nature of marriage and the family in Britain. The later arguments must be considered on their merits, but it is worthwhile to note here that this is by no means purely a personal judgement. It is also the view of some leading members of the legal profession who see the facts and procedures of divorce more clearly and in more detail than the rest of us. As I write, for example (20 January 1972), the legal correspondent of *The Times* reports a 54 per cent increase in the number of divorce petitions lodged in Britain during 1971, as compared with 1970. This, however, resting on the new provisions of the Divorce Reform Act which became operative on 1 January 1971, is, he says, 'not considered alarming', and he thinks that it is one of the new grounds for divorce provided by the act (the five-year separation provision) which is responsible for the sharp increase. (That is to say, it is the legal recognition of marriages broken in fact a long time ago, mentioned earlier.) Commenting on the same figures, Sir George Baker, President of the Family Division (see p. 20), claims that, with the new Act, 'some of the bitterness and public degradation have been taken out of divorce'. It is interesting, too, to see that press reports of divorce no longer carry the salacious and 'adversary' character that many of them once did. One report of the divorce of a baronet by his wife, appearing simultaneously with the publication of these figures, simply records the granting of the decree nisi because of the breakdown of the marriage, and says that the decree was granted to the wife 'on the grounds of the husband's behaviour'. There is no clambering after the vicarious excitement of counter-claims of adultery – with hotel bedroom evidence and the like – which has been for so long a staple of the British 'news'.

Perhaps the most heartening estimation of the new situation comes from a source that could hardly be more reputable and responsible. Addressing the twenty-fifth anniversary of the Marriage Guidance Council (of which he is the National President) Lord Denning, Master of the Rolls, said that the new divorce law was 'entirely beneficial'. Its most impressive result, he claimed, was that contested divorce cases had almost disappeared. He did not feel that its changes would be so disastrous to the institution of marriage as some had foretold, and emphasized that marriage was still recognized by the great majority as a lifelong union not lightly to be dissolved. Those, therefore, who have been most involved in the recent legal debates, and who most understand the detailed legal grounds for all the recent changes, do seem firmly agreed that the removal of the unjust and distasteful obstacles to the termination of marriage is, indirectly, improving the conditions and quality of it.

The 1960s: a historical decade in the law

This raises a second very important point: that the 1960s did, in fact, turn out to be a decade distinguished by a very wide and effective range of legislation on many of the most fundamental matters of behaviour relating to marriage and the family. With the Church of England's publication, *The Family in Contemporary Society* in the background (1958), the decade began with the Legal Aid Act of 1960. From then on, it was filled with intense and important public debate on divorce law reform, on the just provision of financial and property arrangements for all parties following divorce, on legal questions relating to homosexuality, on the rights and wrongs of legalizing abortion, and on many aspects of the status of children and young people, including the illegitimate. Not every Act has been followed by approval (the Abortion Act, for example, has raised grave doubts as to possible abuse, and has given rise to a great deal of further ethical reconsideration), but the success of serious and searching public debate, and of effective legislation on issues as fundamental as these is surely a matter for some public and political congratulation. Indeed, the 1960s might well come to be seen as a decade of considerable historical distinction in these important changes in the law, especially when it is borne in mind that these difficult and deliberate pieces of legislation and subsequent administration were achieved during a period when so many other large-scale problems – in the more immediately pressing fields of economic, political, educational affairs, etc. – were afoot. The list of the more important Acts, all of which carried earlier legislation much further, and on the basis of much prolonged debate, is itself impressive:

The Family Provisions Act (1966)
The Matrimonial Homes Act (1967)
The National Health Service (Family Planning) Act (1967)
The Abortion Act (1967)
The Sexual Offences Act (1967)
The Maintenance Orders Act (1968)
The Family Law Reform Act (1969)
The Divorce Reform Act (1969)
The Children and Young Persons Act (1969)

Each of these did much to improve the status of women both within and beyond marriage; to improve the status of children including reducing the age (to 18) at which they attained responsible adulthood and citizenship; to eradicate many of the most distasteful encumbrances of the previous legal procedures for divorce; to give effect to a more knowledgeable and humane judgement concerning sexual differences; and many other quite specific matters.

This was accompanied, however, by other more general developments of considerable significance. Judgements over divorce, custody of children, etc., were transferred from the former 'Probate, Divorce and Admiralty Division' to a new 'Family Division'; and 1965 saw the establishment of the Law Commission to undertake a thorough-going revision of family law. These legal developments, taking place as the 1960s advanced, substantiate very forcibly the fact that both in changing legal procedures and in the provision for systematic deliberations to consider the need for law reform, there is a very evident concern for the qualities of marriage and the family in society, and a concentration on providing the best legal, administrative and social framework for them. This picture of the law in relation to the family has been excellently presented and summarized by Dr Olive Stone in 'The Family and the Law in 1970'.*

Her own conclusion is quite definite, though by no means final:

... An indication that the law does not contemplate any drastic change in the role of the family in the near future may be found in the many compromises and reformulations that took place before the publication of the Children and Young Persons Act, 1969 ... No substitute for the family in the upbringing of children seems in sight.

New research

A third point that must be noted is that a growing amount of research was devoted to the study of the family during the 1960s, though the most significant of this is only now being reported. There were such studies as *The Family and Social Change* by Rosser and Harris (1965), which repeated, rather more extensively, in Swansea, the kind of study undertaken by Young and Willmott in Bethnal Green, and produced similar findings. The 'extended family', resting chiefly on the relationship between a wife and her mother, was found to be still important – as a basic unit of social identification

* See *The Family and its Future* (a C.I.B.A. Symposium) ed. Kathleen Elliott, p. 87 (Churchill, 1970).

and social support – despite industrial and urban change; and the 'standardization' of this family-type was found among all social classes. But more recent reports are of greater interest, both in their actual findings and in their indication of a breaking of new ground (and new depths) in research.

A major study, so large and detailed that its significance is difficult as yet to judge, is *Separated Spouses*, an investigation by the Bedford College Legal Research Unit (O. R. McGregor, Louis Blom-Cooper, and Colin Gibson), which at last throws much light on the 'submerged' proportion of broken families reflected in separation and maintenance orders rather than in the more conspicuous statistics of divorce. A related (though not similar, and by no means so extensive) development is represented by a few small articles in *New Society** and the *British Journal of Sociology*† which are probing *beyond* the formal statistics (which only record the *legal* termination of marriages, for example) to a better knowledge of the *actual* duration of marriages, and the actual factors involved in family disruptions.

A third, highly significant piece of research is that recently reported by Geoffrey Gorer, *Sex and Marriage in England*. When first writing *The Family and Marriage in Britain*, I was able to draw on Gorer's earlier study, *Exploring English Character*, published in the mid 1950s. Now, his new study compares his findings at the end of the 1960s with those of some fifteen to twenty years ago. This is, therefore, especially relevant to our argument. Also, Rhona and Robert Rapoport have just piloted and published several studies relating to what they regard as the creation of a new family pattern attendant upon the improved status of women and the problems of managing a stable family life whilst both husbands and wives follow careers of their own choosing, and to the extent they desire. This is best presented, despite the

* See, for example, R. Chester and J. Streather, 'Taking Stock of Divorce', *New Society*, 22 July 1971.

† See Colin Gibson, 'A Note on Family Breakdown in England and Wales', *British Journal of Sociology*, Vol. XXII, No. 3, September 1971, p. 322.

fact that it covers only a small number of middle-class families, in their book *Dual Career Families*.

I have taken such research into account in so far as it has seemed necessary in this revision, and again – though some of the shorter articles express a growing concern about the divorce rate – it is worth while to emphasize that the bulk of it supports and reinforces the argument, and the picture of marriage and the family in present-day society, presented in this book. Geoffrey Gorer, for example, shows quite conclusively that a great deal of the denunciation of the modern British family, and especially of the behaviour and attitudes of the young, is simply unfounded. He produces a picture of a widespread desire in modern society for sensitive and seriously considered relationships in marriage and parenthood; of a new, articulate, companionship in married life – a 'marriage of friends', as he calls it. This is a *general* picture; but it is *especially* true of the young, and it is true, too, of men and women in the working classes – so often denigrated or discounted in all this. Gorer pleasantly counters, then, one of the more common sneers at the modern 'nuclear' family – that it is 'bourgeois', or 'middle class'. The significance of his findings is that they rest upon a very carefully designed and country-wide sample. They are, therefore, much more representative than the more localized studies of the past (for example, that of Young and Willmott). The Rapoports' 'case studies', too, show the great amount of reciprocal sensitivity, care and real and persistent effort with which many young men and women today are seeking to make possible a personal fulfilment of both partners in their chosen work in society, whilst jointly sustaining a stable home and family life in which their concern for their children is the most powerful and central factor. The research of the later 1960s, then, is taken into account, and, rather than making necessary any major change, reinforces and fills out in many encouraging ways, the general argument.

I must not dwell on this too much, but it seems important to mention the cumulative force and support of recent research *other* than that mentioned above: that is to say, research which has *not* been specifically directed to the study of the family but has, none the less, produced striking evidence of its continuing importance – for individuals and society alike. It substantiates the historical perspective and the picture of improvement given here, and shows the priority given to the family in terms of current political and administrative concern. A few examples will be enough to make clear what I mean.

Books such as Peter Laslett's *The World We Have Lost* (drawing upon historical sources) and Ronald Blythe's *Akenfield* (drawing upon first-hand accounts of present-day villagers) show graphically how unfounded is the myth of the 'closely-knit community' of pre-industrial times, within which the family has been thought by some to have had its golden age, with all its 'functions' richly intact. The necessitous, impoverished actuality of such communities and families is laid bare in these books. In another direction, all researches devoted to the study of education and educational opportunity in modern society have pointed indubitably and inescapably to the central importance of the family; and not only as a 'mechanism' for transmitting class values and inequalities, but also as the ground for individual growth, advancement, and fulfilment through education, when a child has the sensitive understanding, support and encouragement of its parents. Similarly, researches on the attitudes and patterns of life of industrial workers, on industrial relations, and on the 'social class' orientations and motivations involved in them, have revealed one very clear and conspicuous finding: that, for middle-class professional and modern worker alike, it is the concern for the family's welfare, security, happiness, and advancement, which is the strongest and continuing nucleus of economic motivation. The best example of this is the study of '*The Affluent Worker*' by David Lockwood, John Goldthorpe and others. And in yet another direction, the inquiry of the Seebohm Committee, and its proposals (now just beginning to come into administrative effect) concluded that the whole organization of the social services could be most effective if focused upon the family as the most basic social unit of shared experience and need.

So, when *all* the social researches of the 1960s are considered, not only those on the family as such, the impression given is one of the great and continuing strength of the family in our society.

The present revision, then, is brought up to date to take these several elements into account, and gives a picture of marriage and the family in Britain up to the end of the 1960s. This has the great virtue of leaving us free to think ahead constructively from this basis to the nature and problems of marriage and the family in this present decade. But this, I think, can best form the substance of another book. And here a final and very large consideration arises.

New criticisms of the family – and a new book

Ten years ago, it was necessary to defend the modern family – and the improvements which a great deal of political effort had accomplished – against a host of backward-looking Jeremiahs who saw the scene of the family in modern society as one of disintegration (see p. 33 and Appendix, p. 257). Now, curiously, a new breed of critics has arisen. Far from thinking the family in decline, they see it, on the contrary, as a much too strongly entrenched and conservative unit, standing in the way of a great deal that is enlightened and progressive. They attack the family, not from any recognition of impending destruction, but from an active desire to bring that destruction about. The modern family is, of all social units, the most reactionary upholder of the *status quo*. In short, we are now faced with critics of the 'left' as well as those of the 'right'. In one way or another, these new critics are revolutionaries, so forward-looking that the focus of their vision is out of sight. And they are a very mixed bunch.

Edmund Leach – whose excellence in anthropology (when he is speaking of the tribes of Highland Burma, for example, and the theoretical issues connected with his researches there) no scholar will question – has, aided by mass-communications, become something of an '*enfant terrible*'. He utters a few paragraphs on the family in the Reith Lectures – in common terms and based on evidence of no more than commonsense level – and, lo and behold! – one would think that the state tottered! The journalistic country is agog. Editors use a provocative sentence or two to head their colour-supplement leaders on 'Why Marriage?' Television producers hang all the bright clothes of their educational programmes on this peg of controversy. Colleges of Education quote the sentences in their examination questions, and ask their students to 'Discuss'. All of a sudden, the family is something to be radically changed, to be dispensed with. Far from being in decay, its close network of relationships is now seen as being all too powerful. The suffocating privacy of the family, with its tawdry secrets, is 'the source of all our discontents'.* Films are made to show how it is the nuclear family which destroys us. Women's Liberation, too, in its more extreme forms, is out for the family's blood. One or two expositions claim that women can manage quite well without men – even sexually – and must do so if they are to gain their full freedom and equality. Great arguments go on about 'the rubbing of one clitoris against another' as 'an excellent case for the extinction of the male organ'; 'the myth of the vaginal orgasm'; and other profound matters.

Beyond the Women's Lib argument, however, though having a relation to it, are other specific and serious criticisms of the nuclear family as being productive of various kinds of psychological and social disorder. The work of R. D. Laing (*The Politics of the Family*) and of David Cooper (*The Death of the Family*) are prominent examples. Following this view, and that of the general movement for sexual liberation, there are also those who propose 'group families', 'communes', and uphold 'kibbutzim-type' arrangements, as alternatives to the family. And lastly, there are the extreme left-wing revolutionaries, the radical activists, who maintain that to uphold marriage and the family is to buttress bourgeois society and serve the forces of reaction. An example of

* See 'Ourselves and Others', the third Reith Lecture, *Listener*, 30 November 1967, Vol. 78, No. 2018, p. 695.

this kind of view is Robin Blackburn's in his essay 'A Brief Guide to Bourgeois Ideology' (*Student Power*, 1969). To uphold the modern, freely chosen, democratic family unit is, he thinks, 'domestic mystification', and he himself appears to regard the increase in divorce as a growing rejection of marriage as an institution. It is of no use, in relation to such theorists, to point out that even in collectivist societies, where capitalism has been most completely overthrown, the family is still held in high regard (that, for example, even now, a mother who has ten children in the Soviet Union becomes a 'Mother Heroine'). For revolutionaries of this kind, who think of effective theory as the theory 'of the practice that is changing the world' – which leads you wherever you want the tug-of-war of power, and your expediency of action within it, to take you – do not think that the Soviet Union, any more than any other society, is a truly 'socialist' one. It is of no use to ask them what alternative to the family they propose, or even foresee, for – on principle – they cannot know and do not even wish to ask. It would be, for them, pure unfounded intellectualism to conjecture like this. They might even have to commit themselves responsibly to some specific social objective, and then where would their 'perpetual revolution' be? Such new social forms will emerge only from the practical, dialectical fire of revolutionary processes. Meanwhile, these nihilists in red shirts, these boy scouts of the revolutionary (campus) battlefield, can pour their thin oil on troubled flames, can write their imitations of the Marx and Engels Manifesto in the systematic, pedestrian, superficial style of Joseph Stalin (a good example can be found at the end of *Student Power*): as we said earlier, so forward-looking that the focus of their vision is out of sight.

There is, then, a new – if mixed – breed of critics of the family, and, though some are serious, some not so serious, their arguments should all be taken into account. It is impossible, however, to do this adequately by any simple adaptation of the present book. This really does seem, in many ways, a clear point of arrival and departure. I have therefore decided to revise the present book to fill out and bring up to date the picture it gives of the family up to the end of the 1960s and on the doorstep of the 1970s; to retain, too, the historical perspective and the account of improvements of the family which I take to be a firm ground for any argument; and then to write an altogether new book to take the new criticisms thoroughly into account. The two books together will try to provide grounds of constructive argument for the years that lie immediately ahead.

Ronald Fletcher
Suffolk
January 1972

Introduction*

EVERYWHERE in the world human society is radically and rapidly changing. At the heart of the turmoil is one major factor – industrialization. This, with its commercial, cultural, political, military tentacles, is drawing all the societies of the world into complex interconnection with each other. In doing so – for better, for worse – it is disrupting the traditional order of all communities. Religions are being challenged by new science. A new technology, with the factory and the growing dominance of vast urban settlements, is changing old patterns of work and life. New communications link our minds together in ways we have not known before. No social institution can remain uninfluenced. No society can remain untouched. Ours is the age of the global awareness of mankind and the groping towards some global structure of social organization. In this context, problems of social change, problems of beliefs and values, are an everyday preoccupation. Some argue that all this change is for the best. Some believe that everything of value is being destroyed. We live in an age of dilemmas.

Not the least of our troubles is a universal concern about the family in society, and about those qualities of personal life and personal relationships which are so intimately bound up with it.

What is happening to the family in modern society, that people should regard it with such deep anxiety?

Is it true that in the large-scale, impersonal nature of modern society the family is losing its hold upon us? Is it true that the state and its many agencies have invaded family responsibilities so much that they have removed all

* The Introduction to the First Edition is given in an Appendix: see p. 257.

the family's functions? Is the family in decline? Is it diminishing in importance as a social institution? Is there a 'growing instability of marriage', a 'continual increase of divorce', a 'deterioration of family life'? Is it true that present-day parents are morally lax and irresponsible? Do husbands and wives no longer desire loyalty and fidelity from each other? Do parents no longer love and respect their children, or children their parents? Are the fundamental qualities of mutual care, love, loyalty, which have been the bedrock of human character no longer to be found in the family of today?

What effects have industrial and urban changes, the increase in material wealth, the increased provision of education, the new independence of women, the new affluence and freedom of teenagers, and other aspects of modern society had upon the nature and stability of the family? Are these changes such that we can welcome and encourage them? Or are they to be feared and opposed? Do they constitute a deterioration or an improvement of moral standards and family relationships? Is the family really to blame for all the ills modern society is said to suffer – crime, delinquency, irresponsibility, hooliganism – as many moralists would have us believe? Or are such charges false, unjustified, harmful? What is the truth about such matters?

These are the kinds of questions which torment many people, and clearly the answers we give to them are of considerable importance. Every social policy we devise, every change in the law, every development or curtailment of the social services, will depend upon them. It is a matter of practical urgency, not only of academic interest, that our answers should be correct. If we are to provide satisfactory answers to these questions, some things are clear and important and deserve emphasis.

First – *we must know the facts*. This is a simple point. But it cannot be emphasized too much that most of the arguments about these issues have been, and still are, assertions and counter-assertions of opinion and hot feeling. We are still not sufficiently in the habit of critically examining the facts about a question before arriving at our conclusions about it. It is also important to realize that *the facts are not easy to know*. The kinds of inquiry we can draw upon are relatively few; the kinds of statistical statements at our disposal do not lend themselves to easy qualitative interpretation; the pieces of research being conducted are limited and of a variable nature, so that they are not always comparable. It is still the case with the family, as with so many subjects studied by the social sciences, that we do not possess enough facts. But though it is far short of what we would like it to be, it is still necessary to bring together such historical and contemporary knowledge as is available to us and to organize and analyse it systematically in such a way as to provide a reliable basis for exercising our judgement and evaluation. This is attempted in this book. Without some such arrangements of available knowledge, all argument about social matters is useless.

Secondly – we cannot possibly judge whether the family of our own time is better or worse (in any sense) than that of the past unless we have some reliable historical knowledge and perspective. There is no doubt that, in general, all peoples are greatly ignorant about the past of their own society. This may be the largest single reason why we tend always to glorify it. But we are not altogether to blame. Again, the knowledge is not easily available. It is only recently – a hundred years or so ago – that historians came to think that the social life of ordinary people was worthy of study. We still suffer from the infancy of social history. There is no good social history of the family in British society, for example, to which we can refer. In this study, I have drawn what social historians have had to say about various aspects of family life in the past from their larger treatises about other subjects. But, at least, the findings and views of many historians are brought together here in a form not available elsewhere, and I can only hope that readers may be sufficiently stimulated by this brief taste of their writings to read them more deeply later on. No literature is more fascinating. My crucial point, however, is that a knowledge of history is just as essential to the soundness of our judgement about present-day issues, as a knowledge of contemporary facts.

There is, thirdly, a much broader point which I mentioned at the outset, but which deserves further emphasis.

This book is a contribution to the study of the family and marriage in Britain. It examines the ways in which the family and marriage have changed in Britain during the past two centuries of industrialization; attempts an analysis and evaluation of these changes; and then offers some comments on the ways in which we ought to approach questions of social policy. But there is a sense in which its conclusions may have a wider relevance.

The process of industrial change which Britain has experienced during the past two hundred years is now becoming a world-wide process, and it is giving rise to problems which are common to all societies. This means that what has happened to the family in Britain during the course of industrial development may well be indicative of what is likely to happen elsewhere. What we have seen here may enable us to foresee what might happen elsewhere. The kind of family to which industrial change has given rise in Britain might be the kind of family which is coming into being everywhere in an increasingly industrialized world. In short, it is possible that a careful understanding of the changing family in Britain may give us a useful basis for the understanding of problems encountered by those other societies which are undergoing rapid social change now, and must experience it during the rest of this century. Our experience might possibly help in the formulation of appropriate policies in other communities that might temper the hardship and the indignities which industrial change is always likely to bring in its train. Other recent books – as, for example, *World Revolution and Family Patterns* by W. J. Goode, whose conclusions are very similar to the conclusions of this book – are looking to the study of the family everywhere in the context of industrial change, and the study of the family in our own society can also contribute to this wider comparative field. The time seems ripe for wide comparative research on an international scale, as well as for wide cooperation in the discussion of appropriate social policies. I shall return to this theme in my last chapter on the future of the family, but it is clearly a point to bear firmly in mind.

I think it is important to say, finally, that in the first edition I introduced this book with a fairly strong polemic. At the time I was incensed at the diatribes of a large number of public moralists (whose statements I then documented, but who need not be mentioned again) who were all too ready to denounce the present and glorify the past.* I wrote this book to try to demonstrate that they were wrong; to argue for a more balanced way of looking at our problems; and to try to achieve a more constructive approach to the making of social policy. I wrote what I hoped would be a defence of the modern family, and sought to show that the changes of two hundred years were, in large part, substantial improvements – both material and moral. I believe that the family has *not* declined; that the family is *not* less stable than hitherto; and that the standards of parenthood and parental responsibility have *not* deteriorated. I do not think that the substance of the book suffers from the fairly strong feelings which gave rise to it, but I think readers should know that this was how it came to be written, and I think that they will better understand the form of its argument with this realization.

*

My grateful acknowledgements are due to those authors and publishers upon whose books and articles I have drawn, and whose work I have brought together in a task I hope they will think worthwhile. All of them are mentioned in the notes, and many in the suggestions for further reading. Amongst all these, there is one book especially to which I owe a great deal: that is Dr Ivy Pinchbeck's *Women Workers and the Industrial Revolution, 1750–1850*. This book deals, in fact, with far more than its title suggests and is a mine of information about the domestic conditions of the people of

* See pp. 257–61.

Britain during the period it covers. I would also like, especially, to acknowledge – indeed, to pay tribute to – the many statistical sources, the annual reviews and the commentaries, of the Registrar General, on which I have drawn very heavily. Criticisms are frequently made of these statistics, often on good and useful grounds, but the simple truth is that social scientists would be lost without them; and the changing focus upon issues of topical importance and concern provided in the Part III Commentaries are continually informative, stimulating and helpful. Finally, I would like to express my warm gratitude and indebtedness to my former colleague, O. R. McGregor, with whom I was able to discuss this subject, among many others, interminably and always enjoyably (a rare and pleasant combination) and who was good enough to read and criticize both the original manuscript and the proofs and to suggest many improvements.

1 The Family as a Social Group

THE family is, and has always been, the most intimate and one of the most important of human groups. With qualifications of negligible importance, it can be said to be universal, existing in all known human societies. Indeed, biologists and psychologists have shown that, in a rudimentary form, it exists among other animal species, amongst which mating, procreation, and the care of offspring are largely the manifestations of inherited, instinctive modes of experience and behaviour.

The human family is centred round these same biological propensities and needs: mating, the begetting of children, the rearing of children (especially important because of the long period of dependence of the human infant), and the necessity of providing for the manifold needs of all its members. It can therefore be said to be a 'natural' grouping in so far as it is rooted in fundamental instincts, emotions, and needs serving important biological functions; and a 'socially necessary' grouping in the sense that it exists in all societies for regulating sexual and parental behaviour in order to achieve those relationships and qualities of character which are considered to be desirable.

At first sight, these two aspects of the family seem contradictory. If the family is a 'natural' grouping, why is social regulation necessary? And, indeed, much care has to be taken in speaking of the 'natural' aspects of the family, since it is all too easy to think that this implies that those feelings which are appropriate to the family with which one is familiar in one's own society are 'natural', and those feelings which tend to be disruptive of family ties, or those feelings which are appropriate to different forms of the family in different societies, are 'unnatural'. Further consideration, however, suggests that these two aspects of the family are in fact complementary to each other. Certainly natural instincts and emotions relating to sex, procreation, and parental care are involved in the family; but these propensities do not 'fit nicely' into any particular form of the family, neither are they self-governing. If it were so, sexual immorality, marital infidelity, the unequal and sometimes cruel treatment of children, would not have provided such an inexhaustible vein of material – tragic and comic alike – for folk-lore, legend, poetry, drama, and novel throughout human history. The natural propensities involved require regulation, both with regard to their relationships with each other, and with reference to the wider stability and order of human relationships, and the allocation of claims and duties, in the community. The family is that form of association in which both some degree of *fulfilment* of these natural propensities and some necessary degree of *regulation* of them is combined. As a group it at once entails *both* fulfilment *and* limiting constraint for its members.

This factor of social regulation immediately implies that the *form* of the family in human societies is not determined by biological features alone, but is dependent upon the very variable geographical, social, cultural, and historical circumstances with which particular communities are faced. Thus the family group in some societies is polygamous, in some polyandrous, in some monogamous – but even here, the kinds of polygamy, polyandry and monogamy differ in detail from society to society.

Therefore, though those natural propensities of man which are always involved in the family do not entail any universal type of family group, the idea that man was originally promiscuous (in the sense of having no regulated form of family grouping), and that he *consciously and rationally devised* the family as a necessary regulative social institution, does not appear to be borne out by the evidence. It is truer to say that wherever and whenever we know human society, the family exists and is rooted in natural feelings and in social functions which go deeper than the level of conscious device, and that the various forms of the family have come into being, and continue to come into being, as a result of different and changing social circumstances. Of course, as these changes become increasingly a matter of conscious social policy, rational device enters the situation to a greater degree, but it is never all that is involved.

It is worthwhile to remember that sexual relationships in all human societies are powerfully governed by some form of 'incest taboo'. Relationships amongst kindred are always clearly defined, and between some of them sexual intimacy is rigorously forbidden. The 'incest taboo' cannot yet be said to be fully understood, but it is clear that it is deeply rooted in human psychology and performs important functions of social regulation, ensuring kinds of affection and qualities of relationship between the sexes, and between parents and children, which could scarcely exist if there were complete sexual anarchy. Its universal presence serves to indicate that familial and kinship organization, both psychologically and socially, goes far deeper than the level of conscious device.

Since the family always involves a mating relationship of some regulated degree of permanency, communities always have, also, some appropriate institution of 'marriage' in accordance with which this mating relationship is established and maintained. Forms of marriage therefore vary widely as do forms of the family, and it is important for us, in exercising judgements about the family in contemporary Britain, to remember that marriage has not always been based upon the 'personal love' of the partners – that basis of marriage with which we are most familiar. Marriage has sometimes been based upon capture, on the payment of a 'bride-price', on the decisions of elders, on property arrangements, and on other criteria. Happy and successful, dutiful and dignified marital relationships have therefore been achieved without choice, without the basis of personal love (now termed 'romantic love'), and this is a point to which we shall return later.

Another point of great importance is that the family is not rooted in marriage, but marriage is an institution rooted in the family. This is the conclusion of Edward Westermarck in his book *The History of Human Marriage* (1921). It appears a simple point, but important considerations arise from it, and it is necessary to point out that this conception of marriage is in fundamental disagreement with the teachings of Christian theology which continue to have such a powerful influence upon the regulation of marriage in our own society.

After a very extensive comparative study of the characteristics of marriage and the family in many societies, Westermarck concludes:

. . . it is originally for the benefit of the young that male and female continue to live together. We may therefore say that marriage is rooted in the family rather than the family in marriage. Indeed, among many peoples true married life does not begin for persons who are formally married or betrothed, or a marriage does not become definite, until a child is born or there are signs of pregnancy; whilst in other cases sexual relations which happen to lead to pregnancy or the birth of a child are, as a rule, followed by marriage or make marriage compulsory.[1]

The Christian view of marriage as a sacrament in its own right is clearly very different from this. In the Encyclical Letter of Pius XI on Christian Marriage we find the following statement of doctrine:[2]

. . . let us recall this immutable, inviolable, and fundamental truth: Matrimony was not instituted or re-established by men but by God; not men, but God, the Author of nature, and Christ our Lord, the Restorer of nature, provided marriage with its laws, confirmed it, and elevated it; and consequently those laws can in no way be subject to human wills or to any contrary pact made even by the contracting parties themselves. This is the teaching of Sacred Scripture; it is the constant and universal Tradition of the Church; it is the solemnly defined doctrine of the Council of Trent, which uses the words of Holy Scripture to proclaim and establish that the perpetual indissolubility of the marriage bond, its unity and its stability, derive from God Himself.*

* These statements, and the one on the following page, are theolo-

In the same letter the claim is made that:

It is evident that even in the state of nature and at all events long before it was raised to the dignity of a sacrament properly so called, marriage was divinely constituted in such a way as to involve a perpetual and indissoluble bond, which consequently cannot be dissolved by any civil law.

In the revised edition of *A Catholic Guide to Social and Political Action* (1955), the words of Leo XIII from the Letter of Christian Marriage (1880) are restated as authoritative doctrine.

Marriage has God for its Author, and was from the very beginning a kind of foreshadowing of the Incarnation of His Son; and therefore there abides in it something holy and religious; not extraneous, but innate ... in Christian marriage the contract is inseparable from the sacrament, and ... for this reason the contract cannot be true and legitimate without being a sacrament as well.

It is clear that these two differing conceptions of the nature of marriage entail quite different approaches to the question of divorce. The belief that marriage is a sacrament in its own right, constituting an indissoluble union, necessarily entails the belief that divorce is wrong.

As W. Friedmann puts it:

Implicit in this philosophy is the acceptance of individual unhappiness as part of a status that is ordained by God. 'What therefore God has put together, let not man put asunder.' The shadow of St Augustine still hovers over this conception of marriage. For him all human institutions were essentially sinful, and redeemed only by the grace of God. If men and women have chosen wrongly, let them bear their cross, as a duty owed to God.[3]

---

gical interpretations of facts which have no supporting evidence beyond the particular religious belief itself. In many of the 'primitive' societies and in many of the ancient civilizations marriage was a secular contract only, was very frequently attended by the payment of a 'bride-price', and could be dissolved. Usually a clause providing for divorce, should it become necessary, was included in the marriage contract, and often entailed a part-repayment of the bride-price.

But, for a good account of 'Marriage and Canon Law', see Note 2, p. 265.

On the other hand, the view that marriage is rooted in the fundamental unit of the family and is not a sacrament in its own right clearly entails the position that divorce is not necessarily immoral, and that, under certain circumstances, it may well be justified when the welfare and happiness of all the members of the family are considered.

Friedmann, who is considering these two conceptions of marriage in the context of a discussion of modern family law writes:

There is, however, an entirely different justification for the rejection of the indissolubility of marriage, based on social rather than individual grounds. This philosophy considers the family as an intimate social unit, a community in miniature, which can be disrupted by an unhappy marriage, to the detriment not only of the life and character of the spouses, but of the children. It recognizes that – as has been clearly shown by the social experience of our times – disruption of the marriage may be a prime cause of juvenile delinquency and that, short of criminal actions, it may warp the characters and lives of the children. This philosophy is not, of course, incompatible with that of individual self-fulfilment, but its accent is different. Its central concern is the relation of the marriage bond to the family, and through it, the community.[4]

Barbara Wootton, discussing the issues of modern divorce in an article entitled 'Holiness and Happiness', calls these two differing conceptions of marriage the 'religious' and the 'utilitarian'.[5]

It is not to our purpose to debate these two points of view here, but only to indicate the very great importance of the issues which attend Westermarck's point, and it is a question to which we shall return later. All that needs to be said here is that – whatever the validity of Christian theology for committed Christians – on the grounds of comparative sociology Westermarck's statement holds good. Marriage does not exist in and for itself, but is an institution whose *raison d'être* is the foundation and maintenance of the family. In any society it is one regulation in the whole organization of a particular family type.

The central consideration in this establishment of a

mating relationship is the having and rearing of children, and the family provides for the over-all satisfaction of the needs of children during their years of complete, and then partial, dependence. The family therefore inhabits a common house, a 'home', in which, in conditions of relative privacy and security, this intimate and prolonged provision for the needs of its members takes place. In addition to the care of dependent children, the family usually cares for the dependent aged, and, indeed, for any of its members who may become temporarily or permanently dependent owing to various vicissitudes.

It follows clearly from these characteristics that the family, as a group, is inevitably limited in size. Indeed, it is the smallest of the formal associations in society, and it is just because of this that it is one of the most influential and important. Because its members comprise only a small number of people, living together in great intimacy over a long period of time, the family makes more constant, concrete, intense, and subtle demands upon its members than does any other kind of group. It should also be noted that, for the children especially (but, to varying degrees, for the parents too[6]), the family is an *involuntary* grouping. The particular family of which they are members is not of their own choosing, and they cannot – at least for a very long time (if even then in any real and effective sense of the word) – contract out of it. Consequently, the many compulsive situations of family life must be expected to give rise to frustrations and resentments as well as fulfilments. To use a term familiar in psychology, our experience in the family is necessarily 'ambivalent'. We experience both love and hate, both fulfilment and frustration, both loyalty and rebellion, towards the same people, objects, and situations; and because of this continual – sometimes harmonious, sometimes conflicting, but always intense – complexity of demands in the family, some of the deepest and most abiding human sentiments are set up within it. We know from our experience that these sentiments – whether worthwhile or regrettable, noble or petty, pleasant or painful – prove to be of abiding importance in the characters and personalities of the members of a family; influencing, indeed in great part determining, their directions of taste, belief, interest, and effort throughout their lives.

Enough has been said to show that the family is, in fact, a community in itself: a small, relatively permanent group of people, related to each other in the most intimate way, bound together by the most personal aspects of life; who experience amongst themselves the whole range of human emotions; who have to strive continually to resolve those claims and counter-claims which stem from mutual but often conflicting needs; who experience continual responsibilities and obligations towards each other; who experience the sense of 'belonging' to each other in the most intimately felt sense of that word. The members of a family share the same name, the same collective reputation, the same home, the same intricate, peculiar tradition of their own making, the same neighbourhood. They share the same sources of pleasure, the same joys, the same sources of profound conflict. The same vagaries of fortune are encountered and overcome together. Degrees of agreement and degrees of violent disagreement are worked out amongst them. The same losses and the same griefs are shared. Hence the family is that group within which the most fundamental appreciation of human qualities and values takes place – 'for better for worse': the qualities of truth and honesty, of falsehood and deceit; of kindliness and sympathy, of indifference and cruelty; of cooperation and forbearance, of egotism and antagonism; of tolerance, justice, and impartiality, of bias, dogmatism, and obstinacy; of generous concern for the freedom and fulfilment of others, of the mean desire to dominate – whether in overt bullying or in psychologically more subtle ways. All those values, and all those discriminations and assessments of value, which are of the most fundamental importance for the formation of adult character are first experienced and exercised by children in the context of the family. Furthermore, these qualities are not 'taught' or 'learned' in any straightforward or altogether rational way;

they are actually embodied in people and their behaviour. The child perceives them and appraises them in concrete and demanding situations, and in direct face-to-face relationships with people who matter supremely. In this way, the family is an 'educative' group of the most fundamental kind.

These 'educative' characteristics of the family deserve a little further consideration. As a community, the family is, as we have seen, the earliest and most impressive social situation (or social environment) in the context of which the character of the child is moulded. But the family is not *only* a community in itself, and it is certainly not an *isolated* community. It has its being in the context of a wider grouping of kindred, a wider neighbourhood, and in a wider and more complicated society. For the child, therefore, the family is a kind of 'avenue' through which it comes gradually to an experience of these wider social groupings, and, in so doing, to full adulthood and responsible citizenship. The family provides an 'introduction', as it were, to the wider structure of society – to the knowledge of the wider pattern of kinship; the various groups and characteristics of the neighbourhood; the more detailed economic, governmental, educational, and religious organizations in society. In sociological terms the family is that most important 'primary' group of society which gradually introduces the child to the complicated 'secondary' groups of society – that complicated fabric of social organization with which it will have to come to terms and within which it will have to work out the course and pattern of its life. Through this introduction, the family provides the child with those values and modes of behaviour which are appropriate for life in the wider society. In a fuller sense than we suggested earlier, then, the family is – for the child – the first, and perhaps the most important, agency of education in society.

This might be more clearly illustrated in the diagram overleaf.

Gradually moving beyond his (or her) earliest experience within the family, the child will come to have experience of the other 'primary' (small, face-to-face) groups in the

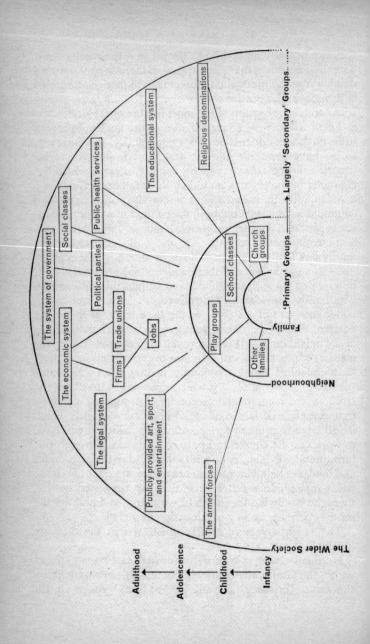

neighbourhood: other families, play groups, school classes, church groups. His experience of these groups will continually broaden during the years of childhood, until, in adolescence, he will have to come to terms with all the demands and activities of adult society and will have to take important and far-reaching decisions with regard to them. He will have to decide the direction and extent of his education and training. He will have to choose a job, and probably join a trade union or a professional association. He will have to decide which political party he will support. He will experience the demarcations, pressures, and curtailments of class, privilege, and status distinctions. He may be compelled to undertake service in the armed forces, and so on. His family background, throughout this experience, will be a central influence in the attitudes he forms and the decisions he adopts.

It is clear, however, that the family is not an 'introduction' to society in any simple sense of the word; neither should it be regarded *only* as an 'avenue' to something beyond it. The family is rather a continuing 'nucleus' of shared experience and behaviour, a 'pooling' of individual experiences, through which medium the impressions, attitudes, beliefs, tastes, of all its members are interdependently being formed. For example, the child's experiences in play groups or at school will be brought back to the family, will give rise to discussion, and may bring changes in knowledge and attitudes. The child's experiences in church may raise arguments in the home and may perhaps give rise to conflicts of belief and loyalty. The father's satisfaction or depression about his work, his degree of security or insecurity in his job, will be issues for the whole family and will affect the experience of all its members. His trade union commitments, his political views and allegiances, will all enter into and colour the experience of the family as a whole. The family is therefore integrally bound up with the life of all its members in the wider society. It is a community which reflects and, in its own particular way, digests, the experiences of its members in all their other forms of association, and it is in the context of this ongoing complexity of experience that children grow up into adulthood and into adult citizenship.

It seems clear that for any wise upbringing of children, neither the 'avenue' nor the 'community in itself' conception of the family should dominate to the exclusion of the other. Both require balanced emphasis. If the family is treated only as an 'avenue' to something beyond it, a child may be treated only as a potential adult, with reference to what it is desired that he should become in future; and he may never enjoy consideration as a person, at the moment, in and for himself; he may never enjoy a child's life, satisfying and important in itself, within a settled home life. But, alternatively, if the family is treated only as a 'community in itself', the child may suffer from too great a degree of family-containment, of dependence upon the family, and he may be handicapped later by never having been brought to terms with the demands of the wider world in which he must live. The home may become too much of a 'retreat'. It is clear that both aspects of the family are of importance and require due consideration, and there are some people, at any rate, who appear to emphasize only one or the other.

It seems possible at this stage to offer a clear summary statement of the more important functions of the family. Bearing in mind all the points we have mentioned, we can say that:

1. The family regulates sexual behaviour in relation to the satisfaction of both sexual needs and the achievement and maintenance of other desired qualities and relationships.

2. The family secures a legitimate and responsible basis for procreation and the rearing of children.

3. The family provides for the sustenance and care of its dependent members – whether children, aged, or those dependent for other reasons.

4. The family provides, in a continuing and detailed fashion, the earliest and most impressive education for the young. In so doing, it introduces the child to those values and modes of behaviour which are appropriate to all kinds of social activity both within and beyond the family. It ac-

complishes what is usually called the 'socialization' of the child. Thus it serves as an important agency in the perpetuation of 'social traditions'.

5. Finally, since the 'titles' of the members of the family – 'husband', 'wife', 'eldest son', etc. – bear specific and different social connotations, the family can be said to invest its members with those rights, duties, customary and legal demands which are recognized and insisted upon in the community in which they live.

It will be seen, from what has been said, that there are two reasons especially why the family is of crucial importance, both for the social scientist (for purposes of social analysis) and for the statesman (for purposes of practical social policy).

Firstly, the family is that association which centres about the *reproduction of the population* and the rearing of new generations of citizens. Any social policy concerned with the quantity and quality of the population must therefore take into account, and operate upon, the families in society. This is, of course, a crucial matter for the very survival and for the sustained quality of the entire political community. Secondly, since it is that association within which the earliest character-formation of individuals takes place – within which the earliest and deepest pattern of sentiments, attitudes, beliefs, ideals, and loyalties is established – the family is one of the most important agencies making for the *continuity of the social tradition*.

There is much (and obvious) evidence to show that this importance of the family is recognized beyond the bounds of social science in the realm of practical affairs. All modern governments which have become aware of population trends have shown concern about the state of the family and the problems which face it, and have undertaken extensive social policies to encourage or limit (depending upon the particular population trends with which they are faced) the number of births in the family. Similarly, it is notoriously true that all social movements wanting to inculcate profound loyalties to themselves try to penetrate family loyalties: either seeking to invest the family with their own beliefs and values, as with the Roman Catholic Church and the later policy of the Soviet Union, or seeking to disrupt the bonds of family loyalties in an effort to replace them by a deeper sense of duty and loyalty to themselves, as, for example, with the Nazi movement in Germany.

This leads, then, to a final point: that the family is demonstrably so important a social group, so powerful a nucleus of interests and loyalties, and so fruitful a source of individual variety, that it is always very conspicuously and strictly regulated by the central agencies of authority and control in society – the state, the law, and religion.

It might be thought, in view of what has been said about the universality, the cohesiveness, and the psychological and social importance of the family, that ideas to the effect that the family is 'dying out' in modern society, that it has become of little significance as a social group, that it has been 'stripped of its functions', seem extremely dubious, if, indeed, they can be seriously entertained at all. And many important scholars are of this opinion. Westermarck, for example, after a searching inquiry in his book *The Future of Marriage*, concludes:

There is every reason to believe that the unity of sensual and spiritual elements in sexual love, leading to a more or less durable community of life in a common home, and the desire for and love of offspring, are factors that will remain lasting obstacles to the extinction of marriage and the collapse of the family, because they are too deeply rooted in human nature to fade away, and can find adequate satisfaction only in some form of marriage and the family founded upon it.[7]

There are, none the less, many who maintain that the family has been so severely disrupted in the modern industrial age, so weakened morally, that it has become socially insignificant and gives rise to grave social problems. In what follows, the grounds for these views will be examined, but perhaps, even at the outset, it may be permitted to mention one actual and striking example of the strength and flexibility shown by the family in meeting the most severe extremes of social disorganization and ideological attack. The example is that of the period following the Russian revolution of 1917, and for purposes of brevity I shall give a few quotations from the study by Maurice Hindus.[8]

The period of civil war in Russia following the revolution of 1917, and the military and political fanaticism accompanying the over-all social confusion, was such as to be disruptive of all tradition and convention and all hitherto normal ties and loyalties:

> Deep and explosive were family conflicts all over the land. Son arose against father, daughter against mother, brother against brother. Political fury submerged all other emotions; social wrath overpowered conventional attachments and age-old loyalties ... Rich is the documentary and powerful is the fictional literature depicting the family cleavages of those times.

Hindus cites instances, for example, of sons, in the company of fellow-soldiers in the Red Army, capturing and executing their fathers. (The widespread disruption and confusion about which Hindus writes is vividly and excellently portrayed in the novel by Mikhail Sholokhov – *The Don Flows Home To The Sea*.[9])

With the end of civil war, governmental policy quickly came into being.

> The promise of leaders to shake the family loose of legal and other external compulsions was quickly and wholeheartedly fulfilled. Divorce was easy and could be obtained for the asking. No cause was necessary. Desire alone counted. There was no limit to the number of divorces a man or woman might obtain. The cost was nominal, within reach of the poorest pocketbook. The procedure was simple. It was easier to obtain a divorce than to buy a new pair of shoes – far easier. If the wife did not care to inform her husband of the legal separation she did not have to. He learned it through the reporter card which '*Zags*' – the registration bureau – mailed to him ...
>
> In the family life the behaviour of the individual was a matter of his own choice or his own discretion.
>
> Registration of marriage was not obligatory, though advisable

for a purely administrative reason, so that the state would have more or less reliable records of marriages and divorces.

Women were favoured with facilities to divest themselves of family obligations. Birth control was fostered, abortions were free and legal. Since there was much prejudice against the common forms of birth control and since, in addition, there was an inadequate supply of reliable equipment, abortions gained wide acceptance as a substitute.

The special disabilities which the laws had imposed on women were now wiped out. A woman was the equal of man in all matters pertaining to individual self-expression and social accommodation. The husband boasted of no prerogatives which were withheld from his wife.

Under the impact of the new freedom, divorce, though chiefly in the cities, was rampant. Families broke up, started again, and once more went on the rocks.

In short, all the previous external compulsions with regard to the establishment and maintenance of the family were removed. And what happened to the family as a consequence of this rapid period of social upheaval and changing regulations? Hindus tells us:

In those days [i.e., the period during which these policies were initiated] endless volumes were written on Russian morality, Russian free-love, Russian desecration of the family. Yet the family remained. Its roots were never shaken and were never in danger of being torn out. Despite easy divorce, the right to free and frequent abortions, the overwhelming mass of Russian humanity, in the village almost all of them, fell in love, married, and even when they did not record the union in the registration office, they stayed married. They raised children. They built a home in the best way they could. Stripped of the family compulsions that their grandfathers had known, they chose of their own accord to continue the ancestral habit and tradition of family life.

And again:

Severe as were these blows to the family, it remained unshaken. Thus, as an institution, the family survived all crises. Its economic foundation was gone. The former taboos were no more. There was no mention of adultery in the legal code. All children were legitimate, whether born in or out of wedlock. Neither father nor mother any longer enjoyed the right to make matches unacceptable to their sons or daughters. Men and women remained the arbiters of their own sexual and moral behaviour. Birth control continued easy, so did abortion.

If a couple wished to go off on a love life of their own for a week or a month the law did not interfere. Nurseries and kindergartens by the thousands were leaping up all over the country. Mothers left their children in one or the other depending on the age of the child, went to their offices or to the fields to work, and on returning called for the children and took them home. More than ever the state participated in the education and the physical and ideological moulding of the child. Yet, contrary to all forecasts and denunciations, the family shook off all assaults and all 'liberations'. Men and women found compensations in home life which transcended the seductive indulgences on the outside. There were transgressions, of course, not a few of them. But the appeal and the hold of the family on the individual, the comradeship, the love, the joy in children and in the common destiny it offered, provided unbreakable bonds of unity . . .

Even those free-minded Bolsheviks who privately and sometimes publicly decried the family as a relic of a dark and bygone age were astonished at the oak-like strength it displayed.

In 1936 and afterwards, the Soviet government completely changed its policies and, both ideologically and practically, supported and strengthened the family, reimposing a set of external compulsions and now arguing completely against the practice of 'free-love and disorder in sexual life'. These now became, as one might expect, completely 'bourgeois', and had (said a *Pravda* editorial) 'nothing in common with socialist principles or with the ethics and rules of conduct of a Soviet citizen'.

We need not go into the details of all these changes. It is sufficient to see that, within a period of nineteen years of the most extreme, radical, and violent social disruption, and in the context of an unprecedented loosening of control over family relationships, the family had powerfully survived and had come, once more, to be completely recognized and supported by the state. So much was this so that, in 1943, having surveyed these changes, Hindus could write:

Unlike religion and the Church, the family has triumphed over all tests and storms to which it has been subjected since the rise of the Soviets on 7 November 1917.

In no other country in the world is the family as an institution so openly and eloquently hallowed as in the Russia of today. In the Press, in literature, on the propagandist's platform, it is accorded high tribute, the very highest. Now it is no less a pillar of society and of individual self-expression than in any other country.

In the present meaning of the word, Sovietism is as unthinkable without the institution of the family as without the institution of collective ownership and control of property! The family is accepted, revered, glorified.

It might be argued that this new glorification of the family was an expedient on the part of the state with regard to its population policies, and this is doubtless true to some extent, but it is clear that the family had shown its stability and resistance to change before these changes of policy came about.

When, in addition to our earlier and general considerations of the characteristics of the family as a social group, we consider also this actual example of the tenacity of the family in surviving such extreme tests, the idea that the family is in danger of disappearing in modern society, that it is breaking down in the face of modern changes, would seem to be a very dubious view, and one difficult to substantiate. One would be more inclined to think with Havelock Ellis that '. . . the family is such an organic part of man's biology and psychology that nothing and nobody can destroy it'.

We must now, however, turn to consider those characteristics and problems of the family in modern society which give rise to such grave fears, criticisms, and moral deprecations; and it is necessary, first of all, to outline some of the sociological generalizations about the trends of family development as a consequence of the processes of industrialization from which, superficially as it seems to me, these views appear to be derived.

2 The Family and Industrialization: Sociological Generalizations

THE central and most pervasive change in society during the past hundred and fifty to two hundred years has been the rapid development of industrialization and the complex changes of social organization which have accompanied it. During this period, Britain has been transformed from a predominantly agrarian and rural society to a predominantly and highly complex industrial and urban society. This 'industrial revolution' has, of course, not been confined to Britain; neither is it at an end. At the present time it is in full flood throughout the world, rapidly affecting more and more societies and transforming the entire human situation. It is worthwhile to remember, too, since industrialization in Britain and the West has been so closely associated with social evils, that if the radical changes it brings about can be adequately dealt with, industrialization is a good and desirable thing. As Professor Titmuss writes:[1]

... the world is increasingly an industrial world and dominated in its values and goals by problems of economic growth. Compared, for example, with the situation only fifty years ago, far more societies – in Asia, Africa, eastern and southern Europe, and Central and South America – are seized with the possibilities and potentialities of economic growth. To these peoples, economic growth spells a higher material standard of life, a release from the age-old passivity of agrarian poverty. Industrialization, as a means of raising the level of living, is thus something to be desired. This, I believe, is one of the most important facts in the contemporary social scene when looked at in international terms: the fact that a substantial part of mankind, compared with only an insignificant fraction at the beginning of this century, is aware or is becoming aware of the benefits of industrialization. In wanting to be industrialized, in thus wanting, as societies, to be radically changed, groups are, in this process of making community aspirations more explicit, becoming more aware of the gulf between what is and what might be in their conditions of life.

As one might expect, since industrialization is so central a factor in the modern world, many sociologists have attempted to make generalizations about the effects of industrialization upon the nature of the family. On the basis of these generalizations, and from a rather uncritical application of them, other, and less reliable, generalizations have been constructed, and moral judgements have been made. In this section we shall see what these generalizations are. The best way of doing this is to examine and compare some of the influential views which have been put forward. For our purposes, it seems sufficient to outline three of these.

(1) Frederick Le Play[2]

In a study of European families, Le Play offered a three-fold classification of family types: the Patriarchal family, the Stem-family, and the Unstable type of family.

The Patriarchal type of family, according to Le Play, depends upon a very stable occupation, and is almost always found in communities based upon an agricultural or pastoral mode of life. This kind of family is very firmly founded, possesses long-standing traditions handed down and shared by many generations, and is very faithful to these traditions, tending to establish its married children near the homestead in order to perpetuate the family and in order to protect the interests of all its members. If harsh fortunes and insecurity are encountered, this family has sufficient strength to resist change and disruption, and tends to migrate as a total unit to seek better conditions. The economic basis of such a family is characterized by stable self-sufficiency, by a simple but durable standard of life.

By contrast, the Unstable family has no permanent attachment to long-founded familial traditions. It has no roots in the past, and consequently can offer little resistance to changes forced upon it by changing external circumstances. This kind of family is characterized by its 'transience' when compared with the Patriarchal type. It comes into being with the marriage tie, increases in size as children are added, decreases in size as they become independent and leave the home, and passes out of existence when the original partners die. Because of the lack of traditional elements, there is nothing to bolster or support this kind of family in times of economic stress and depression. According to Le Play, therefore, it characterizes those societies which are 'suffering'.

The Stem-family is a type mid-way between the Patriarchal and Unstable types and embodies some features of both. The traditional core or 'stem' of the family is perpetuated by the inheritance of property, but to some extent property may be divided and some children of the family have to seek other occupations. The families of these children tend to approximate to the Unstable type, but in times of stress they can still fall back for some degree of support upon the 'stem' family.

Le Play himself was more given to concrete empirical investigation than to large-scale historical generalization. However, from interpretations of his work we gain the generalization that agricultural or pastoral societies, stable in most other respects, possess also stable self-sufficient families which are effective in providing extensive mutual aid amongst their members, and that the change to a complicated industrial and urban society brings into being an unstable kind of family unit which is relatively ineffective in meeting the forces of social change, which drifts, as it were, upon the tide of circumstances, and which is relatively incapable of sustaining any secure degree of mutual aid amongst its members.

(2) *Ralph Linton*

A similar picture has been derived from the work of Linton, in his book *The Study of Man*. Linton offers a classification of two chief types of family: the Consanguine type and the Conjugal type.

The Consanguine type of family is built upon the parent-child relationship (on blood-descent) in connection with which authority is very strongly stressed. The family is a descent-group through the male line which is firmly vested with authority. This family comprises, therefore, a nucleus of blood-relations surrounded by a 'fringe of wives' and others who are only incidental to the maintenance of the family unit. Clearly, such a family can become very large. In Old China, for example, such a family might comprise up to a hundred members. Again, this family possesses very firmly founded traditions and performs some functions very successfully; as, for example, the care of the aged, the general protection of its members, and the perpetuation of property. But this type of family is confined to a stable, agricultural kind of society. It appears to be too large, too self-contained, too clumsy, for modern industrial society which is based essentially upon contractual relationships, individually and voluntarily undertaken, and which requires a high degree of geographical and occupational mobility.

In the Conjugal type of family, the authority and solidarity of the family group reside solely in the conjugal pair. If effective and reasonably harmonious cooperation is to be achieved in this family, *neither* the male *nor* the female can be ignored. This type of family therefore consists of a nucleus of the husband, the wife, and their offspring, who are surrounded by a 'fringe of relatives' only incidental to the functioning of the family as a unit. This type of family is much more isolated from wider kinship relationships and tends to be 'economically autonomous'. That is, it has to try to provide responsibly for itself and has to fend for itself in meeting social problems. It cannot rely on the same degree of mutual aid as can members of the Consanguine family.

There is, clearly, considerable similarity between the points of view of Le Play and Linton. Agrarian communities possess 'Patriarchal', 'Consanguine' families which are firm in their traditions, stable, secure, and self-sufficient. Industrialization brings into being the 'Unstable', 'Conjugal' family which is small, transient, isolated, and relatively insecure. Other sociologists have used the term 'Authoritarian' family to indicate the clear-cut and firmly established authority found in the former types, and the term 'Democratic' to indicate the freer individual discrimination which characterizes the small, conjugal, unstable family.

(3) R. M. MacIver

These views are largely in agreement with, and – for our purposes – can be brought to a head in, the work of R. M. MacIver, and MacIver's views can best be presented by referring to his simple diagram reproduced on page 59.

This diagram makes it clear that MacIver, too, maintains that the family in the stable, traditional, agricultural societies of the past was a 'multi-functional' unit, fulfilling all the functions which he enumerates. This family was to a large extent self-governing, performed its own religious functions, was responsible for the education of its children, and was an economic unit which provided within itself for the health, recreation, sexual, and parental needs of its members and provided a home for them. With the development of complex industrialization, however, and the social policies devised within its context, the functions which he terms 'non-essential' came to be fulfilled by specialized agencies outside the sphere of the family. Agencies of the state increasingly took over governmental functions. Agencies of the Church took over religious functions. The formal system of publicly provided education relieved the family of its educative functions. The family ceased to be an economic unit, and manufacturing industries, with their highly specialized division of labour, removed work from the family and the home. The health of individuals came increasingly to be cared for by public health services of various kinds. Recreation, too, was no longer self-created and enjoyed in the home by the members of the family but was increasingly provided outside the family by agencies such as clubs and the cinema.

The family in modern industrialized society is therefore left with the three functions which seem to be 'essential' to it and which it alone can fulfil: the stable satisfaction of the sexual needs of the marital pair; the secure having and rearing of children; and the provision of a satisfactory home life. MacIver goes on to say that since the modern family is relieved of those functions which are 'non-essential' to it, its members can concentrate much more upon the satisfactory fulfilment of these 'essential' functions, and he thinks that the marital relationship, the care of children, and the provision of a home have been qualitatively transformed and improved in the modern family.

MacIver's analysis of the general historical trends of the changes in the family, as traditional agrarian societies have given place to highly complex industrial societies, is thus closely in agreement with the other generalizations we have mentioned.

In the next section, I want to consider how far these categories and generalizations can usefully be applied to a study of the family in 'pre-industrial' and 'industrialized' Britain, but before doing so there are two preliminary points I would like to make briefly here.

Firstly, from far too superficial an interpretation of these generalizations, and from far too uncritical an assumption that the 'traditional' family-types of the past were morally superior to the family of the present day, a whole plethora of views and moral judgements about the British family – which are, in fact, extremely questionable – have gained wide currency, if not acceptance, at the present time. It is frequently said, for example, that the family in modern Britain has been 'stripped of functions' which were fulfilled by the family of pre-industrial times. Because 'patriarchal', 'stable', 'authoritarian' families are assumed to have been morally superior and preferable to the 'unstable', 'conjugal', 'democratic' family of the present, it is often thought that the family of modern Britain has suffered some sort of 'decline' from the more noble and satisfactory family unit of pre-industrial, and even mid-Victorian times. 'Authoritarian stability' seems to be widely considered morally superior to 'democratic instability'. And thus, society is

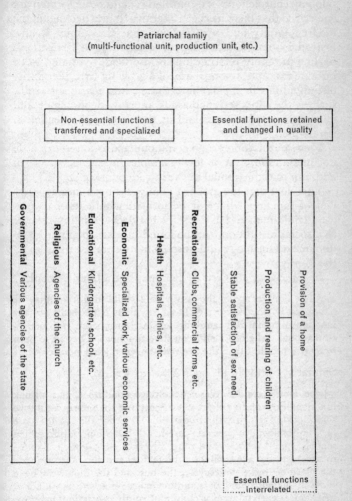

Emergence of the Modern Family Type

Patriarchal family
(multi-functional unit, production unit, etc.)

Non-essential functions transferred and specialized

Essential functions retained and changed in quality

Governmental Various agencies of the state

Religious Agencies of the church

Educational Kindergarten, school, etc.

Economic Specialized work, various economic services

Health Hospitals, clinics, etc.

Recreational Clubs, commercial forms, etc.

Stable satisfaction of sex need

Production and rearing of children

Provision of a home

Essential functions
.......interrelated.........

teeming with moralists – clergymen, social workers, some publicly conspicuous lords and ladies, and others – who are convinced that there has been a serious 'moral decline' in the modern family and who believe that the family is now in need, in some sense or other, of 'rehabilitation'. This moral decline in family relationships is also held, by many, to be but one example among many of a growing 'irresponsibility of individuals in the Welfare State', and many social ills, such as the supposed increase in juvenile delinquency and of crime in general, are laid at the door of the decline in family life.

Views of this kind are so commonplace as to require little documentation, but a few examples might be given in addition to those quoted in the introduction (p. 257).

The view that the modern family has been largely stripped of functions which it performed within itself in pre-industrial times, and in this sense has declined in importance as a social institution, can be found in many popular introductions to sociology and in some more detailed treatises on the family.

In *The Science of Society* by Rumney and Maier we read:

... The significance of the family as a social institution may be measured by the number of basic functions it performs ... the functions of the modern family are few. All but gone are its economic, educational, religious, and protective functions. They have been *transferred* * to the State, the Church, the school, and industry.[3]

Similarly, Sprott in his book *Sociology* writes:

The family, under Western cultural conditions, has shrunk functionally, a matter of greater importance than the quantitative shrinkage in the size of the household ... Gradually ... the state has undertaken to provide pre-natal attention, kindergarten schools, infant schools, and other forms of education; expanded medical services are available; the factory and the office provide the place of work; the bicycle, the bus, and the motor-car have burst the village boundaries and made accessible the new kinds of mechanical entertainment; clubs and youth associations cater for

* The italics in this and the following quotations are my own.

individual members of the household so that a new *anti-family* note is struck.[4]

In a book on *Problems of the Family*, W. Goodsell writes:

Within the last two generations ... the social and economic forces silently at work for more than a century *undermining the unity of the family* have effected transformations in the home dramatic in their rapidity and extent ... and the end is not yet. With a swiftness and inevitability that appals conservative minds, the process of individualization goes on; and, within a generation or two, 'father-power', even now shrunken to a mere shadow, may become little more than a name for an interesting historic phenomenon ... Such a rapid metamorphosis could not proceed without evoking gloomy prophecies from students of social institutions. Since the dawn of the twentieth century certain of these have foretold the doom of the monogamic family – its utter extinction or its transmutation into a form so different as to be unrecognizable.[5]

Another sociologist, Carle C. Zimmerman, in his book *Family and Civilization*, tells us that '... the struggle over the modern family and its *present rapid trend toward a climactic breakup* will be one of the most interesting and decisive ones in all history'. Having spoken of the '*decay*' of the family, Zimmerman continues:

That the family of the immediate future will move further toward atomism seems highly probable ... We are directly bound to reach the conclusion that unless some unforeseen renaissance occurs, the family system *will continue headlong its present trend towards nihilism*. There is as yet no force with sufficient power, knowledge, and interest to prevent this current trend. National states, except when urgently in need of supplies of cannon fodder, *have seemingly little interest in preserving the family*. Their social processes are in the hands of bureaucrats and the atomists. What knowledge exists of the family and its fundamentals is strictly limited to these two social classes and consists solely of a variegated amount of misinformation.[6]

No less a person than Bertrand Russell puts forward similar views. In *Marriage and Morals*, he writes:

The decay of the family in quite recent times is undoubtedly to be attributed in the main *to the industrial revolution*, but it had already begun before that event, and its beginnings were inspired by individualistic theory . . .

The position of the family in modern times has been weakened even in its last stronghold by the action of the state. In its great days, the family consisted of an elderly patriarch, a large number of grown-up sons, their wives, and their children – perhaps their children's children – all living together in one house, all cooperating as one economic unit, all combined against the outer world as strictly as the citizens of a militaristic modern nation. Nowadays the family is reduced to the father and mother and their younger children, but even young children, by the decree of the state, spend most of their time at school, and learn there what the state thinks good for them, not what their parents desire . . . So far from having power of life and death over his children, as the Roman father had, the British father is liable to be prosecuted for cruelty if he treats his child as most fathers a hundred years ago would have thought essential for a moral upbringing. The state provides medical and dental care, and feeds the child if the parents are destitute. The functions of the father are thus reduced to a minimum, since most of them have been taken over by the state . . .[7]

Russell also says:

. . . although the law means to uphold the family, it has in modern times increasingly intervened between parents and children, and is gradually becoming, against the wish and intention of law-makers, *one of the chief engines for the break-up of the family system.*[8]

The same view continues to be expressed in some current sociological writings. Thus Bryan Wilson, in an article on 'The Teacher's Role', says that the family in contemporary society is 'associationally in decline', and has become

. . . a highly specialized agency for affection. It has *lost* the other types of social activity *which were once so much of its activities* – the workplace, the dance hall, the youth club, and other institutions have taken over its economic and recreational functions, and its political and religious functions were *lost long ago.* Even the service-agency aspects of the family have declined now that more meals are consumed in schools and canteens, new materials have all but eliminated stitching and darning . . .

The family, he claims, is *less and less supported as a social entity* ... 'It has lost its mystery, its permanence, its persisting meaning and its appropriateness as a context in which the individual is identifiable.'[9]

As one would expect, the Churches have also been seriously preoccupied with the problems of the modern family, and there is much in their writings to suggest that they too are persuaded not only that the family has declined as a social institution in the ways mentioned above, but also that this decline is accompanied by, and is evidence of, moral deterioration.

The Roman Catholic Church has always maintained that the legal recognition of divorce is both an outcome of, and a subsequent cause of, moral depravity. Pius XII, for example, reiterates the statement of Leo XIII:

Legal recognition of divorce makes all the ties between husband and wife precarious; it wears down their goodwill for each other; it offers a dangerous temptation to infidelity; it interferes with the maintenance and education of children; it undoes all the bonds of home life; it sows the seeds of enmity between one family and another; it worsens and degrades the position of women, who are in danger of finding themselves deserted when the passions of their husbands have been sufficiently gratified. And since corruption of manners is the most powerful of all influences which work for the breakdown of families and for the decay of kingdoms, it is easy to see that divorce is the worst enemy to the welfare of either.[10]

Similarly, in *Casti Connubii* it is argued that since

... nothing contributes so effectively to destroying the family and so sapping the strength of the state as the corruption of morals, it is easy to see that divorce is the greatest enemy of the family and of the state. For divorce is the fruit of depraved public morality, and, as experience shows, it opens the way to the worst vices in private and public life. The seriousness of the situation becomes more evident still if it is considered that when once facility for divorce has been granted no curb will avail to restrict its use within definite and pre-arranged limits. The force of example is great, and the force of passion is greater still. Thus stimulated, the morbid desire for divorce will take hold on the souls of mankind, daily spreading like a contagious disease, or like a mighty flood which breaks its banks and overflows . . . Unless there is a change of heart, family and state must feel themselves in constant danger of a general and complete collapse.

In *Divini Illius Magistri*, on the Christian Education of Youth, also, our attention is drawn to '. . . the unhappy decline in home training at the present day'.

The Church of England has also voiced similar opinions. In the report of the Lambeth Conference of 1948, we read:

The truth is that public opinion in favour of the permanence of marriage has gravely declined, and divorce is ceasing to carry a public stigma . . . it cannot be denied that the effect of making divorce easy has been *to weaken the stability of marriage.*

The report goes on to advocate changes in public opinion and says:

. . . then a halt might be called to the *ever-increasing stream of divorce* which is in large measure due to the mean self-pity of parents who are determined to seek their own happiness even at the price of their children's distress.[11]

The Right Rev. Dr E. J. Hagan, in a chapter in the book *Rebuilding Family Life in the Post-War World*, says:

Though the family is one of the oldest and most fundamental of our institutions, there are manifest signs that it is now exposed to the danger of disintegration. The declining birth-rate, the decay of parental control, the increase of juvenile delinquency, and the growing prevalence of divorce are ominous indications of *a wide-spread revolt against the restraints, sacrifices, and duties of family life.*

The Rev. E. C. Urwin, a Methodist, writes as follows in a booklet on *The Way of a Christian Citizen*:

The searchlight of criticism is turned on the institution of the family and the forms in which it has come down to us. *The family is declared to have failed* both in its primary function of caring for children and as a source of human happiness. Old standards for right be-haviour between men and women are rudely challenged, and a new freedom in sexual relationships is boldly claimed. Religious sanctions of an earlier day are ruthlessly swept aside, and marriage has become increasingly secular, a matter of legal contract which can be dissolved when either party fails to adhere to the conditions laid down . . . Marriages are said to be breaking down at the rate of one for every ten new marriages contracted.

Also:

There is the residual moral problem of the quality of home life . . . *the moral failure of the home* confronts the state with its consequences – poverty induced by prodigality, drunkenness, and the like, juvenile delinquency and all the trail of the 'problem family', and the breakdown of family life by divorce and separation . . .

This list of indictments of the modern family could be extended indefinitely, but enough examples have been given for our purposes. Let us note clearly, however, that all these statements maintain that the modern family has deteriorated in functions, strength, and moral quality from some *better* state of affairs which existed earlier. One of my aims in this book is to suggest, and (I hope) demonstrate, that these views are naïve, insufficiently considered and, in large measure, false.

The second point is that whilst the sociological categories and generalizations we have mentioned are of use when one is comparing societies, and the family types within those societies, over large tracts of history, the uncritical employment of these categories in a study of the very short period from the times immediately preceding the rapid development of industrialization in Britain to the present day is such as to falsify the situation. If, for example, one is thinking of the family in traditional China, in ancient India, in the ancient Greek and Roman civilizations, then categories such as 'patriarchal', 'consanguine', and the like are useful approximations for purposes of classification (though they would need qualification even here). And the categories 'democratic', 'conjugal', 'unstable', do seem, by contrast, to indicate significant differences in modern family developments. But when one is seeking to characterize the family in Britain before the late eighteenth and early nineteenth centuries, the categories 'patriarchal', 'consanguine', 'multi-functional', are very misleading, as I hope to show. In fact, the uncritical use of inapplicable categories serves only to falsify our appreciation of this early 'pre-industrial' situation, and thus falsifies all our assessments of the changes which followed. In short, I shall try to show that the idea that, during the process of industrialization, the British family has been 'stripped' of its 'non-essential' functions turns out to be a spurious assertion. Indeed I shall argue that, on the contrary, the family is now responsible for the fulfilment of *more* functions than hitherto, and that it is more tightly and more responsibly woven into the wider structure of society than was the case before the full onset of industrialization. This view implies that if we have many problems in the modern family it is not because the family has lost many of its functions and has become socially redundant, but, on the contrary, because society now makes far more detailed demands upon it, and expects a responsible undertaking of far more social commitments. It also implies, though this is not clearly apparent at this stage, that these problems are not the outcome of moral decline but the outcome of moral improvements, together with the fact that we have not yet carried these improvements far enough.

I shall be concerned to elaborate and to try and demonstrate these points in what follows. In the next section I shall attempt to describe in sufficient (but by no means exhaustive) detail the specific nature and changes of the family in the context of industrialization in Britain. Only with such a historical perspective can the degree of utility and correct application of the sociological categories and generalizations we have mentioned be adequately shown. Only with such a historical perspective in mind can judgements of the family in contemporary Britain – moral or otherwise – be made with any degree of reliability.

3 The Family and Industrialization in Britain

THE more historians have come to know about the past two or three centuries in Britain, the less they have cared to speak too specifically about a clearly marked and definite period which can be designated as 'the Industrial Revolution'. It is now clearly known that extensive capitalistic enterprise had long preceded the industrial developments of the late eighteenth and early nineteenth centuries. Furthermore, as we have already said, the process of industrialization is, even now, far from being at an end. Historians have therefore come increasingly to question the utility and correctness of using the word 'revolution' to refer to a complex process of development which has lasted during a period of several centuries and which has, as yet, no determinate end.

In his lecture 'The Idea of the Industrial Revolution', for example, George Norman Clark wrote:

When the sequence of the great inventions was studied in its full social context, the late eighteenth century ceased to look like a new beginning. Each step was found to have been prepared for by many antecedent conditions. Mechanization was a response to market-requirements; its pace and range were determined by the state of scientific knowledge and the available skilled industrial man-power. No one industry, no one locality, had an entirely separate history of its own but none went forward exactly in step with the others. There were factories and wholly urban industries before the cotton-mills. When the relevant factors in commerce, in policy, in finance, in the metal-industries, were considered, it proved to be necessary to go back at least as far as the late seventeenth century if the story of the Industrial Revolution was to be told without beginning in the middle. The revolution was dissolved into the aggregate of countless changes, large and small, spread over a long period of time. No wonder historians mislike the phrase: to talk about a revolution which began in the seventeenth century and is still unfinished in the twentieth is making very free with words . . . From the chronological point of view the idea of the Industrial Revolution has collapsed.[1]

In his book on *The Industrial Revolution*, H. L. Beales expresses a similar opinion:

Certain ages in the story of civilization stand out so distinctly that historians have devised special distinguishing labels for them. Such labels are mere summarized descriptions of the most prominent features of these periods. They are never more than superficially adequate. Among these labels is the term 'the Industrial Revolution'.

. . . However appropriate the term revolution may be in the political field, it seems inappropriate in the economic. The changes which are described as revolutionary rose spontaneously from ordinary economic practice, and they were constructive in that they gave an increased power of satisfying wants. It is impossible, too, to find a beginning or an ending of these developments. The inventions on which rested the enlargement of industrial enterprise established themselves only slowly. New economic ideas, revised economic policies, modified economic relationships, all were shaped gradually. The extended probings of scholars who have followed in Toynbee's trail seem to show that there never was an industrial revolution at all. As Unwin put it: 'When, on looking back, we find that the revolution has been going on for two centuries, and had been in preparation for two centuries before that, when we find that both in its causes and its consequences it affects the lot of that three-quarters of the human race who are still farmers and peasants as profoundly as it does that of the industrial worker, we may begin to doubt whether the term Industrial Revolution, though useful enough when it was first adopted, has not by this time served its turn.'[2]

It is therefore completely impossible to speak about the family in Britain 'before' or 'after' the 'industrial revolution' in any clear and definite sense, and any generalization in these terms must obviously be faulty.

All that it seems necessary to say, for our own purposes,

however, is that in the period preceding the more rapid transformation of Britain to a predominantly industrialized and urbanized community, it would have been impossible to specify a 'type' of British family which was uniform amongst all the people of Britain and which was subsequently changed in a straightforward and uniform way by the effects of industrialization. Indeed, with considerable changes in agriculture which affected even the agricultural classes themselves differentially, and with an uneven development of capitalistic enterprise and incipient mechanization in various occupations, it is virtually impossible to generalize about 'the British family' at all during these times.

It is clear at least, however, that it would be necessary to distinguish between the family of the aristocracy and the family of the labouring classes – whether these latter were engaged in agriculture or in domestic industry. In many assessments of the changes subsequently brought about in the family, these earlier aristocratic and labouring families alike have tended to be glorified as the 'stable, consanguine, multi-functional' type of family we have already mentioned, and therefore something must be said briefly about their characteristics.

The Aristocratic Family

The aristocratic family was certainly based upon long-founded traditions, and rested fundamentally upon the custom and law of primogeniture whereby the family property – essentially the landed estate – was kept intact, and perpetuated in the family, by passing to the eldest son.

'The power of perpetuating our property in our families', said Edmund Burke, who rather liked the aristocracy, 'is one of the most valuable and interesting circumstances belonging to it, and that which tends the most to the perpetuation of society itself.'[3]

Not everyone, however, was convinced that the welfare of aristocratic families was synonymous with the wider well-being of society as a whole. John Wade in *The Black Book* expresses a somewhat different opinion:

What right had an assembly of half-civilized men, some five hundred years ago, to tie up the great estates of the country in perpetuity; to enact that, whatever changes of society might intervene, they should never be subdivided, nor severed from their lineal heirs as long as they endured? Was not this creating a monopoly?[4]

On the system of entails, the 'natural consequence of primogeniture', Wade says:

They are founded upon the most absurd of all suppositions, the supposition that every successive generation of men have not an equal right to the earth and to all that it contains; but that the property of the present generation should be fettered and regulated by barbarians who died centuries ago.

Clearly, there were differences of outlook upon the social benefits of primogeniture.

This method of perpetuating the estate raised the problem of providing for the younger children of the family. Chiefly, they found their way into the established professions: the army, the navy, the Church, the law, and the diplomatic and consular service.

The idea that these traditionally based families, constituting the governing classes of society, were models of moral rectitude, however, needs considerable qualification. Writing about their characteristics during the later part of the eighteenth century, when he is discussing a new humanitarianism which was emerging, J. H. Plumb says:

This new moral outlook as yet scarcely touched the aristocracy. For them it remained a golden age of power, privilege, and increasing wealth. And they became a little intoxicated with it all. About many of their lives there is a touch almost of fantasy. Many felt no necessity for restraint and allowed their personalities full indulgence. The more they indulged themselves, the more separated they became from the hardening, purposeful world beneath them. The great Whig families – the Cavendishes, Russells, Bentincks, Manners, and the rest – still had great political empires to rule which gave them a natural position of authority in government. This political responsibility helped to keep the world of society on an even keel and saved it from the utter futility of its

French counterpart, which it resembled more closely than most English historians have been willing to admit. There is the same grotesque extravagance, the same heightened class consciousness, the same feckless attitude to the crises in politics or society. The years before the wars with revolutionary France were the years of England's *ancien régime*.[5]

Writing of the way in which, later, the moral standards of the rising middle classes had their effect upon the 'overt sexual behaviour of the aristocracy', it is O. R. McGregor's view that the new sexual astringency of the middle classes was partly

. . . an evangelical reaction from those free and easy habits of the sceptical Whig aristocracy which led Lord Carlisle to remark, 'I was afraid I was going to have the gout the other day, I believe I live too chaste: it is not a common fault with me.' Nor was it, comments Lord David Cecil, 'a common fault with any of them . . . Even unmarried girls were suspected of having lovers; among married women the practice was too common to stir comment.' Sexual adventurousness was possible for a wealthy, primogenitary class that stuck to the rule of securing a male heir of known parentage; and its members were not often put to the inconvenience and expense of obtaining a divorce by Private Act of Parliament.[6]

McGregor gives the following instances of the 'occasional flickering light' of such aristocratic behaviour in the nineteenth century.

Under the aristocracy's control over appointments to the Queen's Household, the Royal Palaces sheltered easy-going habits of which their mistress never learnt. The Lord Chamberlain, Lord Conyngham, provided for his mistress by installing her as housekeeper in Buckingham Palace, and the Lord Steward, Lord Uxbridge, followed his thrifty example. Lord Palmerston, when Foreign Secretary and the Queen's guest at Windsor Castle, was in the habit of relaxing from cares of state in the bedroom of one of the Queen's Ladies of the Bedchamber. On one occasion he disturbed the wrong lady and her protests roused the Castle. This abuse of royal hospitality was the origin of Victoria's detestation of Palmerston.[7]

Another feature of aristocratic behaviour which accompanied the problem of providing adequately for younger sons was the practice of patronage, and this, at least in the opinion of many, was carried to the point of abuse. Describing the practice of patronage in ecclesiastical circles, John Wade tells us:

One of the greatest abuses in the disposal of patronage is *monopoly* in a few individuals of influence and connection, sharing among them the most valuable emoluments of the Church. In all spiritual offices and dignities there is a great difference in value, and also in patronage; and the great object of ecclesiastical intrigue is to secure not only the most valuable, but the greatest number of preferments. Hence arises the present disposition of Church property. Scarcely any preferment is held *single*, the sees, dignities, rectories, and vicarages being mostly held with other good things, and the most monopolized by the relatives and connections of those who have the disposal of them, namely, the Crown, the Bishops, and Aristocracy. The bishops are frequently arch-deacons and deans, rectors, vicars, and curates, besides holding professorships, clerkships, prebends, precentorships, and other offices in cathedrals. Their sons, sons-in-law, brothers, and nephews are also pushed into the most valuable preferments in the diocese . . .

The late Archbishop Sutton is an eminent instance of the perversion of ecclesiastical patronage. The Suttons remaining in the Church are very numerous; among seven of them are shared sixteen rectories, vicarages, and chapelries, besides preacherships and dignities of cathedrals. Of the *eleven* daughters of the archbishop several had the prudence to marry men in holy orders, who soon became amply endowed. Hugh Percy, son of the Earl of Beverley, married one daughter, and in the course of about as many years was portioned off with eight different preferments, estimated to be worth £10,000 per annum; four of these preferments were given in one year, probably that of the nuptials, and intended as an *outfit*. This fortunate son-in-law is now Bishop of Carlisle, to which see he was translated from Rochester. According to law he ought to have resigned all the preferments he held at time of being promoted to a bishopric; but somehow he has contrived to retain the most valuable prebend of St Paul's, worth £3,000 per annum, and also the chancellorship of Sarum. Another daughter of the archbishop married the Rev. James Croft, who is Archdeacon of

Canterbury, prebendary of Canterbury, curate of Hythe, rector of Cliffe-at-Hone, and rector of Saltwood – all preferments in the gift of the archbishop ... Archbishop Sutton kept a favourable eye towards *collaterals* as well as those in a direct line ...

So the details are enumerated, and Wade deals similarly with many families in the Church (readers will be reminded of Trollope's account of the clergy):

The Sumners, Bloomfields, and Marshes are growing thick in the Church calendar, but ... they have been too recently planted to have yet struck their roots wide and deep in the Lord's vineyard. The death of a bishop causes a movement in the Church, like a change of ministers in the state. Expectations are excited, numerous removes follow, the adherents and connections of the deceased are got out of the way as fast as possible, and all vacancies filled with the followers of the new diocesan. No regard is apparently paid to 'the faithful ordaining, sending, or laying hands on others'; the great object is to secure the dignities, the fat living, the fine living, the noble living to the *next of kin*.[8]

But Wade attacks the consequences of the system of primogeniture even more widely.

Other evils result from this feudal institution. Primogeniture enriches one, and leaves all the other members of the family destitute. Hence they are thrown, like mendicants, on the public for support; but they are unlike mendicants in this, that the public has no option whether they will support them or not. The aristocracy, usurping the power of the state, have the means, under various pretexts, of extorting for the junior branches of their families a forced subsistence. They patronize a ponderous and sinecure church establishment; they wage long and unnecessary wars to create employments in the army and navy; they conquer and retain useless colonies; they set on foot expensive missions of diplomacy, and keep an ambassador or consul, and often both, at almost every petty state and petty port in the world; they create offices without duties, grant unmerited pensions, keep up unnecessary places in the royal household, in the admiralty, the treasury, the customs, excise, courts of law, and every department of the public administration; by these and other expedients the junior as well as elder branches of the great families are amply provided for out of the taxes. They live in profusion and luxury, and those by whom they are maintained alone subsist in indigence and privation.[9]

This may well be a polemical and over-stated view, but it serves none the less to indicate the widespread nature of privilege and patronage attendant upon the form of the aristocratic family and the wide dominance such families enjoyed in the government (in the most detailed sense) of the land.

Little will be said subsequently about the history of the aristocratic family since it is not of central importance for our purpose, but that this family pattern was powerful, long-lived, and able to maintain its character and status relatively little changed throughout the earlier period of industrialization and throughout the greater part of the nineteenth century may be seen in the following facts.

In the New Domesday Book (prepared in 1874–5) it was made clear that a great proportion of the land of the United Kingdom was still in the hands of the aristocratic families and that the law and custom of primogeniture was chiefly responsible for this. The categories of landowners and properties taken into account, however, were such that the findings were open to various interpretations.

In his essay *On the Uses of a Landed Gentry*, Froude wrote:

The House of Lords does own more than a third of the whole area of Great Britain. Two-thirds of it really belongs to great peers and commoners, whose estates are continually devouring the small estates surrounding them. The remaining third, in and about the great towns, is sub-divided, and the sub-division is continually increasing, but the land there also is still falling mainly into the hands of the rich.

George C. Brodrick,[10] writing on 'The Law and Custom of Primogeniture', and having studied the matter in far greater detail, said:

With the new 'Domesday Book' in our hands, we can ascertain how the soil is actually distributed in every county of England and Wales, but how far the Law and Custom of Primogeniture may have contributed to produce this distribution remains even now a speculative question.

He goes on, however, with special reference to England:

Considering . . . that in most counties large estates predominate over small, and that large estates, by the general testimony of the legal profession, are almost always entailed either by will or settlement, while small estates, if hereditary, are very often entailed, there is no rashness in concluding . . . that a much larger area is under settlement than at the free disposal of individual land-owners.

He then gives the following figures:

It appears that although nearly a million persons may own the sites of their own homesteads, 42,524 is the extreme number of properties over 100 acres each, the number of their owners being considerably less; that nearly one-eighth of all the enclosed land in England and Wales is in the hands of 100 owners; that nearly one-sixth is in the hands of less than 280 owners; and that above one-fourth is in the hands of 710 owners. Nor is this all; for it must not be forgotten that among the Dukes and other great noblemen who head this territorial roll, there are several who also derive a vast rental from Scotland, Ireland, or the Metropolis, whereas among the nominal proprietors below one acre there is an indefinite number of mere faggot-voters.

Brodrick also gives figures of particular counties. Nearly three-fifths of Northumberland, for example, was in the hands of forty-four proprietors, the rest being owned by 10,036 owners who possessed, on average, less than one-seventh of an acre apiece. '. . . Nearly half is in the hands of twenty-six proprietors, and far more than one-seventh is in the hands of one proprietor, the Duke of Northumberland, who has also landed estates in other counties.' Similarly, in Nottinghamshire, 9,891 owners possessed, on average, about one-eighth of an acre apiece, whereas nearly two-fifths of the whole acreage belonged to fourteen proprietors, and over one-fourth to five proprietors.

'No other nation', says Brodrick, 'has adopted in its entirety the English right of Primogeniture – a right which could only have grown up in a thoroughly feudalized society, and could only have been perpetuated in a country where the feudal structure of society has never undergone any violent disturbance.'

Arthur Arnold, in his book *Free Land*,[11] begins by noting that according to the New Domesday Book 'we find 525 persons returned as owners of one-fifth of the area of the United Kingdom. These are the nobles, and with few exceptions, they are peers of Parliament.' He then claims, however, that this is an 'imperfect representation of the facts'.

He points out that, amongst other things, all forest lands and all woods, the vast areas of common and waste lands, the area of lands which were not rated for the relief of the poor, and building estates within the Metropolitan area were omitted from the acreage taken into account. Also, single nobles were represented as a number of landowners since their holdings in each county were entered separately. The Duke of Buccleugh, for example, was reckoned as 14 landowners, and 'there are 4 peers who are returned as 44 landowners, because these noblemen – the Dukes of Devonshire and Cleveland, the Earl Howe and Lord Overstone – each appear in the lists of 11 counties'. Arnold claims that, in this way, '525 nobles are in these books made into more than 1,500 landowners'.

Having taken these points into account, Arnold is of the opinion that four-fifths of the soil of the United Kingdom is owned by less than 4,000 persons. He qualifies this to guard against certain possibilities of error and claims finally that the number of owners possessing together four-fifths of the land 'must be much fewer than 10,000 and probably approaches more nearly to 5,000'.

Thus [he says] we arrive at the astonishing result that the representative owners of four-fifths of the soil of the United Kingdom could be placed within the compass of a single voice in one of the great public halls of the country. The landlords of more than 52,000,000 of acres might meet together in the Free Trade Hall of Manchester, and discuss the accuracy of these statements. Of this compact body of perhaps about 7,000 gentlemen, the House of Lords is strictly representative. With the exception of the Bench of

Bishops, who may be said to represent the lands of the Church – an extensive property including 496,046 acres of some of the best and most highly rented land in England and Wales – and of the Law Lords who, by their failures in regard to reform, have faithfully represented the legal system by which this aggregation of property is unnaturally maintained – that House is composed of about 500 of the largest landowners. The fundamental principle of the House of Lords is the representation of the distribution of land peculiar to Great Britain and Ireland. If that House now and then annexes a successful lawyer, or statesman, or soldier, he, as a rule, endeavours to justify the ennobling of his family by providing his less distinguished heir with the proper territorial qualification.

The continued power in the 1870s of aristocratic families, resting upon landed property and the system of primogeniture, is thus well substantiated.

With reference to the occupations of the children of aristocratic families, Helen Bosanquet gives the following figures, based upon an examination of Burke's *Peerage and Baronetage*, 1899.

	Elder sons	Younger sons
Army	325	269
Navy	8	39
Law	24	35
Church	5	30
Medicine	1	5
Civil, diplomatic, and consular service	15	18
Emigrated	1	2
Other professions or business	3	1
No calling	236	475
	618	874
Counted twice	7	7
	611	867

The same pattern of occupations is still to be found, then, towards the close of the nineteenth century. Whether the individuals having 'no calling' were engaged in lives of indolence or in employments of lower commercial status is unsure, but, as Helen Bosanquet puts it:

... the more sanguine view to take is, that many of them have entered into the arena of professional or commercial life in capacities which are not considered sufficiently dignified for the pages of a Peerage.[12]

On a more informal note, and giving this kind of continuity a flavour which brings it into the familiar atmosphere of our own times, Somerset Maugham writes in the beginning of his book, *The Summing Up*:

I have never kept a diary. I wish now that during the year that followed my first success as a dramatist I had done so, for I met then many persons of consequence and it might have proved an interesting document. At that period the confidence of the people in the aristocracy and the landed gentry had been shattered by the muddle they had made of things in South Africa, but the aristocracy and the landed gentry had not realized this and they preserved their old self-confidence. At certain political houses I frequented they still talked as though to run the British Empire were their private business. It gave me a peculiar sensation to hear it discussed, when a general election was in the air, whether Tom should have the Home Office and whether Dick would be satisfied with Ireland.

It might also be of interest to note the particular disadvantages for women in the form of the aristocratic family, which also seem to have continued through the nineteenth century. Helen Bosanquet writes:

But the most characteristic survivals of the feudal family are not the sons but the daughters of the house. In feudal days, as we have seen, there were three courses open to them: marriage, the cloister, or a corner of the eldest brother's house. In families where the aristocratic tradition still prevails, the position is not greatly altered. The main difference is, that at the death of the father it is more usual now for the unmarried daughters, like the young sons, to receive their portions and to seek a life of their own instead of lingering on in the ancestral home. For many of them, in the absence of either family cares or professional work, their solitary lives are little less confined and narrow than they would have been in a convent; and it is perhaps not wonderful that this generation has devised a modernized form of the convent in the great Anglican sisterhoods, where so many women now seek an imitation of the family and industrial life which they fail to find in the real world.

She then makes a comparison with the situation at the same time in France, drawing from the book *Home Life in France* by Miss Betham-Edwards, who claims:

To find out what becomes of the French demoiselle we must refer to statistics. In 1900 no less than sixty-four thousand women were immured for life within convent walls.

The family of the landed aristocracy was therefore very firmly founded in the continuity of property and enjoyed a position of exceptional power and privilege in the land, but to regard this family as the stable, self-sufficient, multi-functional family of the homestead in which all the members lived in close interdependence, performing useful tasks and being mutually responsible for a detailed satisfaction of needs, and – in addition – to regard it as a pillar of morality, is obviously going very far.

Perhaps W. L. Newman has as nice a comment to make on this kind of family as anyone:

It is claimed that entail and primogeniture encourage industry by investing the proprietor with great powers, and, still more, by establishing in the centre, as it were, of each family a magnificently fed and coloured drone, the incarnation of wealth and social dignity, the visible end of human endeavour, a sort of Great Final Cause immanent in every family. It may seriously be doubted, however, whether the ingenious contrivance produces its due effect. The object of adoration lies too often far beyond the reach of his younger brothers. Nor is his magnificent repose less suggestive of elegant idleness than work . . .[13]

The Family of the Labouring Classes in Agriculture

The family of the labouring classes as it existed before the full development of factory-organized industry has also tended to be glorified. It seems true to say that the working-class family, whether engaged in agriculture or in domestic industry, was a closely knit social and economic unit. Both men and women shared the productive tasks of the family and children were put to work at an early age, so that there was a definite division of labour within the family in the context of which the 'socialization' of the child – including such education, moral or otherwise, as may have been available – took place. Furthermore, such a family, in a community which lacked extensive geographical movement, would have its being within a particular locality and within a stable and extensive body of wider kinsfolk.

In agriculture, families with this kind of unity existed among large and small farmers and amongst the cottages, though small farmers frequently found it necessary to blend agricultural work with some form of domestic industry, and the cottagers found it necessary to work as day labourers in addition to working their own land. The lot of the cottagers depended upon the size of their holdings.

Dr Pinchbeck tells us that:

For a few pounds the squatters could build for themselves a hut on the edge of the common, around which they enclosed and cultivated a piece of the waste. The cottagers either owned or rented houses which carried with them certain common rights, such as the pasturing of specified animals and the right to cut turf from the waste; while in some cases common field rights also were obtained. There were therefore certain distinctions among the cottagers as a class. Some who owned or rented a few strips in the common fields were hardly to be distinguished from the small farmers. They worked their own land and only occasionally chose to become wage earners at such times as hay and harvest, when the rate of pay was higher than usual. Others with minute holdings, or merely a garden enclosed from the waste and possessing certain rights of common, were practically day labourers, and worked for wages whenever work was available, leaving their stock and allotment of land entirely to the care of their wives and children.[14]

Sometimes, therefore, the family income of the cottagers, consisting of the man's wages, the proceeds from the working of the land and the keeping of stock, and the earnings from occasional by-employments on the part of the cottager, his wife, or the family as a whole, was satisfactory. Sometimes, however, it was not.

While there were many who gained great advantages from the commons, conditions in the open village were by no means idyllic, and the existence of extensive commons did not necessarily mean that the poor as a class were better off. Contemporary accounts of unenclosed villages show that in addition to the prosperous cottagers, there were often many whose conditions were much less favourable and some living in extreme poverty. Conditions in the open villages varied; some commons were overstocked, particularly with sheep, and the cottager's cow in consequence was almost starved. Again there were many who never managed to afford a cow, and instances of high poor rates in open villages prove the existence of numerous poor even where there were extensive commons which might have been expected to maintain them without assistance. In some cases abuse of the commons indirectly increased the poverty and wretchedness in a village.[15]

To think, therefore, that all families employed in agriculture were characterized by unity and security in any satisfactory sense seems at the very least a one-sided and exaggerated interpretation of the facts.

Furthermore, as Dorothy George writes:

... it must not be forgotten that the agricultural labourer had long been 'the lowest member, the feet of the body politic', that by the great Elizabethan code anyone without means of subsistence could be forced to work for the farmer, and that compulsory apprenticeship to husbandry was the lot of the children of the destitute.[16]

This practice of apprenticeship was obviously and frequently disastrous for children.

Under the Elizabethan Poor Law the children of poor parents were to be apprenticed by being billeted compulsorily upon the ratepayers of the parish, to be farm servants or household servants, the boys till they were twenty-four, the girls till twenty-one or marriage; the usual age of apprenticeship was seven, but it was often younger. But since the chief desire of parish officers was to keep the poor rates low, and since (after 1691) the serving of apprenticeship in a parish for forty days was one of the ways by which a settlement was gained, it became usual to bind parish children to masters living in another parish. As Dr Burn the great authority on the Poor Laws, put it (in 1764), it was the object of the overseer to 'bind out poor children apprentices, no matter to who or to what trade, but to take especial care that the master lived in another parish'.

In an inquiry into the causes of the increase of the poor in 1738, we read:

A most unhappy practice prevails in most places to apprentice poor children, no matter to what master provided he lives out of the parish; if the child serves the first forty days we are rid of him for ever. The master may be a tiger in cruelty; he may beat, abuse, strip naked, starve, or do what he will to the poor innocent lad, few people take much notice, and the officers who put him out the least of anybody: for they rest satisfied with the merit of having shifted him off to a neighbouring parish for three or four pounds, and the duty they owe to every poor child in the parish is no further laid to heart.

The idea [says Mrs George] that the children of the poor shall live with their parents was as remote from the conceptions of the early eighteenth-century philanthropists as from the notions of Elizabethan statesmen.

It must not be forgotten, either, that important changes in agriculture took place during the eighteenth century which, especially, included the extensive development of the 'enclosure' movement. In general, these changes were to the advantage of large landowners and to the disadvantage of the small farmer, but the whole class of cottagers and 'squatters' on the common lands was harshly disrupted.

For large farmers and landowners [writes Dr Pinchbeck] this was a period of great prosperity . . . For others in the rural community came pauperization and acute distress, which might have been greatly mitigated if only those who stood to gain by enclosures had not been blind to a consideration of the rights of smaller men.

An enclosure commissioner reported:

Numbers in the practice of feeding on the commons cannot prove their rights; and many, indeed most, who have allotments have not more than an acre, which being insufficient for the man's cow, both cow and land are sold to the opulent farmer.

Mrs George gives an example of one such family which could not prove common rights.

It is described by William Hutton, who in 1750 lost his way and was benighted in crossing Charnwood Forest, five miles of uncultivated waste without a road. At last he found a building of some sort and induced its unwilling occupant to give him shelter. The man (in the dark) appeared tall and strong-built, but 'his manner was repelling as the rain, and his appearance horrid as the night'. Next morning he was revealed as 'formed in one of Nature's largest and coarsest moulds. His hands retained the accumulated filth of the last three months, garnished with half a dozen scabs; both, perhaps, the result of idleness.' His wife was 'young, handsome, ragged, and good-natured'. Three children and a hideous aunt made up the household, which represented for Hutton the most complete poverty and the most extreme idleness he had ever encountered. Both were at least partly due to a 'mob of freeholders' who had destroyed all the man's outbuildings, and so (presumably) prevented him from keeping beasts to graze upon the common. They had no candle, no fire beyond 'a glow which would barely have roasted a potato'. This truly hospitable family told him 'we have no eatables whatever, except some pease porridge, which is rather thin, only pease and water, and which we are ashamed to offer'. For bedclothes Hutton was given the wife's petticoat: 'she robbed her bed to supply mine.'[17]

Similarly, A. L. Morton writes:

... the cottagers found their rights even more ruthlessly violated. Few were able to establish any legal grounds for the customary rights over the village commons and fewer still received any adequate compensation for the loss of these rights. A whole class that had lived by a combination of domestic industry, the keeping of a few beasts or some poultry, and regular or occasional work for wages, now found itself thrown back entirely on the last of these resources ...

From about the middle of the eighteenth century the improvement in agricultural technique began to make it possible to economize in labour. Wages fell rapidly in relation to prices; in many parts cottages were destroyed or allowed to become ruinous and there was both a decrease in numbers and a decline in the standards of life of the majority throughout the greater part of rural England.[18]

An excellent account of the family conditions of the labouring people who had thus '. . . been reduced from a comfortable state of independence, to the precarious conditions of mere hirelings, who when out of work came immediately on the parish' is given by Dr Pinchbeck. One or two examples might be given from her examination of household accounts collected by Davies and Eden.

None of the families he [Davies] examined ate any fresh meat and few could afford more than one pound of bacon weekly. As for tea, the use of which by the poor raised such an outcry, as being an extravagant luxury, one or one and a half ounces of the poorest quality served a family for a week. Malt was so heavily taxed that small beer, which had hitherto been considered one of the necessaries of life, was quite out of reach, 'except against a lying-in or a christening'. None of the families spent anything on milk, which before enclosures had been a principal article of diet. By the consolidation of holdings many of the poor had been obliged to sell their cows, and the big farmers could not be bothered to retail small quantities of milk. Labourers complained bitterly that the milk they needed was thrown to pigs and calves. Weak tea, therefore, was the last recourse of the poor; without it they would have been reduced to bread and water. According to Davies's estimate a family needed at least £30 5s. a year to live in tolerable comfort and independent of parochial assistance; the average earnings of the families cited by him, however, were only £23, and the deficit had to be made good either by poaching, stealing, debt, or resort to the parish.[19]

Speaking of his parishioners, Davies himself said:

I could not but observe with concern their mean and distressed condition. I found them in general but indifferently fed; badly clothed; some children without shoes and stockings; very few put to school; and most families in debt to little shopkeepers. In short, there was scarcely any appearance of comfort about their dwellings, except that the children looked tolerably healthy. Yet I could not impute the wretchedness I saw either to sloth or wastefulness.[20]

Similarly, Dr Pinchbeck describes the findings of Eden[21] and others:

Eden's budgets and those quoted by other contemporaries tell the same tale of impoverished diet, inadequate clothing, and increasing debt. The accounts of a Northamptonshire family in 1791 show how difficult it was for a labourer to remain solvent even when the efforts of the entire family were exerted to the utmost. By means of task work and extra wages obtained by moving up the country with the harvest, the wages of the labourer and his son amounted to £29 18s., and an addition of £5 4s. earned by the mother and children at lace-making brought the total to £35 2s. 0d., which was considerably above the average of the Berkshire families. By cutting down the weekly expenditure for food, soap, candles, and thread for seven persons to 10s. 3d., or roughly 1s. 5d. per head, the yearly expenses were reduced to £33 16s. 8d., thus leaving a surplus of £1 5s. 4d. 'to lay up or expend in additional cloathes'. But as before, no fresh meat was bought; barley bread was eaten half the year; only 1s. 0d. a week was spent on tea, butter, and sugar; 12s. 0d. only was allowed for wood – the cost of which was £2 8s. 0d. if all had to be bought – and £2 0s. 0d. only was assigned for the clothing of the wife and children, a hopelessly inadequate sum to clothe six persons for a year. When the greatest industry on the part of all members of the family resulted in a bare subsistence and allowed no reserve for sickness, unemployment, and old age, there is little wonder that the labourer was overwhelmed by the hopelessness of his position. Sooner or later, in spite of the exertions of his family, the lack of reserves to tide over a difficult period would drive him to the parish. Faced with this fact, the incentive to continue the struggle for what seemed an impossible independence gradually weakened, and the parish became the first, instead of the last resource.[22]

Such material conditions, Dr Pinchbeck shows, brought about a general hopelessness and moral degradation among the labouring classes, a loss of self-respect and all desire for self-improvement, which had deleterious effects upon the quality of their home and family life.

The decline in housecraft, originally the outcome of economic causes, was aggravated by the general degradation, until finally it became itself a factor in a more complete demoralization. Unable to give warmth, comfort, and any variety of food to her family, the housewife lost interest and the condition of the home went from bad to worse. In despair the labourer sought comfort at the ale-house and his wife the solace of tea-drinking with her neighbours.

Towards the end of the eighteenth century attention began to be directed to the building of cottages, and the reports of the time serve to indicate the deplorable conditions in which the rural labouring-class family lived. In an 'Address to the Landowners of this Kingdom; with Plans of Cottages', the steward of the Marquis of Bath said:

Humanity shudders at the idea of the industrious labourer, with a wife and five or six children, being obliged to live, or rather to exist, in a wretched, damp, gloomy room, of ten or twelve feet square, and that room without a floor; but common decency must revolt at considering that over this wretched apartment there is only one chamber, to hold all the miserable beds of the miserable family.

In spite of some improvement in the provision of cottages on their own estates on the part of some landowners, these shocking housing conditions of the rural labouring families continued during the nineteenth century. Towards the middle of the nineteenth century, Dr Pinchbeck tells us:

Many labourers were still living in dilapidated stud and clay dwellings; the earthen and stone floors of more substantial cottages were frequently below ground level, and were perpetually damp and unwholesome; while in many cases little attempt was made to deal with drainage. It was rare to find more than two bedrooms even in better cottages; the great majority had only one. In the North, where cottages were provided rent free by the employer, they consisted generally of one room in which the whole family lived and slept, while the small recess behind the beds often housed a cow, a pig, and fowls . . .
Bad as these conditions were, they were rendered immeasurably worse by the evils of over-crowding. The pulling down of cottages, and refusal to build new ones to avoid settlements, resulted in several families crowding into the accommodation previously intended for one. At the same time young people who in earlier days would have lived in the farms as servants in husbandry or apprentices now remained in the cottages with their families. The Report of 1843 showed the extent to which the evil had grown. So

many cottages had only one sleeping apartment that it was a common thing for a big family to share a tiny room; in one case at Studely there were twenty-nine people living under one roof; and in a few rare cases, neighbours were found sharing their cottages – the females of two families sleeping in one, the males in the other. As a concrete example of what over-crowding at this period really implied, one of the Commissioners quoted the case of a family at Stourpain, in Dorset. Here in a room ten feet square, roofed with open thatch and only seven feet high in the middle, with one window of about fifteen inches square, slept a family of eleven in three beds; in one the mother and father and two young children; in the second two grown-up daughters and a younger girl, and in the third, four sons. This, he pointed out, was no exceptional case, but the *ordinary accommodation* of a labouring family in that district. Practically every room in the village was similarly crowded as a result of the lack of cottages. Until such conditions could be remedied it was useless for critics to speak of the demoralizing effects of field labour. The morality of women workers was very much the same as that of the agricultural classes generally, and if the standard was not very high, it was owing to poverty, the lack of education, and the housing conditions to which they were accustomed from infancy.[23]

It would be too long a story even to summarize here the changes in the employment of women and children due to this new position of the labouring families in agriculture; to describe, for example, the 'gang system' which developed in the eastern counties, where gangs of men, women, and children of seven years of age (and sometimes four, five, and six years of age) were accompanied to their work and supervised by an overseer, sometimes walking seven to eight miles each way and working from 8.30 a.m. to 5.30 p.m., and where 'by threats, and not infrequently by blows, women and children were urged beyond their strength, whilst the accounts of some gang-masters are sickening in their description of brutality and licence'; and to describe the other forms of women's employment.[24] It is sufficient to note, for our purposes, that these new patterns of employment, coupled with poverty and deplorable housing conditions, were such as to make a satisfactory family and home life impossible.

The long hours of labour of women outside the home, the inability of such families (because of economic pressure) to take advantage of such limited education as was available, the continual struggle against poverty and limiting material conditions, meant that there was both a prevailing ignorance among the rural labouring classes and a lack of opportunity to provide a satisfactory home for members of the family.

Writing of the standard of comfort of domestic life, Dr Pinchbeck tells us:

When a woman arrived home in the evenings after a long day in the fields there was housework, cooking, mending, and the children to look after. Sometimes the home was neglected and, if not, it often meant that the woman was over-worked. No hard and fast rule can be made about the neglect of the home. A married woman often did not start until 8 a.m. and returned before her husband to get the evening meal. Sometimes she had one day a week at home to attend to family affairs. There was certainly little time for cooking, but the lack of fuel and the low wages which provided little more than bread and potatoes did not in any case allow much to be done. Those who blamed women's agricultural work for the lack of domestic comfort failed to realize the actual position; *among the labouring classes generally there was the greatest ignorance of domestic economy*, and management in the homes of domestic workers was not generally better than that of those who were out all day. The lack of comfort was due, not so much to neglect – for many field workers were among the most industrious of their class – but to ignorance and long years of low wages and mean diet. Until the income of the labourer was raised there was little chance of improving the domestic comfort of the family.[25]

And, having pointed out the pressures which made it impossible for members of the family to take full advantage of educational provisions, she writes:

The result of this desultory attendance was that few women in the agricultural classes could read fluently or write correctly. The knowledge gained by many was so imperfect that it was quickly forgotten, and even those who were able to read and write a little were generally in a state of ignorance with regard to needlework, cooking, and domestic economy. Their homes for the most part were too poor to give any training in these matters, and the result was that only field work and the poorest kind of domestic service were open to them. Prevented by ignorance and lack of training from improving their position, the lives of too many children in the agricultural classes proved to be a mere repetition of those of their parents. More than anything else the lack of education was responsible for the continued exploitation of the labour of women and children.[26]

So much, then, by way of qualification of the notion of the 'stable, independent, self-sufficient, closely knit, multi-functional' family unit of the agricultural labourer with its high moral qualities. Now, what of the labouring family engaged in domestic industry?

The Labouring Class Family in Domestic Industry

Any detailed study forces upon us the same kind of qualification. It is true that the family engaged in domestic industry possessed a certain degree of independence and was a closely knit unit, but the hard conditions of family life and work, and the fact that this 'closely knit' character entailed a lack of independence of and consideration for its members – indeed, frequently a direct exploitation of some of its members – is often overlooked.

In the early nineteenth century, in various reports, comparisons were made between the conditions of domestic industry and those of factories, and these were frequently to the disadvantage of domestic industry. We can conjecture what family life was like amongst people engaged in such domestic industry from the reports concerning the crowded living and working conditions in the home, the long hours of labour, the degrees of poverty experienced by these families, and, perhaps especially, the employment of children, since it is too often, and incorrectly, thought that the harsh employment and exploitation of children began with the factory system.

In the Hand Loom Weavers report of 1840 we are told of the conditions of domestic workers in the silk trade:

In some parts of Bethnal Green and Spitalfields, inhabited by weavers, every house ought long ago to have been condemned and razed to the ground. Ruinous buildings, streets without sewers, overflowing privies and cesspools, and open ditches filled with a black putrefying mass of corruption infecting the air for miles around render the district the abode of disease and death. There are streets and alleys from which typhus fever is never absent the year round.

With regard to health, having seen the domestic weaver in his miserable apartments, and the power loom weaver in the factory, I do not hesitate to say that the advantages are all on the side of the latter. The one, if a steady workman, confines himself to a single room in which he eats, drinks, and sleeps, and breathes throughout the day an impure air . . .

And with reference to work in the Lancashire cotton trade:

Weaving as a domestic occupation, among the hand-loom cotton weavers, is carried on in circumstances more prejudicial to health, and at a greater sacrifice of personal comfort, than weaving in any other branch. The great majority of hand-loom cotton weavers work in cellars, sufficiently light to enable them to throw the shuttle, but cheerless because seldom visited by the sun. The reason cellars are chosen is that cotton requires to be woven damp . . . Unhappily the medium which might be preserved without injury to the constitution and which is preserved in the best power-loom factories, the impoverished hand-loom weavers are obliged often to disregard. I have seen them working in cellars dug out of an undrained swamp; the streets formed by their houses without sewers and flooded with rain; the water therefore running down the bare walls of cellars and rendering them unfit for the abode of dogs or cats. The descent to these cellars is usually by a broken step ladder. The floor is but seldom boarded or paved . . .

One commissioner reported that

. . . domestic happiness is not promoted but impaired by all the members of a family muddling together and jostling each other constantly in the same room.

Dr Pinchbeck, having pointed out that domestic circumstances may have deteriorated to some extent with the increasing population of the early-nineteenth-century towns, none the less claims that 'the deplorable state of housing and the almost complete lack of sanitation must have prevented the conditions of domestic work from ever having been really good'. In the late eighteenth century, she tells us, labourers' cottages were completely unsuitable for industrial work, and were 'so constricted in size they "seemed to be built as discouragements to industry", and were "fit for nothing but eating and sleeping places".'

Again, she writes:

In the eighteenth century they [the hand-loom weavers] appear to have worked long though irregular hours; the standard of living was simple and diet extremely frugal. Meat was not part of the regular fare until the prosperous days at the end of the century, and then only for a brief period. Close confinement in the loom must always have rendered the trade an unhealthy one, although among country weavers the effects were probably mitigated by outdoor exercise. But housing conditions were such that a family of six to eight persons often inhabited a two- or three-roomed cottage which had to serve as workshop as well as home. A weaver's cottage in the West Riding described in 1842 consisted of two rooms and a pantry for a family of man, wife, and nine children . . . In the room above where the weaving was carried on in a space about twelve feet square were three looms, three old oak stump bedsteads, three chests, 'one oak chest used as a child's bedstead', and a quantity of lumber. Five of the children worked as weavers in this restricted space and yet this was not the home of a weaver in poor circumstances. As for the weavers in the towns, many of them lived and worked in a single room amidst horribly insanitary surroundings.

Long hours of work in living and working conditions such as these were bound to have grave consequences for the health of domestic workers.

It has been said [writes Mrs George] that the domestic worker produced what he liked and worked when he liked. Of course he was more of a free agent in many ways than the factory worker. When he worked at home his hours were his own concern, but if he was to earn a living wage they were certainly long. Arthur Young remarked in 1767 that the Witney blanket-weavers could make from 10s. to 12s. a week – high wages for weaving, which was a badly paid occupation – but their hours were from four in the morning to eight at night, and in winter they worked by candle-light. This working by candle-light must have had disastrous effects on the eyesight of the workers. Hutton notes that stocking weavers all go to the workhouse 'when they cannot see to work'.

Dr Pinchbeck also writes that

Confinement in small, low, over-crowded rooms, not only in childhood, for adults frequently assembled together for company and to share light and warmth, was in itself often a prelude to disease; but this was not all. Injurious effects often resulted from the actual occupation.

She goes on to give details of the widespread diseases of the eyes, of the lungs, and of physical deformities due to the posture of the workers such as the 'slight distortion of the spine' which was 'almost universal' amongst lace runners. Injurious results also followed from the position adopted by the hand-loom weaver: 'consumption and diseases of the stomach frequently resulted from the constant pressure against the beam of the loom.' Weavers frequently worked in a bad atmosphere since to open their windows might allow the air to affect the colours of their work, and one old weaver, speaking of her own childhood, said: 'I have often been tied to the loom all day and ate my meals as I sat there.'

Some idea of the unhealthy conditions of work endured by domestic workers might be gained from the evidence of Elizabeth Sweeting, an embroiderer, given to the Children's Employment Commission, 1843:

Has worked at the trade twenty-one years; when she first began it was a very good business; begins at 7 a.m., and leaves off about 10 p.m. but oftener later than earlier; often works till between 11 and 12, has done so all the winter round; in the summer generally begins between 5 and 6, and works as long as it is light, often till 9 p.m.; often does not go to the bottom of the yard for a week; can earn by working hard 7d. a day ... Finds her sight very much affected, so much so that she cannot see what o'clock it is across her room; the work affects the stomach and causes a pain in the side; often makes her light-headed; generally the lace runners are crooked, so that the right shoulder is higher than the other . . . Her candles cost her about 8d. a week.

The difficulties of achieving anything approaching a satisfactory family life under domestic conditions of this kind may be seen in the following report on married women working in their homes as embroiderers when their wages were low:

One of the most appalling features connected with the extreme reduction that has taken place in the wages of lace runners, and the consequent long hours of labour, is that married women, having no time to attend to their families, or even to suckle their offspring, freely administer opium in some form or other to their infants, in order to prevent their cries interfering with the protracted labour by which they strive to obtain a miserable subsistence.

The practice, which is most common, usually is begun when the child is three or four weeks old; but Mr Brown, the coroner of Nottingham, states that he knows Godfrey's Cordial is given on the day of birth, and that even it is prepared in readiness for the event. The extent to which the system is carried may be judged of by the fact, expressly ascertained by this gentleman, that one druggist made up in one year 13 cwt of treacle into Godfrey's Cordial – a preparation of opium exclusively consumed by infants. The result of this terrible practice is that a great number of infants perish, either suddenly from an overdose, or, as more commonly happens, slowly, painfully, and insidiously. Those who escape with life become pale and sickly children, often half idiotic, and always with a ruined constitution.

The evils of child labour are often associated only with the factory system, but they were already present in domestic industry. In knitting and embroidery, glove and button making, children were regularly employed at the age of six and seven, and sometimes earlier. In straw-plaiting, children began work at four and were earning a regular wage at the age of six. In work on pillow lace children were employed at the age of three. Commenting on these facts, Dr Pinchbeck writes:

In one extreme instance . . . a child of four years had been drawing lace for two years, and was then working twelve hours a day with only a quarter-of-an-hour interval for breakfast, dinner, and tea, and never going out to play. Two other children in the same family, aged six and eight, were working fifteen hours a day. Among the little embroiderers some were so young when they began that they could not reach the regular frame on which the work was stretched and were therefore obliged to stand.

She concludes:

The exploitation of child labour in the early factories has probably caused more horror and indignation, and rightly so, than any other feature connected with the industrial revolution; but it is not so often realized that the same sort of thing was equally characteristic of the older domestic industries. Hidden away in cottages, where they attracted no attention, thousands of children in rural areas worked factory hours every day, under conditions which were often no better than those which aroused so much feeling in industrial centres.

Dunlop, in *Apprenticeship and Child Labour*, writing of child labour in domestic industry, said: 'The creatures were set to work as soon as they could crawl and their parents were the hardest task-masters.'

In the *Life of Crompton* by French, we are given the following description of the boyhood experience of Crompton:

I recollect that soon after I was able to walk I was employed in the cotton manufacture. My mother used to bat the cotton wool in a wire riddle. It was then put into a deep brown mug with a strong ley of soap and suds. My mother then tucked up my petticoats about my waist and put me into the tub to tread upon the cotton at the bottom. When a second riddleful was batted I was lifted out, it was placed in the mug and I again trod it down. This process was continued till the mug became so full that I could no longer safely stand in it, when a chair was placed beside it and I held on by the back . . .

The truth is that in the closely knit unit of the family engaged in domestic industry, in which every member had his or her own 'economic function', women and children were often harshly exploited. L. C. A. Knowles claims that:

... it must be remembered that family work and the family wage often meant that the members of the family were sweated by their parents or the wife by the husband.

And again:

Much of the success of the domestic worker depended on the fact that he could control a cheap labour supply in his wife and children or apprentices. This laid the work of wife and children open to considerable sweating and very long hours were worked.

In the report of the commission which inquired into the conditions of children in factories, in 1833, it was said:

It appears that, of all the employments to which children are subjected, those carried on in the factories are amongst the least laborious and of all departments of indoor labour amongst the least unwholesome. Hand-loom weavers, frame-work knitters, lace runners, and work people engaged in other lines of domestic manufacture are in most cases worked at an earlier age for longer hours and for less wages than the body of children employed in factories.

J. H. Plumb also writes:

The worst conditions, long hours, irregular payment of wages, truck, gross exploitation of female and child labour, were to be found in small-scale and domestic industry.

And a report of 1866, supporting legislation with reference to the employment of children, claimed:

... more especially would such legislation be a protection and benefit to the great numbers of very young children who in many branches of manufacture are kept at protracted and injurious labour in small, crowded, dirty, and ill-ventilated places of work by their parents. It is unhappily to a painful degree apparent through the whole of the evidence that against no persons do the children of both sexes need so much protection as against their parents.

It is worthwhile to remark that this complete preoccupation with work in the home made anything approximating to education in the family almost impossible.

Attempts to establish ordinary schools in districts where domestic industries were carried on [writes Dr Pinchbeck] frequently ended in failure, and most children depended entirely on Sunday Schools for such education as they received. The result was that for the most part they grew up in complete ignorance of everything but their particular industry. The popular outcry against the factory system, that it prevented girls acquiring any knowledge of domestic duties, was a mere repetition of an argument that had long been used against all domestic industries in turn. The girl who had been perpetually spinning from infancy knew nothing, it was asserted, but how to turn her wheel; in straw districts girls were 'ignorant of everything but straw plaiting'; buttonmakers were 'so ignorant as scarcely to know how to wash and mend their own clothes', and lacemakers were 'helpless' and 'good for nothing else'.

It appears then that, far from providing the basis for a satisfactory family life, the conditions of domestic industry were such as positively to produce an ignorance of even the most rudimentary arts of homemaking.

By and large, the above illustrations are all with reference to domestic industry in the textile trades, but conditions were equally bad in other domestic industries such as nail making and the metal trades. Hutton, describing the shops of nail makers in the region of Birmingham in 1741, said: 'In some of these shops I observed one or more females, stripped of their upper garments, and not overcharged with their lower, wielding the hammer with all the grace of the sex. The beauties of their faces were rather eclipsed by the smut of the anvil . . .' and he goes on to describe the extreme poverty of families so employed. A sub-commissioner, reporting on the nail makers in 1840, said: 'I never saw one abode of a working family which had the least appearance of comfort or of wholesomeness, while the immense majority were of the most wretched and sty-like description.' He gave the following description of their conditions of work:

The best kind of these forges are little brick shops of about fifteen feet long and twelve feet wide, in which seven or eight individuals constantly work together, with no ventilation except the door and two slits, or loop-holes, in the wall; but the great majority of these work-places are very much smaller (about ten feet long by nine feet wide), filthily dirty, and on looking in upon one of them when the fire is not lighted presents the appearance of a dilapidated coal-hole or little black den. They are usually ten or twelve inches below the level of the ground outside, which of course adds to their slushy condition, since they can never be cleaned out except by a shovel, and this is very seldom, if ever, done. In this dirty den there are commonly at work a man and his wife and daughter, with a boy and girl hired by the year. Sometimes there is an elder son with his sister, and two girls hired; sometimes the wife (the husband being a collier, or too old to work, has taken to drinking, or is perhaps dead) carries on the forge with the aid of her children. These little work-places have the forge placed in the centre generally, round which they each have barely standing-room at an anvil; and in some instances there are two forges erected in one of these shops ... The effluvia of these little work-dens, from the filth of the ground, from the half-ragged, half-naked, unwashed persons at work, and from the hot smoke, ashes, water, and clouds of dust ... are really dreadful.

Conditions were similar in other metal trades and the level of home life was deplorably low. Writing of conditions in the Black Country, Dr Pinchbeck says:

... here, too, Godfrey's Cordial, the drug indispensable to working mothers, was freely administered to quieten young children. Throughout the district 'Godfrey's' stood 'in a great jug' on every chemist's counter.

The family in domestic industry was thus no bed of roses, and it is difficult to see how anyone could regard it as being an embodiment either of closely knit stability in any desirable sense of the word, or of high moral qualities. And in what sense such a family could be regarded as a 'multi-functional' unit is extremely difficult to see.

It is true that, with some qualifications (since the work of many such families was to some degree dependent upon the merchant or capitalist for whom it was undertaken), this family could be regarded as an economic unit. But, as we have seen, the characteristics of this 'economic unit' were far from being such as to provide the basis for a satisfactory family life. And what of the rest of the 'non-essential functions' which were mentioned earlier? In what sense could such a family seriously be said to 'govern' its own destiny and its own affairs? What 'religious functions' were performed within it? How far could this family seriously be said to provide for the 'health' and 'recreation' of its members? And to turn to the 'essential functions': how is it possible to maintain that this family provided a satisfactory home for its members; satisfactory upbringing for its children; the achievement and maintenance of a satisfactory marital relationship between man and wife? And what of the 'educative' functions of this family?

Gaskell (1833), who is inclined to idealize the domestic family, echoes what we have already said and tells us that the domestic worker could 'seldom read freely or write at all' and was 'in ignorance of almost everything but the common arts of life'. Gaskell, however, appears to approve of this state of affairs, and dislikes the urban artisan who 'shows a very high order of intelligence, seeking his amusement in the newspaper, the political union, or the lecture-room . . .' and whose factory conditions give him 'every facility for secret cabal and cooperative union . . .' The educative functions of the family in domestic industry could have been little more than a harsh initiation through early employment into the narrow confines of an impoverished and unhealthy mode of life. The 'socialization' of the child, far from giving it values and modes of behaviour appropriate to any kind of independent citizenship in the wider society, could have done nothing but press the child, without choice, into the miserable and inescapable conditions which faced it.

And what of the variety and interest of the work of the domestic family which is sometimes compared favourably with the dull monotony of later factory routines? What of the joy and pride taken in his work by the domestic craftsman? Dorothy George gives us the following answer:

Many people seem to assume that the hand-loom weavers of the old days were in the position of the modern hand-loom weaver. It would be as reasonable to suppose that an Elizabethan ale-house resembled the modern inn or tea-shop which calls itself 'Ye Olde Englyshe Hostelrye'. The weaver as a rule was achieving mass-production by dint of unremitting bodily effort. He worked to a standard, often on warps given out by his employer. The element of design did not even come into the work of the Spitalfields brocade weavers, though these were highly skilled men. The employers, who were usually the mercers, gave out the patterns, sometimes copied from French materials, sometimes supplied by the professional pattern-drawers of Spitalfields . . .

The theory that the domestic weaver felt a creator's pride in his work started, I think, in the days of Ruskin and William Morris. Doubtless some did – pride in work, mercifully, is not uncommon – but it seems unlikely that the average weaver, toiling hour after hour, throwing the shuttle backwards and forwards on work which was monotonous and exhausting, had the reactions which would satisfy a modern enthusiast for peasant arts.

When we think of joy in work as being the happy lot of the domestic worker of the past it is as well to remember Francis Place's account of the 'sickening aversion' to his work which periodically overcame every working-man, and drove him to idleness and drink, a phenomenon which explains a good deal of the social history of the eighteenth century, and which is to be explained at least in part by the normal monotony of work.[27]

Enough has been said to show that the picture given to us by social historians of the family of the labouring classes before the full development of large-scale industrialization is not one that can be held up as a paragon of morality and happiness from which our contemporary family has suffered a depressing 'decline'. This kind of family does not fit at all happily or satisfactorily into the general categories of the 'patriarchal', 'consanguine', 'multi-functional' family types which were outlined earlier. Those functions which are held to be 'non-essential' now must also have been 'non-essential' then, for the family could not, by any stretch of the imagination, be said to have performed them in any satisfactory sense, and even the 'essential' functions must have been sadly lacking in their degree of fulfilment.

Bearing these characteristics of the 'pre-industrial' family in mind, what now can be said of the more immediate impact upon the family of nineteenth-century developments?

THE IMMEDIATE EFFECTS OF INDUSTRIALIZATION

During the nineteenth century there was a growth in the scale of industrial enterprise, accompanied by the development of factory organization in industry, and a rapid, continuing growth in the size and congestion of industrial towns situated about the sources of power and raw materials. Some consequences for the family of this expansion of industry and urbanization seem fairly clear. Little will be said about the aristocratic family, as this was probably the least affected. It seems plausible to say that the aristocratic families suffered no serious lowering of status and power in the face of the rising influence of the manufacturing middle classes until at least the 1870s and 1880s when the nature of property settlements was probably affected in the context of the growing importance of commercial capital and falling farm rents; but enough has been said earlier to show that the pattern of the aristocratic family was but little changed even by the end of the nineteenth century.

The immediate consequences of industrialization were most marked in connection with the family of the rising middle classes and the family of the wage-earning classes.

The Middle-Class Family

A qualitatively new kind of family – that which we now call the 'Victorian Middle-Class Family' – came into being among the manufacturing middle classes. The new manufacturers and entrepreneurs enjoyed a considerable advance in wealth, social status, and influence, and, with the changing franchise, a growing degree of power and importance in government. The development of factory organization led to a separation of the business establishment from the home. The business establishment was the 'undertaking' of the man, and the woman was relegated to domesticity.

With increasing wealth and the easy availability of labour, there was an extensive employment of domestic servants in the middle-class household. Desiring to give their children an education which was not then provided by the state, the middle classes supported and, in supporting, changed and extended, the 'public school system' (which, as we now know it, was essentially a nineteenth-century development) and sent their children to boarding schools to receive an education and 'finish' befitting the new 'leaders of society'. In the context of these developments, the husband and father became the central economic provider, the supreme, dominant, authoritative figure of the family. The wife and mother, no longer intimately involved in the business 'undertaking', was confined to domestic life, and, with domestic servants, became more and more of a 'functionless' member of the household – one ornament amongst others in the pattern of conspicuous consumption – totally subjected to the authority of her husband. She had, with slight qualifications, no rights to property, education, or occupation. Children, too, were expected to be submissive to the authority and dignity of father and home and the respectability of the family station. They were to be obedient, to be 'seen and not heard'.

L. C. A. Knowles writes as follows:

It is interesting to speculate on the effect of this increase in numbers and wealth of the middle classes on their women-kind. Among the bigger merchants, manufacturers, and shop-keepers the place of business became divorced from the home. The man began to sleep in one place and work in another. When the home was over the shop the wife helped to run the business and marriage was as much a business partnership for the shop-keeping and trading class as it was for the artisan or farmer classes. With her isolation from the business the woman lost touch with affairs, her life became narrowed, if less strenuous. When the children went to a boarding school 'to finish', or grew up, she was often condemned to a tea-drinking, fancy-work, district-visiting existence after a few crowded years of child rearing.

With the growth of capital it became far more difficult for a woman to set up in business for herself, and as she was deprived of any training in business, widowhood often meant ruin. She could not 'carry on' when the man died. It is often not realized how prevalent widowhood is. According to the Census of 1901 one woman in every eight over the age of twenty was a widow.

While many women no doubt lost greatly by being 'out of business' others probably greatly preferred the gentility of being a 'real lady' with nothing to do. This explains the early Victorian women, the viragos and the sugary nonentities as portrayed for us in Dickens, Thackeray, or Miss Austen. The viragos were women who had not sufficient outlet for their energies, and the Esthers and Amelias were so genteel and amiable and futile because they had never been brought into contact with real life.[28]

In an invaluable book on family law (1857–1957), Professor Graveson writes:

The English family in the years following Waterloo differed in many ways from the family of today. The husband was in a real sense the authoritarian head of the family, with very extensive powers over both person and property of his wife and children. But his right to inflict personal chastisement on his wife had greatly declined in importance since Blackstone had described it half a century before as one which the lower orders took seriously and cherished dearly. On marriage husband and wife became for many purposes one person in law . . . In the words of a late nineteenth century lawyer, 'The Creator took from Adam a rib and made it Eve; the common law of England endeavoured to reverse the process, to replace the rib and to re-merge the personalities.' On marriage all the wife's personal chattels became the absolute property of the husband, while the husband could dispose of the wife's leasehold property during his life and enjoyed for his own benefit her freehold estate during her life. Subject to the institution by the Court of Chancery of what was known as the wife's separate estate in equity, the married woman, both physically and economically, was very much in the position of a chattel of her husband.

Commenting on this position of women, John Stuart Mill had asserted:

. . . there remain no legal slaves except the mistress of every house.[29]

These authoritarian characteristics of the family were

firmly cemented by religious beliefs. The family was almost a 'religious corporation' within which the dignified authority of the father and the submissiveness of wife and children were sanctified and sustained. The life of the family was attended by regular family prayers. The unity of the family was written into the source of its sanctity – the family Bible. And the outward dignity and responsibility of the family was manifested in the Sunday occupation of the family pew. As O. R. McGregor puts it with reference to the status of husband and wife:

Outside the family, married women had the same legal status as children and lunatics; within it they were their husband's inferiors. By marriage they moved from dependence on fathers or male relatives to dependence on husbands. To the Pauline conclusion that they two shall be one flesh, the Victorians added the explanation: 'and I am he'.

These social distinctions and religious beliefs entailed very specific sexual ideas and discriminations. The husband was expected to be sexually virile; such virility was an essential ingredient of the nature of the 'male' (it is worthwhile remembering the wide practice of prostitution which was a concomitant of these sexual proprieties, an aspect of Victorian life which is often forgotten). On the other hand it would have been morally repugnant to the Victorians to think that women themselves also had sexual feelings and sensual needs. A woman submitted herself to a man in marriage because this was, if somewhat shameful and certainly unmentionable, none the less the divinely ordained way in which babies had to be produced. But that women had actual sexual desires which ought to be taken into account in what we would now call 'marital compatibility' was an idea foreign to these family relationships.

It is very largely on the basis of an idealization of this Victorian middle-class family (which has lived with us until recently, and the ghost of whose drawing-room we can enter occasionally even now), just as upon an idealization of the 'pre-industrial' family, that many adverse criticisms of the contemporary British family are made. It is therefore important to see that it possessed many shortcomings. The 'stable and authoritative' characteristics of the family, though possessing some virtues, were far from denoting an altogether morally defensible state of affairs.

The Family of the Wage-Earning Classes

The conditions of labouring families in agriculture and domestic industry had been so poor materially and morally that it has been much disputed whether factory organization and urbanization in the nineteenth century lowered these standards at all. Indeed, the new industrial methods were such as, in the long run, to improve them. But, as McGregor insists, the emphasis here must be on the term 'long run'.

In the long run mechanization offered an emancipation permanently denied to the domestic worker. But it was a long run advantage. If industrialism gave workers, especially skilled workers, rising wages and improving standards of life, it brought with it also new insecurities and a new environment. The rapid growth of towns posed problems of health and housing, government and police, on a scale that no community had ever faced before. Industrialism did not, as Gaskell, Disraeli, and Engels thought, impoverish and demoralize workers whose lives and families had been secure and carefree in an earlier age. In 1850 it was keeping alive three times as many people as in 1750 at a standard of living certainly no lower than that endured by their progenitors. The real disaster was that too many of the old ways of life and working survived to be carried forward, together with those that had been revolutionized by machinery, into the age of great cities.[30]

Writing about conditions in the early years of the nineteenth century among the bulk of the population which fell within the category of the 'labouring poor', J. H. Plumb comments:

It is difficult to judge whether their lot grew better or worse with the intensification of the industrial revolution . . . But the poorest working men today would have found the lives of their ancestors almost unbearable. The hours of work were fourteen, fifteen, or even sixteen a day, six days a week throughout the year except for

Christmas Day and Good Friday. That was the ideal time-table of the industrialists. It was rarely achieved, for the human animal broke down under the burden; and he squandered his time in palliatives – drink, lechery, blood-sports.

It was impossible [he concludes] for most of them to live a life of more than bare subsistence and the natural disasters of their personal lives – unemployment, sickness, death of the bread-winner – left families in utter destitution, for the state had little conception of social service; its only answer for unemployment and poverty was the workhouse.[31]

The conditions of life and work in the new factories, in the mines, and in the growing industrial towns were so unbelievably bad, by modern standards, that even to read about them is a harrowing and nauseating experience. They have been so well chronicled that there is little need to dwell upon them. A few instances will suffice.

The working and social conditions of men, women, and children employed in mines were known to be deplorable long before the nineteenth century. Wesley, for example, writing of the people round Huddersfield in 1743, said: 'A wilder people I never saw in England. The men, women, and children filled the street as we rode along, and appeared just ready to devour us.'[32] Of the colliers in an area near Newcastle, he wrote that they were 'such as had been in the first rank for savage ignorance and wickedness of every kind'.

In the early nineteenth century, R. Ayton[32] described a visit to the Whitehaven mines in 1813, writing that he saw a horse drawing a line of baskets

... driven by a young girl, covered with filth, debased and profligate, and uttering some low obscenity as she passed by us. We were frequently interrupted in our march by the horses proceeding in this manner ... and always driven by girls, all of the same description, ragged and beastly in their appearance, and with a shameless indecency in their behaviour, which awe-struck as one was by the gloom and loneliness around one, had something quite frightful in it, and gave the place the character of hell. All the people whom we met with were distinguished by an extraordinary wretchedness; immoderate labour and a noxious atmosphere had marked their countenances with the signs of disease and decay; they were mostly half naked, blackened all over with dirt, and altogether so miserably disfigured and abused, that they looked like a race fallen from the common rank of men, and doomed, as in a kind of purgatory, to wear away their lives in these dismal shades.

The workers, says Ayton, were regarded as

. . . mere machinery, of no worth or importance beyond their *horse* power. The strength of a man is required in excavating the workings, women can drive the horses, and children can open the doors; and a child or a woman is sacrificed, where a man is not required, as a matter of economy, that makes not the smallest account of human life in its calculations.

The Report on Mines of 1842 revealed the conditions of employment in the mines in all their horrifying detail. At the age of six many girls spent the entire day in darkness attending to ventilation doors. Young boys, girls, and women dragged heavy loads of coal along passages to the bottom of the pit shaft. 'Chained, belted, harnessed like dogs in a go-cart, black, saturated with wet, and more than half naked, crawling upon their hands and feet, and dragging their heavy loads behind them – they present an appearance indescribably disgusting and unnatural,' wrote one commissioner in describing some examples of this kind of work. In some pits girls were working in passages no more than 26 inches high, and some adult women worked in passages no higher than 30 inches. The commissioner claimed that, in Lancashire, workers pulled their loads – often in passages no higher than 20 to 30 inches – for an average distance of four to six miles a day. In East Scotland girls and women between the ages of six and sixty or more carried to the surface of the pit, on their backs, burdens of coal varying in weight between $\frac{3}{4}$ cwt and 3 cwt. One woman, giving evidence, said that she made forty to fifty journeys a day to the surface carrying 2 cwt as her burden, 'Some females carry $2\frac{1}{2}$ to 3 cwt but it is over-straining.' The commissioner wrote: 'However incredible it may appear, I **have** taken the evidence of fathers who have ruptured themselves from straining to lift coal on their children's backs.'

Long hours of labour in such wretched conditions resulted in such desperate fatigue that time spent at home was chiefly time spent in recuperation. A woman working in the West Riding said: 'The work is far too hard for me; the sweat runs off me all over sometimes. I am very tired at night. Sometimes when we get home at night we have not power to wash us, and then we go to bed. Sometimes we fall asleep in the chair.' Many girls and women claimed that Sunday (their one day of rest) had to be spent in bed. Needless to say, physical deformities and diseases were common. The quality of family life of many mine-workers may be conjectured from the effects of the harsh conditions of work upon childbirth. Many women suffered distortions in the spine and pelvis which led to great difficulties in childbirth. Many pregnant women worked in the mines up to the day of the birth of their children. One woman stated that she 'had a child born in the pit' and brought it up the pit shaft in her skirt. Many said that a high proportion of the children born while they were in the pits were still-born. One, after thirty-three years of employment in the mines, said that a vast number of women

. . . have dead children and false births, which are worse, as they are not able to work after the latter. I have always been obliged to work below till forced to go up to bear the bairn, and so have all the other women. We return as soon as able, never longer than ten or twelve days; many less, if they are much needed. It is only horse work, and ruins the women; it crushes their haunches, bends their ankles, and makes them old women at forty. Women so soon get weak that they are forced to take the little ones down to relieve them; and even children of six years of age do much to relieve the burden.

Such conditions of work unavoidably led to a widespread brutalization of social life. Dr Pinchbeck writes:

Deplorable as were the effects of underground employment on women's health, the brutalizing conditions and vicious depravity with which they came in daily contact had moral results which were far more serious in so far as they affected not only the character of the women themselves but the standards of the whole mining community. Of the women in the West Riding the commissioner wrote: 'They are to be found alike vulgar in manner and obscene in language: but who can feel surprise at their debased condition when they are known to be constantly associated, and associated only, with men and boys, living and labouring in a state of disgusting nakedness and brutality . . .?' All classes of witnesses, indeed, bore 'the strongest testimony to the immoral effects of their employment'. The tragedy was that 'the savage rudeness' of the upbringing of girls in the pits was not counteracted by any system of education. Introduced into the pit in early childhood before any correct ideas of conduct could be formed, they gradually grew accustomed to obscene language, vice, and debauchery, and knew no impropriety in them.

Concerning child-labour in the factories, one writer said:

In stench, in heated rooms, amid the constant whirling of a thousand wheels, little fingers and little feet were kept in ceaseless action, forced into unnatural activity by blows from the heavy hands and feet of the merciless over-looker, and the infliction of bodily pain by instruments of punishment invented by the sharpened ingenuity of insatiable selfishness.[33]

Gibbins, the author of a popular educational text late in the nineteenth century, wrote that children

. . . were fed upon the coarsest and cheapest food, often with the same as that served out to the pigs of their master. They slept by turns and in relays, in filthy beds which were never cool; for one set of children were sent to sleep in them as soon as the others had gone off to their daily or nightly toil.* There was often no discrimination of sexes; and disease, misery, and vice grew as in a hot-bed of contagion. Some of these miserable beings tried to run away. To prevent their doing so, those suspected of this tendency had irons riveted on their ankles with long links reaching up to their hips, and were compelled to work and sleep in these chains, young

* Readers may be reminded of similar conditions in Zola's *Germinal*, the account of a mining community in France.

women and girls as well as boys suffering this brutal treatment. Many died and were buried secretly at night in some desolate spot, lest people should notice the number of the graves; and many committed suicide.[34]

Lest these statements might be thought too severe, we might also take the word of a reformer who generally stands in high repute among modern readers. Lord Shaftesbury, speaking to the House of Lords in 1873, said:

Well can I recollect in the earlier periods of the factory move-ment, waiting at the factory gates to see the children come out, and a set of sad, dejected, cadaverous creatures they were. In Bradford especially the proofs of long and cruel toil were most remarkable. The cripples and distorted forms might be numbered by hundreds, perhaps by thousands. A friend of mine collected a vast number together for me; the sight was most piteous, the deformities in-credible. They seemed to me, such were their crooked shapes, like a mass of crooked alphabets.

Writing to a Mr May (1 March 1833) about factory labour, Southey remarked: '. . . the slave trade is mercy compared to it.'

And Gibbins commented:

The spectacle of England buying the freedom of black slaves by riches drawn from the labour of her white ones, affords an interest-ing study for the cynical philosopher.

The conditions of the rapidly expanding towns, too, were almost unbelievably bad. L. C. A. Knowles writes:

People massed in numbers on the coal and iron areas, the new canals enabled them to get food and fuel even in regions like the North where the food supply was scanty. As there were no building restrictions houses were run up in any fashion, often back to back. There were no regulations to prevent over-crowding or cellar dwellings. There were no arrangements for disposing of the house refuse which always accumulates, ash-pits overflowed and spread a 'layer of abomination' about the courts and streets; there was no system of main drainage and no system of sanitation. An adequate or clean water supply laid on to the houses was rare until after 1850. The wells and pumps were quite insufficient for the numbers who wished to use them and the river and canal water was polluted and disgusting.

Needless to say, in these conditions, diseases – typhus, small-pox, fevers of all kinds – were rampant, and, says Knowles, 'on top of the dirt and disease came the great difficulty of the disposal of the dead'. Two instances are given from the Report on the State of Large Towns and Populous Districts, 1844.

Of Clerkenwell, it was stated positively that 'the shallow well water of the parish received the drainage water of Highgate cemetery, of numerous burial grounds, and of the innumerable cesspools of the district'.

The burial ground in Russell Court, off Drury Lane, where the whole ground by constant burials had been raised several feet, was a 'mass of corruption' which 'polluted the air the living had to breathe and poisoned the well water which in default of other they often had to drink'.

The new characteristics of factory employment and urbanization, then, although not necessarily reducing their material standards of life, were such as to compel the families of the labouring classes to live in working, housing, and sanitary conditions of the utmost squalor.

Another point of importance to be noted is that, in the context of these conditions, the working-class family also suffered a new disunity resulting from the fact that, now, men, women, and children had to go out of the home to undertake their separate kinds of work. To go out to work, in terms of modern standards, does not seem a sufficient factor to cause any disunity of the family, until it is remembered that in these early times men, and those women and children in employment, alike worked for very long hours – as many as sixteen hours a day, sometimes more – and with no regulated meal-times or 'break-times' as we now know them. It is difficult to see, therefore, how the 'home' could have been more than a place in which to eat and sleep. Also, because of this plentiful supply of labour, wages were low and poverty persisted.

It is, of course, impossible to generalize about the standards of morality of the people doomed to live in these wretched conditions, but it is feasible to suppose that among many members of the working population they were very low. Describing some of the districts of London later in the nineteenth century, the author of *The Bitter Cry of Outcast London* wrote:

'Marriage,' it has been said, 'as an institution, is not fashionable in these districts.' And this is only the bare truth. Ask if the men and women living together in these rookeries are married, and your simplicity will cause a smile. Nobody knows. Nobody cares. Nobody expects that they are. In exceptional cases only could your question be answered in the affirmative. Incest is common; and no form of vice and sensuality causes surprise or attracts attention. Those who appear to be married are often separated by a mere quarrel, and they do not hesitate to form similar companionships immediately. One man was pointed out who for some years had lived with a woman, the mother of his three children. She died and in less than a week he had taken another woman in her place. A man was living with a woman in the low district called 'The Mint'. He went out one morning with another man for the purpose of committing a burglary and by hat other man was murdered. The murderer returned saying that his companion had been caught and taken away to prison; and the same night he took the place of the murdered man. The only check upon communism in this regard is jealousy and not virtue. The vilest practices are looked upon with the most matter-of-fact indifference. The low parts of London are the sink into which the filthy and abominable from all parts of the country seem to flow. Entire courts are filled with thieves, prostitutes, and liberated convicts. In one street are 35 houses, 32 of which are known to be brothels. In another district are 43 of these houses, and 428 fallen women and girls, many of them not more than 12 years of age. A neighbourhood whose population is returned at 10,100, contains 400 who follow this immoral traffic, their ages varying from 13 to 50 . . .[35]

Those who bemoan the immorality of the present day might ponder a little upon such an account of the past.

The rapid developments of manufacturing industry and urbanization, then, did not bring about, for the wage-earning classes, a total worsening of an earlier family life which had been altogether more satisfactory, so much as a new and terrible aggravation of existing evils. There was a new degree of family disunity in a situation where new insecurities, new harshnesses of work and environment, new miseries, were added to the old.

SUBSEQUENT CHANGES AND SOCIAL REFORMS

The early evils attendant upon the extension of industrialization and urbanization, together with the continuation of the evils of domestic industry within this context, forced themselves increasingly upon public attention, and social policies of various kinds were gradually formulated to deal with them. These policies, reflected in reports, parliamentary debates, and legislation, together with other political, economic, and social changes, and together with significant changes in knowledge and currents of opinion, all had their continuing effects upon the nature of the middle-class and labouring-class family alike, and were responsible for gradually shaping the family in Britain as we now know it. The central fact to be borne in mind throughout this analysis is that most of the policies which will be mentioned constituted *reforms* of earlier and undesirable conditions; they were *improvements* of a wretched state of affairs. The characteristics of the modern family will thus be seen to be the result of these considerable moral improvements, and more will be said about this later.

Clearly it is impossible in a short space to trace the history of these policies and changes in anything like full chronological detail, and in any case this is not really necessary for our purpose. I propose, therefore, simply to enumerate as clearly and briefly as possible those elements of change and reform which have taken place during the nineteenth and twentieth centuries, and which can be supposed to have had the most important influences upon the characteristics of the family.

Woman and Child Labour

The appalling conditions of the employment of women and children were perhaps the first major evils to engage public attention. Regulations were gradually introduced limiting their hours of work and, indeed, removing children to a considerable extent from the labour market. During the first thirty years or so of the nineteenth century a series of measures improved matters to some extent in the cotton factories, but a commission set up in 1832 revealed the continued existence of many abuses: for example, that some children (many of eight years of age) worked for as long as nineteen hours a day (3.00 a.m. to 10.30 p.m.); that if they were five minutes late they lost a quarter of a day's pay; that there was no compensation for accident; that factory conditions resulted in the considerable malformation of children; that many overseers used whips; and many other repelling details. The first genuine factory act, providing among other things, a new and effective inspectorate came in 1833. The employment of children under the age of nine was prohibited. The working time of children under thirteen was limited to forty-eight hours, and that of children under eighteen to sixty-nine hours a week. Ten years later, the hours of work of women, and of boys under the age of eighteen, were limited to eleven hours a day, and later still there was a reduction to ten hours. After the Ten Hours Act, and with the Acts of 1850 and 1853 which established a normal day for woman and children in the textile trades, the ten-hour day became a reality. During the same period, the horrors of woman and child labour in mines and collieries were fully exposed. Henceforth it was forbidden to employ women in the mines, and children could not be employed before the age of ten, and then with a regulation of the number of hours worked.

Women and children of the labouring classes were thus to some extent freed from burdensome toil, and this, surely, must be regarded as a substantial moral improvement. They were now given a certain amount of leisure during which attention could be paid to home-making and family life; and it is worthwhile noting that this was made possible by industrialization whereas it had been impossible under the domestic system.

Like all improvements, however, this, too, had its problematic side, in that women and children became economically dependent upon the husband and father of the family to a far greater degree, reducing the extent to which they contributed to family resources, since their wage-earning capacity was now greatly diminished. It had the effect, also, of placing the burden of provision for the family chiefly upon the wage of the man. Both the degree of dependence of the wife upon the husband, and the degree of responsibility for family maintenance on the part of the husband, were therefore enhanced.

Education

The illiteracy and ignorance of the labouring classes, and the great need for a publicly provided system of education were also matters of concern early in the nineteenth century. Education began in a very limited way with the activities of the voluntary (church) societies, but the proposals for a national system of education were feared by many and were bitterly opposed by the Churches throughout the nineteenth century[36], so that substantial reform was much delayed. In 1870, however, locally elected school boards were set up which, after 1880, could compel attendance to the age of thirteen, and the age of compulsory school attendance, as we know, has been continually extended to the present school-leaving age of fifteen.* This process of educational reform, considerably extended during recent years (i.e., since the 1944 Act), clearly reflects one of the most important changes brought about during the past hundred years, and that is *the greatly improved status of the child* in British society: a decided improvement which, presumably, no one would deny. But, again, this extension of the period of compulsory school attendance has had the effect of increasing the extent to which the child is an economic liability to the family; it has

*Now (1972) raised to sixteen.

increased the 'maintenance costs' of the family which have to be borne by the husband's wage. It might also be mentioned that by an Order of Council in 1870 patronage was abolished and recruitment to almost all branches of the Civil Service became, compulsorily, subject to competitive examination. (A year later the purchase of commissions in the army was abolished.) Thereafter, recruitment depended upon demonstrated merit rather than privilege, so that the provision of education for their children became of more urgent importance for members of the more privileged classes of society.

The Status of Women

A third important change and reform which has gradually been brought about during the later nineteenth and early twentieth centuries is the considerably improved status of women.

We have seen that in the Victorian middle-class family women were the inferiors of men, were subjected to their authority in many ways, and were confined to a domesticity in which, with the easy availability of much domestic service, they were rendered practically functionless. Both within and beyond the home their range of activities was extremely limited. Women increasingly rebelled against this subservient position and the enforced narrowness of their lives. Increasingly, they voiced their desire to be considered as equal partners in marriage with their husbands. They insisted upon their right to equality of status with men in educational and occupational opportunity, and demanded recognition as responsible citizens of the community. Growing more articulate and forceful, this rebellion gave rise to the Feminist Movement. After much struggle, aided by the demands and experience of the First World War, in which the contributions of women were positively needed and valued, women ultimately achieved political equality with men, and, at least to a greatly increased extent, a measure of effective social equality with men. Women have thus come to possess recognized rights in own-

ing and managing property, in educational opportunity, in
entry to many occupations, and in sharing to the full extent
that their inclinations, abilities, and circumstances will
allow in public, social, professional, and wage-earning work.
Women now enter marriage on a completely voluntary
basis and on an equal footing with their male partners. This
improved status has meant, of course, that many women no
longer wish to be confined to a life of child-bearing, child-
rearing, and domesticity, but wish – sometimes instead,
sometimes in addition – to go out to work and to pursue
whatever aims and interests they might have.

Improved Standards of Living

Although it cannot be said that the nineteenth and twentieth
centuries have witnessed a consistently improving standard
of material well-being, continuously progressive and uni-
formly shared by all sections of the population, there
is no doubt that the later developments of industrialization,
increasingly guided and controlled by government policy,
have made possible and have actually brought about a
substantial improvement in the material standards of living
for the large majority of people in society, if not for the
whole community. These improved standards of living
have also had their effect upon the family and upon family
attitudes.

Firstly, with an increased standard of living, with a
growth in the competitive spirit of 'getting on', and with
the widening of opportunities which people possessed, the
handicaps of a large family became increasingly apparent.
Married couples realized – especially in view of the increased dependence of women and children upon the man's
wage which was mentioned earlier – the extent to which a
large number of children handicapped them in achieving
the new standards of which they were becoming increasingly
aware. They came to realize the improved standards of life
they could themselves enjoy if they limited the number of
children they had. This may be considered a selfish attitude,
but clearly unselfish considerations were also involved. With

the improving standards of living, the expectations and concern of parents for the future of their children also became more demanding. Parents aimed at providing for their children better opportunities than they themselves had enjoyed, and this they could do only if they limited their number of children in accordance with their circumstances. It seems plausible to argue, also, that as the standards of life enjoyed by young men and women during their *single* life improved, the higher became the standards they desired in their *married* life.

If young people become accustomed to high standards of clothing, entertainment, and the like, when they are single, they will obviously be reluctant to enter upon a married life which entails a sudden reduction in these standards. Young married couples will therefore be inclined to limit the number of children they have. This consideration, too, clearly constitutes a motive on the part of the woman to go out to work as soon as possible to maintain her accustomed standards. Furthermore, it also gives the husband a motive to approve of this action on her part, and there is little doubt that husbands are now far less reluctant that their wives should go out to work than they have been in the past.

Though young people, as well as others, may be inclined to limit the size of their families, it would be a great mistake, however, to think that their desire to marry and found families has at all diminished. On the contrary, the increasing prosperity of the past few decades has been paralleled by an astonishing and continuing increase in the proportion of the population who are married, and particularly is this true of the younger age-groups. In the Statistical Review for the year 1957,[37] for example, the Registrar General wrote:

As a result of the maintenance of relatively high marriage rates generally and in particular of an increase in the numbers of marriages at young ages, the proportion married has increased in all age-groups except the oldest where the effect of mortality in terminating marriages operates to a material extent. The following figures are illustrative:

Proportion married per 1,000 in each age-group

Age	Males			Females		
	1931 (census)	1951 (census)	1957 (estimate)	1931 (census)	1951 (census)	1957 (estimate)
15–24	70	125	149	140	272	305
25–34	640	720	748	658	798	844
35–44	855	862	869	752	820	857
45–54	847	877	882	720	759	786
55–64	795	850	862	619	624	650
65 and over	619	664	685	341	352	342

In the youngest age-group 15–24 the proportion married has been, since 1931, doubled for men and more than doubled for women.

In the latest detailed statement of this kind (Statistical Review 1964, Part III, p. 17) this picture of more and earlier marriage is given even stronger emphasis. The Registrar General comments:

During the last thirty years there has been a striking change in the marriage of British and other Western European women. For centuries Western Europe had the lowest and the latest marriage rates of the world, but since about 1935 the pattern has changed.

And to illustrate this, he compares, in the following table, the proportions of women of different ages who had ever been married at the 1921 and the 1961 censuses.

Proportions of women ever-married per 1,000 population, England and Wales

Year	Age-group						
	Under 20	20–24	25–29	30–34	35–39	40–44	45–49
1921	18	274	590	740	796	821	832
1961	66	579	844	890	902	903	895

In 1964, the age of marriage was also compared for women and men. Over thirty years, the marriage rate for spinsters at all ages had risen markedly, but (for example) for women under 20, it had increased to over $2\frac{1}{2}$ times the rate experienced in 1938. For men, too, the rate had increased over-all, but for men under 20 it had *quadrupled*, and for men between 20 and 24 it had increased by 80 per cent.

The following table and graph are of interest in showing very clearly the details of both women and men between the ages of 16 and 30.[38]

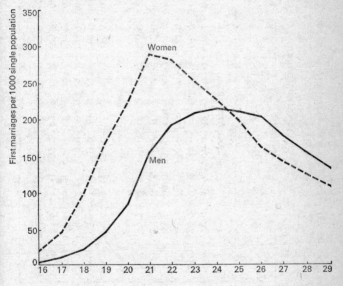

First marriage rates of men and women under 30 years of age, 1964, England and Wales

The graph shows particularly clearly the younger marriage pattern of women, and also its much more well-defined peak.

The Registrar General also commented on the decline in the rate for women under 19 between 1963 and 1964, suggest-

First marriage rates per 1,000 by sex and single years of age 16 to 29, 1951, 1956 and 1961-64, England and Wales

| Year | Age at marriage | | | | | | | | | | | | | |
| --- | 16– | 17– | 18– | 19– | 20– | 21– | 22– | 23– | 24– | 25– | 26– | 27– | 28– | 29–30 |
| BACHELORS |
1951	0·2	2·0	8·6	19·9	48·9	109·0	143·0	177·2	192·4	190·4	179·0	169·2	159·1	146·8
1956	0·4	3·5	14·3	28·7	65·8	137·9	172·6	206·9	216·0	214·8	203·6	177·7	165·9	151·1
1961	1·0	5·9	18·9	45·3	83·5	152·2	175·6	207·2	222·9	213·2	199·7	178·3	155·8	135·8
1962	1·0	6·0	19·5	43·5	82·5	154·9	179·6	202·7	221·0	214·6	195·3	173·2	155·3	133·2
1963	1·1	6·3	20·8	45·6	80·9	156·1	184·1	205·3	218·0	215·4	194·6	172·3	152·3	135·0
1964	1·1	6·5	21·3	46·7	83·2	156·0	191·0	207·7	216·0	213·6	202·7	178·6	154·8	134·5
SPINSTERS
1951	5·8	22·9	64·7	120·5	171·4	250·0	241·9	235·3	218·5	193·6	171·3	148·7	133·9	114·6
1956	9·8	34·3	86·5	153·5	213·2	299·6	290·3	277·2	242·6	217·8	198·5	155·0	135·7	116·0
1961	19·1	47·3	100·0	170·4	222·6	304·9	282·3	262·2	233·1	208·8	178·5	153·2	131·2	112·9
1962	18·5	47·8	100·3	166·6	222·3	295·3	287·5	260·5	232·7	201·7	171·7	150·7	129·5	112·0
1963	18·2	46·9	100·9	167·6	217·5	297·7	273·2	257·4	229·2	199·3	167·3	147·0	127·2	114·5
1964	18·1	45·5	98·2	168·4	224·7	289·0	283·9	251·9	227·6	197·4	166·6	145·9	124·6	109·6

ing that changes in the rate of population growth were beginning to have some influence:

The fall in marriage rates for the youngest group of women may well be associated with the demographic history of these age-groups. Women aged 16–19 in 1964 were born in 1945–48, years which included the post-war 'baby boom'. An analysis of 1961 showed that brides aged 16–19 were then marrying men aged 21–23 on average (i.e., 4–5 years older than themselves). In 1964, men aged 21–23 were the survivors of the considerably smaller number of births than those which produced the women aged 16–19 in 1964 . . .

The suggestion is, therefore, that these young women are likely to experience lower marriage rates than their predecessors because of the comparative shortage of husbands of what has been hitherto the most popular age. It will be necessary to follow a larger part of the marriage history of these generations before a full assessment can be made of the way this basic lack of balance is resolved.

In 1967, describing the changes that have occurred in marriage patterns since the 1930s as 'fundamental', the Registrar General again wrote:

In this country . . . marriage age has fallen to a point lower than at any time since the beginning of civil registration. Propensity to marry has also increased very markedly. In England and Wales in 1961 almost 90 per cent of the female population aged 45–49 years were currently or had been married and this proportion is bound to increase since in later years this figure has already been exceeded in the younger age-groups. Further, the mean age at marriage for spinster brides fell by about two years from 24·41 to 22·54 years between 1951 and 1966; this compares with little or no change in the mean age marriage during the period 1901–1935, when it stood between 25·37 and 25·81 years.

And since 1966, with slight variations, the number of marriages each year, and the rate of persons marrying per 1,000 of the population, has consistently increased. The following figures are taken from the Annual Abstract of Statistics (No. 108), 1971:

Marriages in the United Kingdom, 1966–70*

Year	Total Number of Marriages	Persons marrying per 1,000 population
1966	437,083	16·0
1967	439,092	15·9
1968	462,758	16·7
1969	451,627	16·3
1970	470,189	16·9

Professor Titmuss wrote, towards the end of the 1950s:[39]

Never before, in the history of English vital statistics, has there been such a high proportion of married women in the female population under the age of forty and, even more so, under the age of thirty. Since 1911 the proportion at age fifteen to nineteen has risen nearly fourfold; at age twenty to twenty-four it has more than doubled. Such figures as these hardly support the conclusion of the Royal Commission on Marriage and Divorce that 'matrimony is not so secure as it was fifty years ago'.

The figures given above make it quite clear that, as we enter the present decade, this statement is still true, and that if one thing is certain, it is that the desire for marriage and the family has by no means diminished – indeed, exactly the opposite is the case – and that marriage is now being contracted at an earlier (*and* at a later) age than previously. Throughout all age-groups, marriage and the family have never been more popular.

Voluntary Family Limitation

All the reforms and changes mentioned so far – the removal of young children from the labour market, the extended period of compulsory education and economic dependence of the child upon the family, the improved status of women, and the improvements in the standards of living with their

* See note 39, p. 267–69, for additional statistics for England and Wales.

accompanying motives – have brought about what is perhaps the most conspicuous feature of recent family development, and that is the almost universal growth and acceptance of the idea and practice of voluntary family limitation: the conscious control by parents of the number of births in the family with reference to the conditions and opportunities they can provide for their children, and the kind of life they themselves wish to lead. The effect of birth control has been a considerable decrease in the *size* of the family from Victorian times to the present day. The average number of children in the family in mid-Victorian times was between five and seven, whereas now it is (statistically) just over two.

This decline in family size may be seen in the following table (p. 124).[40]

The growing preference for the smaller family is clearly indicated in the following figures taken from the Papers of the Royal Commission on Population.[41]

Distribution of women marrying in 1870–79, 1900–1909, and in 1925, with varying numbers of live births

Number of live births	Proportion of women (per 1,000) with specified number of births who were first married in:		
	1870–79	1900–1909	1925
0	83	113	161
1 or 2	125	335	506
3 or 4	181	277	221
5 to 9	434	246	106
10 or more	177	29	6
All	1,000	1,000	1,000

The general practice of birth control, supported by the motives already mentioned, was furthered during the late nineteenth century by the increased knowledge and discussion of birth control, and by the improved manufacture of

Mean ultimate family size of marriage cohorts since 1861, all marriage ages under 45, England and Wales

Calendar year of marriage	Mean ultimate family size (*actual*)	Calendar year of marriage	Mean ultimate family size (*actual*)	Calendar year of marriage	Projected mean ultimate family size *using fertility rates for*	
					1951–5	1960–61
1861–9	6·16	1910	2·95	1930	2·09	2·09
		1911	2·83	1931	2·08	2·08
1871	5·94	1912	2·80	1932	2·08	2·08
		1913	2·81	1933	2·06	2·06
1876	5·62	1914	2·73	1934	2·03	2·03
1881	5·27	1915	2·43	1935	2·04	2·04
		1916	2·43	1936	2·01	2·01
1886	4·81	1917	2·44	1937	2·02	2·02
		1918	2·45	1938	2·06	2·06
1890–99	4·13	1919	2·57	1939	2·05	2·05
1900–1909	3·30	1920	2·47	1940	1·99	1·99
		1921	2·38	1941	2·03	2·03
		1922	2·28	1942	2·08	2·08
		1923	2·23		1951–5	1963–4
		1924	2·21			
		1925	2·17	1943	2·15	2·14
		1926	2·14	1944	2·19	2·18
		1927	2·09	1945	2·20	2·19
		1928	2·08	1946	2·20	2·19
		1929	2·08	1947	2·22	2·21
				1948	2·24	2·22
				1949	2·25	2·24
				1950	2·27	2·26
				1951	2·27	2·27
				1952	2·32	2·32
				1953	2·36	2·37
				1954	2·38	2·41
				1955	2·41	2·45
				1956	2·45	2·51
				1957	2·46	2·55
				1958	2·48	2·61
				1959	2·48	2·65
				1960	2·47	2·69
				1961	2·45	2·73
				1962	2·41	2·74
				1963	2·40	2·76
				1964	2·36	2·76

the means of practising it effectively, which took place especially after the well-known trial of Bradlaugh and Mrs Besant which was purposely contrived by their re-publication of a book on the subject. Voluntary family limitation, as one would expect, appears to have been first practised by the more educated classes, but has since permeated all sections of the community. This trend in contraceptive practice is shown by the following table.[42]

Percentage of married women in different occupational groups using any form of birth control, by date of marriage

Year of marriage	Percentage of wives of men in the following groups who had used birth control			
	Higher occupations and all non-manual workers	Skilled manual workers	Other manual workers	All classes
Before 1910	26	18	4	15
1910–19	60	39	33	40
1920–24	56	60	54	58
1925–9	58	60	63	61
1930–34	64	62	63	63
1935–9	73	68	54	66
1940–47	67	53	47	55

Of course, none of this means that the average size of the family in Britain will continue to be completely unchanged whatever the circumstances. Indeed, during the sixties, there has been evidence of a slight increase, and it seems clear that generally improved social and economic circumstances, together with a sense of long-term security, may weigh against the extent of family limitation we have so far seen. The Registrar General, however, writes very guardedly on this (1964):

Some knowledge is being gained on the factors which influence family size . . . It can reasonably be suggested that factors such as the probability of a continuing rise in the standard of living and better housing, the falling age of puberty and the 'fashion' for larger families are likely to work towards the increase of family size while the effect of cheaper and more effective contraceptive methods may well work in the opposite direction. To arrive at a forecast of family size it is difficult to make anything but a subjective judgement of the balance of these factors.

Having mentioned projections based upon the assumption of continuing family increase, he none the less qualifies this by the proviso that the increase will proceed 'more and more slowly as time passes'. Whatever the improvement in circumstances enjoyed by varying sections of the community within the foreseeable future, the over-all economic problems of the country, the population problem itself – together with increasing urban congestion, and the availability of abortion as well as contraception, all suggest that, though there may be a slight average increase, and some class variations, the small family pattern is likely to be here to stay.

Changes in Knowledge and Opinion

The rapid development of industrialization and technology during the nineteenth century was paralleled by the increasing intellectual and social importance of science. The scientific method of establishing knowledge, which had already demonstrated its value in intellectual spheres, was also shown to be of great utilitarian and social value by the success of its application to industry, and science increasingly came to be extended to the study of man himself. The science of biology – the systematic study of the species of organic life (including man) on the earth – was successfully established early in the nineteenth century, and chiefly (but by no means only) following the publication of Darwin's *Origin of Species* in 1859, a new body of knowledge about man and his place in the nature of things rapidly developed. Sociology, anthropology, psychology all began to provide a picture of man, nature, and society which radically transformed human perspectives and human attitudes. This knowledge was such as to clash intractably with orthodox religious views, and ideas which had previously gone unquestioned were now forced to face the challenge of criticism. The scientific attitude towards man as one biological species amongst others now made it possible, indeed necessary, to recognize and discuss facts about human nature which, before, would have been considered improper. The idea that sex was a natural desire and not something darkly rooted in sin; the idea that women as well as men had sexual feelings and needs which should be considered in the relationship of love and marriage; the idea that sexual experience itself – apart from its utilitarian end, the production of children – was desirable, enjoyable, even beautiful, and not something to be taken illicitly under a cloud of guilt; ideas such as these could now emerge. The central importance of sexuality in the love relationship between a man and woman could now be taken out of the dark cupboard in which urban Victorian respectability had hidden it, and love – especially, for example, in the work of Havelock Ellis – came to be conceived and written about as an art. The relationship between a man and woman in marriage came to be thought of in new and improved terms of mutuality – of mutual consideration, mutual compatibility, and mutual dignity. The gradual loosening of the older religious views also led to an increased questioning of the Church's view that marriage was essentially a 'sacrament', and the idea (very old in the history of human society) grew and gained force that marriage could be considered purely as a civil and secular matter, entailing a set of rights and contractual duties between men, women, and children.

But the new scientific modes of thought had even wider effects. Variously influential in the work of important thinkers and writers – Spencer, Mill, Marx, and many others – they gave rise to a whole ferment of desired and purposefully contrived social change. Of course, not all thinkers agreed with 'purposefully contrived' social change. Many, like Spencer, adopted *laissez-faire* principles. But all were affected by scientific modes of thought, and as the nineteenth century proceeded the more positive approach towards purposefully undertaken governmental intervention and reform became dominant. Increasingly, people were no longer ready to resign themselves to their 'station' in a social order traditionally and even divinely sanctified. Government commissions and some surveys of the conditions of the poor clearly demonstrated the existence of nauseating social evils. The new trends of thought were such as to encourage the belief that man could now establish reliable knowledge of his own nature and his own society, and – on the basis of this knowledge – could, by consciously undertaken social and political action, positively *change* the institutions of society in order to approximate more closely to the ideals of social justice. These ideas themselves were not new; they had permeated the theories of many thinkers and the activities of practical statesmen before and during the French Revolution, but they gradually became more forceful, more effective, and were worked out in greater detail, as the nineteenth century proceeded; and they have, during the past fifty years, become the common assumptions underlying government.

Men came increasingly, therefore, to think it right to take upon themselves, on the basis of knowledge and reason, the responsibility for changing society (including the nature and conditions of the family) in such a way as to achieve a state of affairs morally and materially better than their experience of the past.

Sanitary and Housing Conditions

Another series of reforms which has vitally affected the situation of the family has been the considerable improvement of the sanitary and general physical conditions of town and country alike which were so lamentable during the nineteenth century.

A report of 1842[43] revealed the nature and extent of these conditions, and by 1848[44] a general Board of Health had been appointed to supervise health functions given partly to borough corporations and partly to *ad hoc* local public health authorities. Since that time continuing progress has been made in improving water supplies and general sanitary conditions. Similarly, though it was late in coming, much improvement has been made in the housing conditions of the population. The provision of adequate housing has never, even to the present day, really caught up with the numerical increase and the increasing urban congestion of the population, and, latterly, the demand for houses has been further accentuated by the improved standards of living. The enormous and still unsatisfied demand for houses which has been felt since the Second World War, for example, is not only an outcome of housing demands which were inadequately satisfied *before* the war, neither is it merely a demand for the replacement of houses destroyed during the war; it is due also to the increased 'effective demand' of people who have enjoyed higher incomes since the war and can now afford, and therefore entertain the idea of, a separate house for their families – a 'luxury' which many could not contemplate before the war. In spite of the late and inadequate provision of houses, however, the development of the public building of houses during the present century has considerably improved the situation, and now a greater number of families are separately housed than before.

Recently, all these tendencies of reform have culminated in extensive 'town and country planning', and great efforts are made to secure good living conditions in existing residential areas, and to plan totally new residential areas – the New Towns – which are well provided with local employment, amenities, neighbourhood centres, and social services of various kinds.

The Family and Wider Kindred

Industrialization brought with it an increasing degree of geographical and occupational movement, and an increased degree of social mobility (i.e., movement between social classes, and changes of social status between the generations). Geographical and occupational movement was made possible by the development of mechanized modes of transport and communication during the nineteenth century, and the increased availability of means of transport – the motor-bus, the motor-car, the motor-cycle, and the bicycle – during the twentieth century. These latter developments in transport largely promoted the growth of suburbs, since people could now live at greater distances from their work. It seems plausible to maintain, therefore, in spite of some recent criticisms of this view, that these forces must have had the effect of loosening the ties between the individual family and its wider kinship relationships, and diminishing the degree of social life which the family shared with groups of wider kindred. The family would no longer live within a particular locality and within a stable and wide network of kinship relationships to the same extent that it did before industrialization.

It seems plausible, also, to suggest that the two great wars of the present century – involving the 'masses' of the civilian population – must have accentuated this 'geographical dispersion' and this distance between families and their earlier localities and kin-groups. Families, during both wars, were compulsorily disrupted. The young men and women of a whole generation – a generation just arriving at maturity, just moving from their family and school experience into adulthood, just setting out upon their careers – were suddenly removed from the contexts of their settled family lives, taken away from the localities with which they were intimately acquainted, and plunged into totally different and exacting experiences for many years, during which they formed new relationships and developed new, though perhaps unsettled, ideas for the future. None can have returned to their old localities, to the 'bosoms of their families', unchanged. Many must have married, obtained employment, and settled elsewhere. One cannot be sure of the over-all effects of such wide-scale disruption as that brought about by the two recent wars, but surely it must have been very far-reaching and must have been such as to enhance the degree of distance between families and their wider kindred which had already been brought about by the more ordinary circumstances of industrialization.

It has always seemed to me that the wars of the present century can explain *much* – both at the widest social level, and at the most intimate level of individual personality – and it seems odd that the consequences of these wars should receive such little attention, if they are not sometimes altogether forgotten. In exercising judgement on contemporary problems, many people seem to forget the major disasters of their recent history, and, instead, go in for a kind of clinical dissection and moral denigration of individual souls. It is as though an earthquake suddenly disrupted the entire people of a small island, forcing upon them unexpected and totally new situations and problems, mixing up their personal lives and their personal relationships until they were like a nightmarish dream, and then, in sorting out their ensuing problems, the people forgot all about the earthquake and looked for the causes of their troubles in the consciences of individuals. It is all very curious, perhaps absurd.

It seems undeniable, therefore, that these vast and complex changes of industrialization and war alike must have rendered the family, as a unit, more isolated from wider and settled groups of kindred than was the case in an earlier, predominantly rural community when people – as it is still said in some areas – 'knew their forty-second cousins'; when families were so intimately related to kin-groups of the same name that they had to be distinguished by 'nick-names' of various kinds.

In addition to these kinds of mobility attendant upon industrialization, however, the increase in general prosperity, especially during the past two decades, must have had its effects upon the relationships between the individual family and its wider kindred. In this sense, the individual family has become not so much 'isolated' from its wider kindred as increasingly 'independent' of them. With full employment and a greater degree of economic security, families are not so dependent upon each other for mutual aid as they once were.

It will be noted that I am not saying, in making *this* point, whether this kind of change can be considered an altogether good or an altogether bad thing. We shall come to this later (see pp. 192–8). Here, I am only claiming that it is plausible to think that this change has occurred.

Social Services

Another widespread change of the twentieth century, developing earlier policies and extended especially since the last war, has been the increasing role of government in maintaining economic stability, full employment, and social security, and in providing a wide network of social services. Owing to economic action on the part of government, booms, slumps, and periods of large-scale and chronic unemployment have been increasingly avoided, so that families now enjoy a new degree of security in their work and in their standards of economic well-being. National Insurance, the National Health Service, the extension of the public provision of education, the improved provisions for the aged and the handicapped, the regulation of rents, and many other government measures and services have all considerably improved the basis of family life – the basis of security, well-being, and opportunity upon which the members of the family can develop their lives and potentialities to a far greater extent than ever before.

Political Citizenship

A final point which is rarely, if ever, mentioned in considerations of the family – which is somewhat taken for granted, but surely a very fundamental matter – relates to the extension of the franchise. We have already said that women achieved a considerable improvement in status which included, though but recently, their effective recognition as responsible voting members of the electorate. But it must not be forgotten that, though rather more long-lived, this right of recognized political citizenship was only made effective for *men* relatively late in the nineteenth century. The 1832 Reform Bill which enfranchised certain copyholders, leaseholders, and occupiers, and gave representation to towns which had gained new importance through industrialization, to some extent met the wishes of the middle classes, but was still wholly unsatisfactory for the artisans. Only in 1867, and improved and extended thereafter, was the vote given to the majority of artisans. This extension of the franchise meant that the working people shared, for the first time, an effective degree of responsibility for those subsequent policies of government which affected their families, as, indeed, they affected every other question of state. Mackenzie writes:

Fifty years before, a few great families had guided the destinies of the nation. The people had exercised no shadow of control over the actings of their government, and had little knowledge regarding them, except such as they had gained from the tax-gatherer, the policeman, or the press-gang. Their attitude had been that of spectators, their feeling one of dumb acquiescence . . . They had looked on in silence while men – sometimes able and good, more frequently weak and unscrupulous – expended their scanty substance in enterprises which had no reference at all to their welfare. When the Reform Bill of 1867 passed into law, the reversal of all these conditions was complete . . . The platform and the press provided the people with the most ample means for the communication of their sentiments on all public questions . . . The voice which could speak decisively at the polling-booth was a voice whose authority no man dared question. It became the care of the politician to discover the wishes of the people, and he was the most successful who was earliest to detect and cherish the yet hidden tendencies of opinion.[45]

In some respects this statement is obviously too extreme. It was not until long after the act of 1867 that the working classes possessed any real and effective political power. Even so, the point which is true, and which it is most important to see here, is that by this extension of the franchise to men, and subsequently to women, the men and women of the labouring classes have gradually come to possess a responsible voice in the actual government of all those affairs which, amongst other things, determine the conditions of their family life. The various welfare policies we have mentioned, though not formulated by the people, have had to be formulated in such a way as to take account of their desires, to meet with their approval; and this has been necessary, if only at the very lowest level of political expediency, to succeed in securing their voting power.

Though it is too long a story to embark upon here, precisely the same kind of point could be made with reference to the growing recognition and power of the trade unions during the later nineteenth century, and especially during the present century. By supporting trade union activity in industry itself, and by pressing, through the trade unions, political measures which have had to be taken into account by the political parties, and especially, of course, by the Labour Party, working people have come to possess an increasing degree of power in determining the various conditions of their employment, and, thereby, the conditions of their family life.

Summary

We are now in a position to summarize the effects of these changes and reforms in altering the characteristics of the Victorian middle-class family and the family of the labouring classes as they existed during the earlier period of industrialization, and the ways in which, consequently, they have come to shape the modern British family.

First of all, it is clear that in the context of these changes the Victorian middle-class family has suffered a complete eclipse. It is no longer with us. Compared with their position relative to the working classes during the nineteenth century, the middle classes are now no longer in such a dominant position of expanding wealth and increasing power and social status. Their domestic establishments are therefore not so widely and conspicuously distinctive from those of wage-earning people (though they are still different). Working-class wives no longer curtsy to the larger rate-payers when they leave church on Sundays. (Indeed, neither group is so conspicuous nowadays in this vicinity.) With the opening of other and more lucrative and more liberative avenues of employment, domestic servants are no longer easily available, and, when employed at all, are employed certainly only on a much diminished scale. The middle-class wife and mother is therefore no longer able – even if she so wished it – to remain encapsulated within a prettily-cultured but ill-educated gentility and harmless idleness. But (although she would like more domestic help) the middle-class wife no longer wishes to be confined in this way. She is a responsible citizen, equal in status to her husband. She has the right and opportunity to enjoy the education and career of her choosing. Great concern is also shown by middle-class parents for the well-being, education, and future careers of their children, and consequently (coupled with the desired freedom on the part of the mother) control is exercised over the number of children born into the family. Voluntary family limitation is therefore practised in the middle-class family – more consistently, carefully, and effectively, it seems, than among families of lower income-groups – so that the family is small in size. The 'authoritarian' family of the earlier middle classes has gone, and in its place has developed the small, planned, democratically managed family.

Since it seems that many people misconstrue the nature of this change, it must be emphasized that although there has certainly been a 'decline' of the Victorian middle-class family, this cannot on any count be characterized as a *moral* decline. If anyone doubts this, let him ask himself whether he does or does not approve of the improved status of women, the extension of their opportunities, and the new mutuality of consideration in the marriage relationship; whether he does or does not approve of the careful consideration of the kind of life that can be offered to the child, and the control of the number of births with these considerations in mind. Let him consider whether he would think it morally right to return to a 'stable, authoritarian' situation which entailed that inferiority and subjection of women which generations of women (and of men) have struggled to overthrow.

When, secondly, we consider the effects of all these changes upon the earlier family of the labouring classes, the moral improvement in the trends of family development are made even more clear, and are surely beyond doubt.

The working-class family – as a result of all those policies which, cumulatively and taken together, we now call 'Welfare State provisions' – has achieved a new condition of stability, well-being, security, and opportunity for the development of all its individual members, which is unprecedented in our history. Here, again, men and women alike are responsible citizens, having a voice in the acceptance or rejection of public policies, and, if they are active, a voice in the actual shaping of these policies. They, too, are becoming equal partners in a voluntarily undertaken and democratically managed marriage. They have a new degree of security and prosperity in their work, and enjoy a relatively improved degree of security for themselves and for their children when they encounter the vicissitudes of unemployment, accident, ill-health, old age, and even death. Their housing conditions, and the general conditions of neighbourhood and environment – though leaving much to be desired in some areas – are considerably improved when compared with those of the past. Their children are given opportunities of health from their very conception onwards, and are given greatly extended opportunities in education and the pursuit of careers. The family of the wage-earning classes, having these widened horizons of opportunity, can now, itself, plan ahead with some secure expectations of achievement. Voluntary family limitation is therefore common here also, and the average size of the family – though somewhat larger than that of the middle classes – is small. The number of births is controlled with reference to the attainment of what is considered an enjoyable life for all its members.

It will be seen, from what has been said, that there is not now such a great degree of difference between the family of the middle classes and the family of the wage-earning classes as there was during the nineteenth century. It seems to be the case that, with the changes and reforms mentioned, the same social forces, engendering the same expectations and attitudes, have increasingly come to fall upon middle-class and working-class families alike. Some differences continue to exist, but the degree of difference is considerably diminished, and the chief characteristics of the family in both classes seem to be very similar. This leads us to the conclusion that whereas, in earlier times, it would have been necessary to distinguish between the characteristics of the family in different social classes, now, in contemporary Britain, it *is* possible to speak of *the* British Family as a type of family unit which is fairly uniform throughout society. In short, the many adjustments of the family to the new conditions and requirements of a complex industrial and urban society, and the many attempts to improve the status and relationships of members of the family in accordance with the principles of social justice, have brought about a certain 'standardization' in the form, or the characteristics, of the family.

THE CONTEMPORARY BRITISH FAMILY

It now seems possible, therefore, to offer a reasonably clear definition of the contemporary British family in such a way as to summarize all the points made earlier.

The contemporary British family can be said to be:

1. contracted or founded at an early age, and therefore of long duration,
2. consciously planned,
3. small in size,
4. to a great extent separately housed, and in an improved material environment,
5. economically self-responsible, self-providing, and therefore (a) relatively independent of wider kindred, and (b) living at a 'distance' from wider kindred, sometimes geographically, but also in terms of a diminished degree of close and intimate social life shared with them,
6. entered into and maintained on a completely voluntary basis by partners of equal status,[46] and therefore entailing a marital relationship based upon mutuality of consideration,

7. democratically managed, in that husband and wife (and frequently children) discuss family affairs together when decisions have to be taken, and

8. centrally concerned with the care and upbringing of children – to such an extent that it is frequently called 'child-centred'.

Finally, we might add:

9. that the importance of the modern family is widely recognized by government and by the whole range of social services, and is therefore aided in achieving health and stability by a wide range of public provisions.

When these points are considered, there can surely be little doubt that the characteristics of the family in contemporary Britain manifest considerable moral improvements upon the family types of the past. How, then, does it come about that the modern family is said to be in a condition of 'instability'? Why is it said that the family is 'declining in importance as a social institution'? On what grounds can it be argued that there is evidence of 'moral decline'? What are the problems experienced in the family of the present day which give rise to this kind of charge?

In order to answer these questions, I want, in the next section, to consider each relationship in the modern family in turn, to examine the 'stresses and strains' characterizing these relationships. I shall do this in such a way as to try to show that, far from being the outcome of moral decline, these problems are the direct if not the inevitable outcome of the moral improvements we have mentioned. I shall then go on to suggest that this different kind of analysis of the roots of present-day problems leads us to very different conclusions as to what our attitudes should be towards the devising of social policies for their resolution.

4 Relationships in the Contemporary Family

IN the modern marriage, both partners choose each other freely as persons. Both are of equal status and expect to have an equal share in taking decisions and in pursuing their sometimes mutual, sometimes separate and diverse, tastes and interests. They live together permanently and intimately in their own home and in relative independence of wider groups of kindred. They base their choice in marriage and the maintenance of their subsequent relationship on personal love. With equality of status and mutuality of consideration they desire full 'compatibility' in marriage. The marital relationship has thus come increasingly to be considered as something worthwhile in and for itself.

It is clear, therefore, that the modern relationship between husband and wife must be an extremely intense affair, and, as such, is potentially unstable. This is not to say, however, that modern marriage is *actually* characterized by instability, and we shall return to this point later. What I mean is that if we have so improved the marital relationship that it depends entirely upon free choice and personal responsibility, we have made it at one and the same time potentially more rewarding and potentially more unstable. But this is a good, not a bad, thing. An increase in freedom and responsibility in any aspect of social life necessarily entails difficulties. Freedom is not to be had easily, and certainly does not bring about an automatic resolution of problems. The successful working out of relationships and problems depends more and more upon continual individual effort, but what is achieved by individuals in this context is, correspondingly, much more rewarding. The modern marital relationship, to a far lesser degree than the Victorian, has no authoritative 'blue-print' in custom, morality, and law of expected family relationships. One cannot know what is involved in marriage until one has actually entered into it. It is therefore a matter of personal initiative, exploration, and creativity, and calls for a great degree of personal adjustment and for continual care and mutual consideration. As such, it can be most rewarding and enriching if it is successful, but perhaps the most miserable and intolerable of human experiences if it is a failure. But it is important to see that its potential instability is a direct entailment of extending personal choice and personal responsibility.

The changed position of women is of particular importance here. With the improvement in the education and in the occupational opportunities of women, with their equal right to pursue their interests and develop their talents, with the practice of birth control, and also with the extended expectation of life, the position of the woman in the family has been changed more fundamentally than many realize. Nowadays, if a woman marries fairly young, and in the few following years has the number of children she and her husband want to have, by the age of forty she has more or less done with caring for children and (bearing in mind the increased expectation of life) has almost half of her life still before her.[1] If a woman has completed her education and secured qualifications for a career before marriage, when her children are over the age of early dependence she is in a position to undertake part-time employment, and, later, can participate as fully as she wishes to do in wider social activities. She has also, of course, far greater opportunity for active companionship with her husband. The changed position of women, then, an outcome of moral improvement, makes the working out of a successful marital relationship a more demanding and intricate affair than it has been hitherto. To mention a specific matter in order to indicate the concrete difficulties that are involved, it is probable that more difficulty arises in the mutual working out of the monetary problems of the family when both partners, of equal status, are independently earning an income, than when there is only one wage (or salary), earned by one person of dominant authority, coming into the family.

All this amounts to the fact that the demands made by women, both within and beyond the family, have considerably increased, and this itself has brought about new 'stresses and strains' within the family.

Since personal love is the important basis of the modern marital relationship, something should, I suppose, be said about certain current conceptions of love. But this is a difficult subject, and I shall say little about it for fear of talking nonsense. I see no reason to suppose, however, that the ideality of love is not still a real and important element in human experience. When, for example, Shakespeare writes:

> Let me not to the marriage of true minds
> Admit impediments; love is not love
> Which alters when it alteration finds,
> Or bends with the remover to remove:
> O, no! It is an ever-fixed mark,
> That looks on tempests and is never shaken;
> It is the star to every wandering bark,
> Whose worth's unknown, although his height be taken.
> Love's not Time's fool, though rosy lips and cheeks
> Within his bending sickle's compass come;
> Love alters not with his brief hours and weeks,
> But bears it out even to the edge of doom.
> If this be error and upon me proved,
> I never writ, nor no man ever loved.

I think we know quite well what he means. But perhaps it is unwise to try to speak of this conception of love unless one has the tongue of a Shakespeare. Something, however, might be said at a less exalted level. It appears to be a very widespread conception at the present time that love is something one 'falls into'; that it constitutes an immediate and high sublimity of experience which is the central *raison d'être* of, and which should be perpetuated in, marriage; and that if it begins to be somewhat dimmed in the day-to-day stress of family life then the relationship has failed and one should terminate it by divorce. Clearly there is some truth in the notion of 'falling in love' (it happens), and clearly the continuation of love in marriage is a desirable thing (it helps). But, apart from the obvious comment that marriage is for the foundation of the family, for the begetting and rearing of children, and thus entails far more than the maintenance of personal romantic feelings, all one would tentatively suggest is that perhaps love also has other qualities; that it is perhaps something which can grow and become more profound and satisfying as ordinary problems, difficulties, duties are shared, as mutual concern for children is experienced, and as qualities of character come to be more deeply appreciated. It may be, then, that – with the enhanced emphasis upon *marriage* as something in and for itself – the 'glossy magazine' notion of 'romantic love' is in danger of spreading an altogether superficial and inadequate conception of those qualities of love upon which a successful and happy marital relationship can rest.

It is here that one of our introductory points is worth reconsidering. We noted at the outset that marriage was rooted in the family, not the family in marriage, and that marriage as an institution did not exist in and for itself. In recent times there has been, rightly, this greater emphasis upon a mutually worked out marital relationship as being worthwhile in itself, but it must be remembered that the central core of concern in the *family* is the having and responsible upbringing of children. Even if full 'compatibility' is not successfully achieved by the partners in marriage (and, whatever it is, can it ever be?), and even if 'love' becomes somewhat dimmed amongst the vacuum cleaners and the electric washing machines, this in itself cannot be held to cancel out the duties which parents have towards their children, nor does it obliterate the love and concern they have for them. Finally it does not constitute a supreme ground for dissolving the marriage. Parenthood involves *duties* to children which must be taken into account whatever the personal relationship of wife and husband.

In short, while it is right and proper that the marital relationship should be considered as being worthwhile in itself, there is perhaps a danger at the present time that this emphasis is being taken too far, and that the other central relationships and duties in the family are receiving too little emphasis. In discussing the intricacies of modern marriage, Dr Peters has recently commented[2] that since the founding of the family is such a responsible affair it is rather odd that, whilst we continue to make it a difficult contract to get out of, it is still the easiest thing in the world to get in to; and he suggests that we might consider making entry into marriage more difficult than it now is. There are many and obvious difficulties in the way of such a proposal. What, for example, would be the appropriate qualifications for marriage? (And how many of us would possess them?) All that need be said here, however, is that, under some circumstances, the recognition of family duties would seem to justify making marriage more difficult to get out of. As Mr McGregor has clearly, and to my mind rightly, emphasized on various occasions,[3] petitions for divorce should be clearly distinguished, and differently treated, in accordance with whether or not the marriage is childless. If there are no children to a marriage, there seems no reason why divorce should not be by mutual consent,[4] since no one is affected but the two partners themselves, and a mutual settlement of their affairs can be worked out. But when there are *children* to the marriage, the parents are responsible for the fulfilment of duties to their children whatever may have happened to their own personal relationship, and it is arguable that divorce here should be made very difficult indeed. Of course, divorce between parents could not be entirely excluded, for some families may be better broken than sustained for all the members concerned; but the overriding consideration as to whether or not the marriage should be dissolved should be the well-being of the children, and the grounds for divorce should be made very astringent in such a case. Parents should at least have to satisfy the court that divorce is in the best interests of the children.

With the improved emphasis upon the personal relationship of *marriage*, then, new problems have arisen, and it now
seems necessary to stress more emphatically the central concerns and duties of the *family*.

It is possible, too, with the intensity and many-sidedness
of the modern marital relationship, that an ill-considered
conception of 'romantic love' might be in danger of becoming a choking, limiting, possessive thing. Love, while it is
one of the most enriching, unselfish, and liberative human
experiences, can, when insufficiently governed by intelligence
and care, become perhaps the greatest of tyrants. The
family, instead of being a basis for the full and free development of the individual lives of its members, can all too easily
become a narrow, self-contained, little den in which people
suffocate each other with their possessive, stagnant, and
petty emotions.

I have tried to show, then, that the stresses and strains
in the present-day relationship between husband and wife
are the outcome of moral improvements, and I have claimed
that this relationship has thereby been made potentially
unstable. But since there are many who are inclined to make
much of the word 'instability' as being evidence of moral
decline in the family, it is necessary to give, though briefly,
some facts concerning divorce[5] in order to show that, although potentially unstable, the modern marital relationship does not *in fact* appear to be characterized by instability.

Frequently, for example, it is said that divorce has been
continually increasing during the past few decades. Although,
since 1961, the number of divorces has been rising continuously, this wider statement is simply not true, and the figures
of divorce – especially as being indicative of the stability of
the family, or of any moral deterioration of it – require very
cautious interpretation.

If we take roughly the past fifty years, the incidence of
divorce began to increase sharply just before and continued
to increase until just after 1918; then it declined (but not to
the pre-war level) and remained fairly steady until just before
1939. It increased again during the war years until shortly

after 1945 (the peak being in 1947). Then there followed another decline until about 1950 when legal aid for divorce was effectively introduced. Here the incidence of divorce slightly increased (in 1952) and then again gradually

Annual numbers of petitions for divorce and of decrees nisi made absolute, 1909 to 1923 and 1936 to 1950, England and Wales[6]

(Suits for both dissolution and nullity are included)

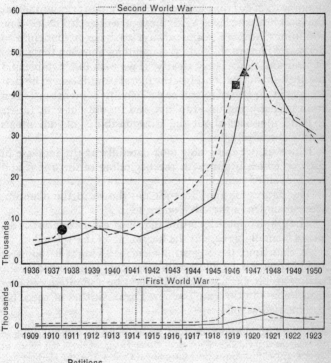

- - - - - - Petitions
———— Decrees absolute
● Matrimonial Causes Act 1937
▪ Matrimonial Causes (Decree absolute) General Order 1946
▲ Matrimonial Causes (Special Commission) (No. 2) Order 1946

decreased until about 1960. Although there has been a large quantity of divorce, therefore, it is quite wrong to say that divorce has been continually increasing. And, before going further, there is one fact which never seems to be given sufficient emphasis: that the sharper increases in divorce in Britain occur during and immediately following periods of war. The reasons for this are obvious, yet, to reiterate a point made earlier, few people seem to realize how extensively the major wars of our time have disturbed human relationships at the most intimate level. With the return of settled peace-time conditions, divorce seems always to have a tendency to decrease. The graph (p. 145) is useful for showing these facts of 'war and peace' very clearly. If we wish to see stable and happy human relationships, the moral would seem to be that we would do better to try, ceaselessly, to prevent statesmen from perpetrating the stupidity and insanity of war, rather than to moralize about the irresponsibility of individuals within the family.*

However, we must now look carefully at the increase in divorce which began with the beginning of the 1960s and has continued since.

The figures for 1951 to 1961 not shown in the diagram, were as shown in the table opposite.

The graph opposite, continuing the previous one on p. 145, shows a small increase at the beginning of the 1960s.[7]

At that time, the Registrar General thought it too early to interpret the significance of this, and, as indicated in the earlier graph, suggested that it might be a sensitivity to new legislation – in this case the new Legal Aid Act of 1960. He commented as follows:

* War is, of course, not the only, though probably the chief, cause of the increased incidence of divorce. Other factors such as the effects of Poor Persons' Procedure, the Matrimonial Causes Acts, the Herbert Act, the Legal Aid Act, etc., have to be taken into account. Griselda Rowntree and Norman Carrier (see Note 5, p. 271) undertake a detailed analysis of the causes of the increased incidence of divorce during particular periods, and, when all factors have been considered, it is found that a considerable degree of importance must be attributed to the effects of war.

Divorce petitions filed and decrees absolute granted, 1951 to 1961, England and Wales[8]

Year	Petitions filed		Decrees absolute granted	
	Number	Per 1,000 married women aged 20–49	Number	Per 1,000 married women aged 20–49
1951	38,382	5·23	28,767	3·92
1952	34,567	4·69	33,922	4·60
1953	30,542	4·14	30,326	4·11
1954	29,036	3·93	28,027	3·79
1955	28,314	3·83	26,816	3·62
1956	28,426	3·83	26,265	3·54
1957	27,858	3·74	23,785	3·19
1958	26,239	3·52	22,654	3·04
1959	26,327	3·52	24,286	3·25
1960	28,542	3·80	23,868	3·18
1961	31,905	4·25	25,394	3·38

Dissolutions and annulments of marriage: new petitions filed and decrees made absolute per 1,000 married women aged 20–49, 1931–61, England and Wales

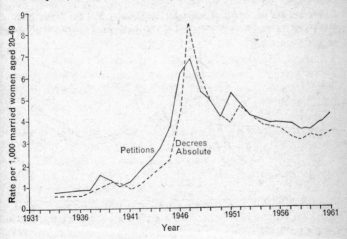

The rise in the number of decrees absolute granted in 1959 may be partly due to the operation of the Matrimonial Causes (Decree Absolute) General Order 1957 which applied to petitions filed on or after 30 April 1957 and which increased the normal interval between the granting of a decree *nisi* and the making of it absolute from six weeks to three months.

The number of petitions and dissolutions rose in 1960 and this rise continued in 1961. The 1961 figure for decrees absolute granted reflects the earlier rise in petitioning which may be linked with a change in the income limits for legal aid which became effective from 1 April 1960 under the terms of the Legal Aid Act (1960). In the past the incidence of divorce appears to have been sensitive to changes in the provision of financial assistance to litigants.

When taking this into account in the first revision of this book, I myself commented: 'It will be interesting to see whether, subsequently, the gradual decline of the post-war years will be resumed (as it was after a similar temporary increase after 1951).' Well, this gradual decline has not been resumed. The 1964 graph showed the continuity of the increase as follows:[9]

Dissolutions and annulments of marriage: new petitions filed and decrees made absolute per 1,000 married women aged 20–49, 1936–64, England and Wales

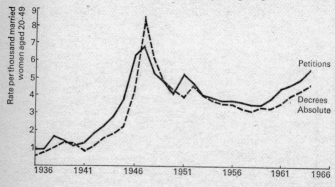

In 1964, the Registrar General thought that:

... the start of the latest rise may well have been associated with the introduction of the Legal Aid Act (1960) which changed the income limits for legal aid, though the continuing increase, which has now lasted for five years, seems too persistent to be accounted for solely by the effects of that Act.

The increase in both the petitions and the decrees absolute has been sustained since 1960, although petitions appeared to have started to move upwards in 1959 and decrees started to increase in 1960. By 1964 the number of petitions filed was 45 per cent higher than in 1960, while the number of decrees absolute granted was higher by 46 per cent. Since 1961, the rise in the number of decrees absolute is nearly 38 per cent and ... the 'all ages' divorce rate has risen by the same amount. This indicates that the increase in the number of divorces has not been associated simply with a rise in the numbers in the married population ... the proportional rise has been greatest for young men and women.

At the same time, it was thought that since the rise in the divorce rate was evident among all age-groups, this was consistent with the influence of new, generally available, terms of legal aid. However, the most recent graph (p. 150) shows the trend as still increasing, and it may be of interest to show, also, the rate per 1,000 married women (p. 151).[10]

Figures available up to 1970 confirm that the trend is continuing as we enter the seventies.[11]

Year	Petitions filed	Decrees Absolute granted
1965	42,981	37,785
1966	46,609	39,067
1967	50,956	43,093
1968	55,007	45,794
1969	61,216	51,310
1970	71,661	58,239

A number of points, however, must be borne in mind in the

difficult task of interpreting these facts. Firstly, they must still be seen against the large continuing increase in the number of marriages, the fall in the age of marriage (which we shall come to in a moment), and, therefore, the considerably larger number of people 'at risk'. The Registrar General writes (in 1967):

> With the strong propensity to marriage and falling age at marriage, the recent increase in the number of marriages that fail, measured by the number of decrees absolute, is brought into proper perspective and the task of seeking the cause of the increase is made somewhat less difficult.

Secondly, the 1960s has been a decade during which marriage, the family, the reform of the divorce law – and, indeed, many other related issues on sexual relations, abortion,

Dissolutions and annulments of marriage: new petitions filed and decrees made absolute, 1910–66, England and Wales

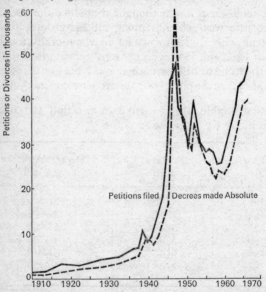

Decrees made absolute per 1,000 married women, 1910–66, England and Wales

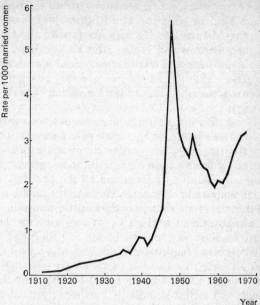

etc. – have been matters continuously in the spotlight of public discussion, and this in the most conspicuous way: in books and journals, on radio and television; with prominent pronouncements from the churches, the law, academics and journalistic feature-writers alike. *The Family in Contemporary Society*, the report of a group convened by the Archbishop of Canterbury, appeared in 1958, and thereafter a whole literature came into being. The campaigning for the reform of the Divorce Law grew and became more influential. In 1964, the Archbishop of Canterbury appointed a group to study 'A Divorce Law for Contemporary Society', and in 1966 its report – *Putting Asunder* – was published. The debate continued hotly, inside and outside Parliament, and then, gradually, more and more agreement was achieved until the Divorce Reform Act was passed in 1969. In addition to this there was much other legislation within the context of the same kind of concern. The Matrimonial Homes Act (1967), the Maintenance Orders Act (1968), the Children and Young Persons Act (1969), the Family Law Reform Act (1969), all effected clarifications and improvements in the status of children and spouses which were a furthering of earlier movements of reform and legislation. The Abortion Act (1967), the Sexual Offences Act (1967) were culminations of long, difficult, and often heated debates on some of the most basic issues in the most intimate of human relationships. The sixties, in short, was a decade of acute debate and legislative achievement on almost all the issues surrounding marriage, the family, divorce, and all the personal, social, financial conditions involved. Perhaps it should also be added that the establishment of the Law Commission (under the chairmanship of a High Court judge of the Divorce Division) in 1965, began a deliberate and thorough review of the whole of our family law. These were all very substantial strides.

Two things, surely, can be said. Firstly, that this undoubtedly (a) reflected, and (b) further sensitized a wide public desire for some change in the existing law; some change which was in the direction of 'liberation' from what were felt by many to be anomalies, inequalities, and injustices. And it was this, of course, that gave rise to the label of the 'Permissive Society' – about which there has been, and continues to be, so much dispute.

The second point, however, is equally firm: that most of the concern shown throughout these public debates, and embodied in this legislation (whether subsequently thought to be wise or misguided), was – far from being a reflection of an increasing family instability, and a set of casual attitudes about it – especially and exactly to the contrary. It was a concern to ensure the *stability* of the family, in so far as this can ever possibly be ensured by public policies, and to ensure the best quality of *desired* reciprocal relationships within it; those relationships, indeed, which seemed morally justifiable.

The Divorce Reform Act (which embodies most of these attitudes) could not be clearer about this. Whilst undoubtedly making divorce easier through removing certain obstacles to it, it also made other things very clear. For example, (1) that the removal of the obstacles would (hopefully) minimize the hitherto 'adversary' nature of divorce petitions and defences, and wrangles over the custody of children; (2) that the changes in the law would provide for genuine attempts at reconciliation (if desired) without this constituting a subsequent legal bar to divorce if, despite the efforts, this turned out to be thought necessary; (3) that it would be possible formally to terminate many marriages which had, in fact, broken long ago (and in which spouses and children of old and new allegiances alike were living in a legally insistent irregularity); and (4) that it would open the way, by formal remarriage, to the legal recognition of the subsequent families which, again, had for a long time actually existed; it was hoped, too (5) that within this context an approach to the financial and property arrangements which would be best for all parties concerned might be achieved. And, above all, (6) its criterion (with its several indicative conditions) of the 'irretrievable breakdown' of marriage, made it clear that its primary concern was the existence of stable and wanted families, and the termination of those which had, in fact, ceased to exist, without the forced odium of the 'matrimonial offence'. In short, a large part of its aim was to see that the formally recognized marriages and families in society should be those which (*de facto*) existed, and which were *wanted* by their members, not those which (*de jure*) had to continue in legal pretence, though they did not exist in fact at all. It was a change such as to bring the law closer to social actuality.

This means that the increased resort to divorce which the statistics portray, though no doubt resting on changed attitudes towards the termination of marriage, by no means indicates, in any simple and definite way, any change in the stability of the family, in the desire for such stability, or in attitudes of responsibility in seeking it. Indeed, on the contrary, it could indicate (a) a bringing out into the open, a recognition, in and through the law, of a social actuality (whatever its unsatisfactory aspects) which had long existed but which had hitherto been prevented from formal resolution, and (b) a *raising* of the standards expected of marriage, and an active will to end the unsatisfactory and move towards the more satisfactory. It could, like the changes in the law itself, be an active pursuit of personal and social truthfulness about the conditions of marriage and the family. It is, when one comes to think about it, a curious interpretation of the increase in divorce that people casually and deliberately seek, or casually do not mind, the difficulties and miseries of dissolving broken family ties; of disengaging from, and disentangling such close and intimate bonds (whatever they may have been like). It makes the entering into marriage and the breaking of it seem like a light pleasure and an inconsequential abandonment; but this, surely – whatever some may say – it can never be.

There are, however, other considerations best discussed in relation to other distinct points, before we even try to come to any conclusion. For the moment, it is enough to see that it is not true that divorce has been continually increasing 'this century', or 'since the war'. The incidence of divorce has moved up and down – sometimes in clear relation to major social facts, like war, its enormous disturbances and aftermath, sometimes in relation to the effects of specific pieces of legislation. And even the increase over the past ten years is so intricately entangled with changes in legal aid, the changing rate and age of marriage, a new range of public debate and education, and other factors, that – though we must be acutely sensitive to it, conscious of it, and see it as an extremely important social problem – it can on no account be easily or glibly interpreted as an increasing instability (in any sense of moral decline) of marriage and the family.

A second generalization frequently encountered is that the increase in divorce is evidence of a growing degree of irresponsibility in entering into marriage. Again, there is no good evidence for this view, and the facts are hard to interpret.

During the past fifty years or so approximately 60 per cent of divorces each year have been in marriages which have lasted for ten years or more. Indeed, many divorces are in marriages which have lasted for more than twenty years. There is thus no evidence of irresponsibility in entering marriage and subsequent casual divorce in the early years of marriage. It is true that there seems to be a long-term correlation between divorce and the age at which marriage is contracted. That is, there is, in the long run, a higher incidence of divorce amongst women and men who marry very young, but this may be due to immaturity, to the uneven level of maturity of wife and husband, or even to the relatively longer period of marriage involved. What is certain is that it cannot simply be put down to an irresponsible seeking of divorce during the early years of marriage.

Table showing the incidence of divorce in relation to the duration of marriage, 1957[12]

Duration of marriage (completed years)	Divorces and annulments	Percentage
0–4 years	2,601	11
5–9 years	7,281	30·6
10–14 years	5,079	21·3
15–19 years	3,807	16
20–24 years	2,374	10
25–9 years	1,499	6·3
30 and over	1,144	4·8
Total:	23,785	100

It will be seen from this table that, in 1957, just over 58 per cent of divorces were of marriages which had lasted for ten years or more. It is interesting to see, too, that there were twice as many divorces in marriages which had lasted twenty years or more than there were in those which had lasted four years or less.

However, again, the later statistical information that is now available does not allow any simple conclusion, and is certainly such as to prevent any setting aside of the problem – as something easy to discount.

Dissolutions and annulments of marriage made absolute in 1966 by wife's age at marriage and duration of marriage per 1,000 married women, England and Wales

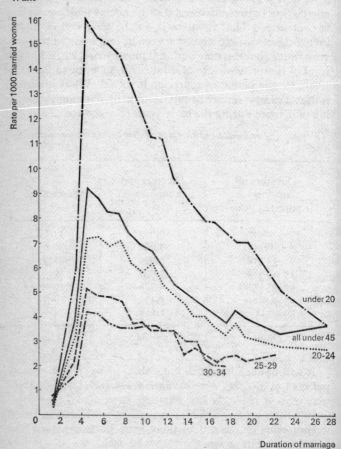

The over-all spread of divorces over marriages of all lengths of duration still remains much the same. But what has emerged as the most striking fact is the conspicuously higher rate of divorce among those – women and men alike – marrying in the younger age-groups. The average duration of marriages dissolved in 1966 was 13·05 years. For women marrying at under 20 years of age, it was 11·57 years; whereas for those marrying between 20 and 24 it was 13·81 years; for those between 25–29 – 15·44 years; and for those between 30–44 – 13·77 years. The pattern of distribution of the divorce rates is interestingly shown in the accompanying graph, and can be seen to be the same for all age-groups, though the preponderance of the under-20s is very clearly marked.[13]

The diagram shows that the duration of 4 to 6 years is the most critical for all age-groups. Bearing in mind (a) that normally a petition for divorce could not be filed within 3 years of the date of marriage, (b) the lower age of marriage, and (c) the very preponderant peak of divorces of the lowest age-groups during this 4- to 6-year duration period – it is clear that a large proportion of the increased quantity of divorces does come from those who marry early. Further, when one bears it in mind that this duration marks the period to the date when the dissolution of marriage is made absolute – *not* the date when the marriage in fact broke up – it is clear that some of these marriages may very quickly have become casualties. It must be noted, too, that pre-marital conception, as well as age at marriage, has been found, according to the Registrar General, to exert some influence on the divorce rates, and this has recently (though it is not of basic relevance here) been connected with the type of marriage ceremony. For example, in over 50 per cent of dissolutions where spinsters under 20 were married according to civil ceremonies, they were pregnant. And for men who married under 20, the rate of pre-marital conception was higher than for marriages of women who married at the same age – *whatever* the type of ceremony.

Beyond any doubt there is a problem here which needs much further investigation. However, it is still far from being the case *either* that this incidence of divorce can be explained as an *irresponsibility* in entering marriage on the part of the young, *or* that it indicates any over-all increase in the instability of the family. In times past, much of this divorce would not have taken place – because of a much smaller rate of marriage, especially among the lower age-groups, because of the sheer inaccessibility of resort to the law for the vast majority, because of lack of legal aid, etc. – but broken families in plenty may still have been there. But also, it is to be borne in mind that the pattern of divorce and the duration of marriage is *the same for all age-groups*. There is likely to be something much more generally at work here than the irresponsibility of the young (or, indeed, of any age-group). It is to be noticed, for example, that in all age-groups there is a *second* peak (at the duration, roughly, of 18 years) as well as a first (at the duration of 6 years). This may well be connected with the problems of reorientation of husbands and wives when their children are 'off their hands'. One's suspicion, anyway, is that common *situational* factors are at work in all age-groups, which are more marked among the under-20s because of immaturity, and perhaps the *sheer availability to them of responsible marriage now* – at a younger age of (socially and legally recognized) adulthood, and with an economic basis which is, at least, much more apparently affluent and secure, and buttressed by provisions of social security, than hitherto. It is worthwhile to bear in mind, too, that 'pre-marital conception' occurred in *nearly* half (47·9 per cent) of *all* the dissolved marriages with civil ceremony in which there was a child to the marriage; that this proportion was 38·6 per cent of dissolved marriages with a Roman Catholic ceremony, and 18·3 per cent for those married in the Anglican Church. It is not only the young, and not only the secular, who stumble into accidents, and who may not be able to work out a subsequent marriage, though they have tried.

Perhaps one of the most central points to consider in all this is the possibility that behavioural problems stem not so much from the irresponsibility of the young (though no doubt this exists among some, and perhaps to some extent in all – which could, by the way, be said of all ages) as from those many aspects of modern social life which are continuously pressing children into a new kind and degree of personal and social *responsibility* (i.e. of citizenship and economic independence; of educational provision, expectation, and effort, etc.) at an age when they are perhaps not ready? Is it a possibility, perhaps, that we are not so much creating a 'youth culture' as *obliterating* youth? Is it the case that – far from giving care to an adolescent period during which a youthful 'bridge passage' may be experienced in the many-sided, difficult task of coming to terms with adult society – we may be forcing a premature adulthood upon children in their early teens? And all this in a society so complex in its citizenship involvements, and so hurried and harried in its supposed education, as to give no satisfying personal orientation of meaning, value and purpose. Our problems, in short, may be due not to irresponsibility but to a forced behavioural disorientation (an imposed *lack* of orientation) when young people are under pressure to make a pretence of maturity and responsible choice.

These are large and grave issues, but they cannot be known and judged fully, let alone solved, by any easy charge and condemnation on grounds of irresponsibility.

A third statement, frequently made, is that there is, as a consequence of increasing divorce, a continual increase in broken homes and, therefore in the numbers of deprived children. Again, the facts necessitate a considerable qualification of this view. Fairly consistently during the past few decades a third of the total number of divorces have been of marriages which are childless; a third have been of marriages which have only one child; and the remaining third have been of marriages which have more than one child. No one would wish to underestimate the degree of suffering which children may experience in broken homes, but the facts suggest that the number of children who suffer from broken homes (at least, as indicated by the rates of divorce) is not so large as is commonly supposed. This conclusion is enhanced when one remembers that the age of the children of marriages is not given in divorce citations, so that many of the children accounted for will not be dependent infants, but may (especially in the high proportion of marriages which have lasted over twenty years) be quite mature; some will indeed be adult. A note of the Registrar General makes it clear how large a category this is: 'These children', he writes, 'are those alive at the date of petition irrespective of their age, and may include children legitimated by the marriage, and adopted children, as well as children of the dissolved marriage.'[14]

The 23,785 marriages which were dissolved or annulled in 1957 had altogether 30,765 children who were alive at the date of petition: 7,995 of these marriages (about a third) were childless and 7,309 (nearly another third) had one child; 1,567 (less than seven per cent) had four or more children. The proportions in each marriage age-group are shown in the following table.[15]

Percentage distribution of marriages, dissolved or annulled, by number of children, 1957, England and Wales

Age of wife at marriage	Number of children					
	Total	0	1	2	3	4 and over
All ages	100	33	31	21	8	7
Under 20	100	21	32	25	12	10
20–	100	31	32	22	9	6
25–	100	43	30	19	5	3
30–	100	58	27	11	2	2
35 and over	100	81	13	4	2	0

The figures for 1961 were: of all marriages dissolved during the year, 32 per cent were childless, 30 per cent had one child, 31 per cent had two or three children, and 7 per cent had four or more children.

It may be, indeed, that childlessness and differential fertility may be a factor underlying some divorces. Calculations for 1950, for example, had shown that divorce rates were highest for childless couples and declined with increasing family size.

Divorce* rates per 1,000 married women at risk, by wife's present age and size of family, 1950, England and Wales[16]

Present age of wife	Number of children						
	0	1	2	3	4	5–6	7 and over
Under 25	3·3	3·8	2·9	2·8	0·8	–	–
25–29	10·6	6·8	3·4	2·8	2·3	1·6	–
30–34	11·7	5·6	2·7	2·4	2·5	2·5	0·6
35–39	9·2	4·5	2·5	2·1	2·0	2·0	1·4
40–44	5·3	3·2	2·1	2·0	1·8	1·5	1·3
45–49	3·1	2·2	1·8	1·6	1·7	1·4	0·7

*Decrees absolute for dissolution and nullity of marriage.

And in the Statistical Review for 1961 it was stated '. . . the incidence of divorce for childless couples may be about twice as high as the average for the marriage age-group concerned'.

In 1964, the extremely interesting table on the next page was provided, comparing the average family size and the proportion infertile between married women and women divorced.[17]

It goes without saying that no argument should lead us to diminish our concern for the children who suffer from broken marriages, or to be less acute in our consideration of how great a problem this is, in discovering its real magnitude, and what might most effectively be done about it. At the same time, we must be equally careful in not allowing such a concern to exaggerate the significance of the problem, or to lead us to make unwarranted generalizations about the 'instability' of marriage and the family among the great majority of people, and in society at large.

Mean family size and proportion infertile of women divorced in 1964; comparison with married women at the 1961 Census, England and Wales

Age of wife at marriage	Mean family size		Proportion infertile	
	Women divorced in 1964	Married women 1961 census (Standardized for duration)	Women divorced in 1964	Married women 1961 census (Standardized for duration)
All ages	1·44	1·80	0·30	0·18
Under 20	1·67	2·30	0·22	0·08
20–24	1·41	1·92	0·31	0·13
25–29	0·83	1·66	0·36	0·20
30–34	0·92	1·43	0·41	0·29
35–39	1·07	1·18	0·48	0·42
40–44	0·84	1·05	0·59	0·54
45 and over	0·57	1·31	0·74	0·51

In addition to marriages dissolved by divorce, there are also, of course, homes which are broken by separation. Indeed, the problems attending separation are probably far worse than those attending divorce. But little is systematically known of the conditions of such families, and the matter requires a good deal of research before anything at all reliable can be said. Such research has, however, been very substantially embarked upon, and a first large report has recently been published. *Separated Spouses* (1971, produced by the Legal Research Unit, Bedford College, London) shows that in the five years from 1961 to 1965, 69 broken marriages resorted to the magistrates courts for every 100 resorting to the divorce courts. This clearly indicates the size of the problem, and it is significant that the broken marriages turning to the magistrates courts (for separation) come from the lower income groups. About half of these, it seems, later petition for divorce, so that the calculation of the number of 'broken homes' in society – as indicated by the number of wives who apply for maintenance orders and the divorce statistics combined – is made more difficult by this kind of overlap. We are still far from having an accurate estimation of the problem. A national random sample conducted by the same research team showed, however, that about 165,000 maintenance orders are now (1971) being enforced in England and Wales.

In very recent years, social scientists have become more acutely aware of the insufficiency of the statistics at our disposal, and also their *limitation* for exploring all the dimensions of social *actuality*. For example, the divorce statistics show the duration of marriages to the dates of petition and decrees absolute granted, but the actual duration of marriages may be quite different from this in many respects – each carrying a different significance. The marriages for which divorces are granted during the 4–6 years duration may well have foundered very early – within the first year or two of marital experience. They may never have got off the ground. But, at the other end of the scale (e.g., of marriages terminated after, say, 18 years), divorces may have been delayed for many years for the benefit of the children of the marriage. Indeed, the marriage may well have been stable *with* children but have become vulnerable *without* them (without all the shared experiences, problems, concerns, and intricate family involvement which they entail). And such conditional elements of interpretation make it clear that the termination of a marriage may not indicate an instability of the *family* in any simple sense at all. Furthermore, the overt statistics of *broken* marriages do nothing whatever to indicate the condition of marriages which endure. It is at least arguable that the qualities of life of some of those which endure – in terms of harmful consequences for spouses and children – are more questionable than some of those which are responsibly ended. Also, we do not know how many broken marriages do *not* resort to the divorce courts or the magistrates courts.

The picture derived from the statistics is therefore a very vexed, uncertain, indeterminate one, and is not such as to bear the weight of any dogmatic generalization. One thing above all that we should remember, however, is that at least at the present time – with the many changes in the law and in legal aid – the facts are increasingly *overt*. Until very recently, the social actuality concerning marital conditions and the extent of enduring or 'broken' marriages were almost entirely hidden for the very simple reason that they could not be expressed. Now, at least, they can. Historically speaking, then, a greater quantity of legally recorded 'facts' is far from being an index of worsening social actuality. As with many human problems – to bring them into the open, to make them fully known, is a first step towards an attempt to deal satisfactorily with them; though, of course, it is also wise to remember that it does not *guarantee* this. Frankness, alas, is not all!

Although, then, we have spoken of the modern marital relationship as being *potentially* an unstable thing, the figures of divorce do not show that there is *in fact* any decline in the stability of the family. Actually, something like 93 per cent of marriages do not end in the divorce court. In 1950 the estimated percentage of marriages terminated by divorce was 7·3. Indeed, the 'cohort analysis' of divorce recently presented by Griselda Rowntree and Norman Carrier seems to suggest (though the authors are most emphatic that it is too early to speak with any certainty) that the rate of divorce may well decline still further in the near future. 'What is more surprising', they write, having commented on the not-surprising effects of the war upon marriages contracted during and immediately preceding it, 'is the persistent and by no means negligible downward trend shown for the post-war cohorts.' 'Since more recent cohorts have shown greater stability it may perhaps be argued . . . that in the absence of a war a substantially lower proportion of more recent marriages will ultimately end in divorce, and one may speculate how near the proportion will come to the 3 per cent shown by the cohorts of the early 1920s.'[18]

As we have seen, the downward post-war trend has not continued, but the increase in the sixties has been so closely related to better terms of legal aid and new legislation, that the speculation might still be allowed to stand. Indeed – it is very tempting to speculate still how far, in terms of cohort analysis, this increase may be reflecting the disturbance of war and its aftermath. For the marriages being broken during the sixties, and as the sixties advanced – and especially the peak of those having married in the younger age-groups – would be those of children born not only just before, during, and just after the war, but also born of some marriages which were themselves contracted during the war, and experiencing conditions and problems of resettlement immediately after it. During the sixties, speculations were advanced about the 'peak' of juvenile delinquency – attributing this to the disturbing conditions experienced by children during and immediately after the war. It would, of course, be absurd to equate delinquency with divorce, and I hope it is very clear that I am not doing so; but, at the same time, it is interesting to speculate that there might be a 'bulge' of divorces among that generation whose childhood took place in conditions of domestic and social disturbance, and who may have been well into adolescence before the families from which they sprang had become satisfactorily settled.

However, I say only that it is tempting to speculate. There is one important reason, perhaps, why we should not be continually looking over our shoulder for some kind of *excuse* for an increased degree of resort to divorce. And it is simply that if – to make the resolution of marital difficulties formally clear, to make the law more equally accessible to all, to remove anomalies and injustices, and the like – we have provided a new law and new conditions for divorce proceedings and their resolution, then we should surely *expect*, at least for some time, a greater amount of use of these facilities. If the new fabric of the law is a way of dealing more responsibly and more effectively with marital breakdowns, and more equitably in relation to the needs and claims of all involved than has been available hitherto, then we must surely expect an increased use of it. In short, an increased use of divorce procedures is not, and should not be assumed to be, necessarily a bad thing, for which some kind of excusing explanation is required. We have got into the habit of thinking like this, but perhaps we should break it. And there are further considerations – such as, for example, that with an improved divorce law and its increased accessibility to all, there might well be a movement *away* from magistrates courts (and judicial separations) *towards* termination by divorce. And this might be better, in terms of ensuring the best and most stable conditions of social actuality.

However, in all this, I say 'might'! Clearly, we should not cease to try and understand the truth about marital and family matters underlying the facts of divorce, and a thorough-going causal explanation would help us in both personal judgements and social policies. All I am saying is that we should perhaps temper our too-ready assumption that the increased quantity of divorce that now exists is necessarily indicative of a worsened social situation.

At any rate, it is too early, with all the provisos which complicate the issue, to say whether this recent increase is a firm long-term trend. It should be noted, too, that this increase is almost certain to continue in the early seventies – and *still* without firmly indicating long-term trends; for in 1971 petitions were being filed under the new Divorce Reform Act (1969), and yet a great many of these divorces were no more than a late formal recognition and legal regularizing of a social actuality that had already existed for many years. The increased quantity of legally recorded facts will in very large part be only an overt acknowledgement of the nature of our society as it has existed for quite a long time. In one sense, nothing will be new but the figures. In another sense, however, what will be new in social actuality will be the far larger number of families (so far hidden in illegitimacy) now possessing the overt status of legally constituted families – which they have long wanted to enjoy. And this, surely, will be a great gain, and can be said to be more of a movement towards the improvement of family stability than a statistical indication of the contrary. It will be some time, therefore, before the significance of the increase of the sixties, and its continuity into the early seventies can be reliably clarified.

Neither, as we have seen earlier – and this is very certain –

can marriage and the family be said to have declined in popularity, since more people are now married than ever before, and people enter marriage at a younger age than previously. It is also to be noted that marriage appears to be very popular amongst divorced people. In the Statistical Review for 1946–50 it was stated that: 'At all ages a much higher rate of marriage is shown for divorced men and women than for the other marital conditions,' and, in the Review for 1956, 'it seems likely that the proportion of divorced persons who ultimately remarry is in the region of three-quarters, so that the net loss to the married population is only a fraction of the total number divorced.' The actual figures (given from 1951–6 by way of illustration) are as follows:

Annual number of divorced men and women remarrying, as a percentage of those divorced in the same period, England and Wales[19]

Period	Percentage of divorced people remarrying		
	Persons	Men	Women
1951	76·8	80·3	73·2
1952	67·9	69·9	66·0
1953	72·5	74·4	70·7
1954	74·9	76·9	72·9
1955	79·6	81·3	77·9
1956	77·3	78·9	75·7

The same proportions were in evidence in the figures for 1961 and 1964, though in 1964 the remarriage rates were slightly lower than in 1951–6. In the latest review containing such figures (1964), it was also shown that, on average, divorced men remarried at the age of 40, and divorced women at a slightly younger age (over half remarrying under the age of 35), and that remarriage took place on average within 3 or 4 years of divorce. The Registrar General's comment is: 'The rates of 364 per thousand for men aged 30–34 and 398 per thousand for women aged 25–29 both imply an average interval between divorce and remarriage of well under two years.' From all this, it is clear that though some people find it desirable to terminate *one* marriage, it is not marriage and family life itself from which they are wishing to escape – since so many of them choose it again within so short a time.*

The statistics of marriage and divorce, then, do not suggest that people in general are succumbing to the 'stresses and strains' of modern marriage. The institution of marriage remains firm and stable for the great majority of people, and, whatever the condition of modern marriage may be, more and more people appear to desire it. Statistical information, however, is not the only evidence now at our disposal. There are other, more 'qualitative' studies that give us information of the greatest interest.

It might be thought, for example, that the companionate marriage which, I have argued, constitutes a great improvement in family relationships has in fact only been achieved by the more enlightened middle classes (I use the words which are often used), and has not yet become the 'normal' marital relationship throughout the population. To some extent this may be true, but, to give one example, the study of the family in Bethnal Green undertaken by Michael Young and Peter Willmott shows that this improvement in the nature of marriage is quite conspicuous, and quite conspicuously realized, among the people there. Complaining about the confusion due to the fact that the 'image' of the working-class family with its 'absentee husband' has been carried over from earlier studies, and that

The one aspect of that family which has been amply described is its failure. Study has been piled upon study of all the things that have gone wrong, of juvenile delinquency and problem families, broken homes and divorce, child neglect and Teddy Boys, which together have created an impression that working-class families are disunited, unsocial, and unhappy . . .[20]

the authors tell us that

There is no confusion in Bethnal Green. People are well aware of the change which has come upon them in the course of a few decades.

* See also table on p. 242.

Having described improvements in economic security, housing, and other material conditions, the fall in the death-rate, the reduction of disease, Young and Willmott go on to describe the changes in the nature of marriage. The emancipation of women which has come about, they say, 'has depended upon husbands even more than upon wives'.

. . . the younger husband of today does not consider that the children belong exclusively to his wife's world, or that he can abandon them to her (and her mother) while he takes his comfort in the male atmosphere of the pub. He now shares responsibility for the number of children as well as for their welfare after they are born . . . Many husbands acknowledge that, when their wives also go out to work, they have a responsibility to do more to help in the home.

This new mutuality of consideration in marriage is also seen in the spending of the family income.

The man's earnings may still be his affair, but when it comes to the spending of the money, his part of the wages as well as hers, husband and wife share the responsibility . . .

The sharing of responsibility is nowhere more obvious than over the children . . . Nowadays the father as well as the mother takes a hand in the care of the children . . . Not only do fathers, as well as mothers, have more money; they also take a pride in their children's turnout. Both of them now share in the hopes and plans for their children's future.

Having given much more evidence of this kind, Young and Willmott conclude:

These . . . impressions suggest that the old style of working-class family is fast disappearing. The husband portrayed by previous social investigators is no longer true to life. In place of the old comes a new kind of companionship between man and woman, reflecting the rise in status of the young wife and children which is one of the great transformations of our time. There is now a nearer approach to equality between the sexes and, though each has a peculiar role, its boundaries are no longer so rigidly defined nor is it performed without consultation . . .

Similarly, findings of great interest are presented by Geoffrey Gorer in the sections on the attitudes of the English to love, sex, and marriage, in his book *Exploring English Character*. Earlier, we said that the 'glossy magazine' notion of 'romantic love' might be in danger of spreading too superficial a conception of the qualities of love and of character necessary for a happy marital relationship; and that this could entail some naïvety and irresponsibility in entering marriage. Gorer's findings, however, suggest that this is a misplaced fear.

The English pattern of love [he writes] which leads to marriage can be briefly summarized as follows. A young man meets a young woman, becomes attracted to her, courts her for between one and two years, and then may have an engagement lasting less than a further year. If the young man is a working lad from the northern regions his future wife is likely to be the first girl by whom he was seriously attracted; if the girl is of the middle classes and from the big cities or the southern regions she is more likely to have considered other young men before allowing herself to become seriously attached. There is little here of whirlwind romance, or of playing around before finding Miss or Mr Right; there is also little of the in-group marriage of old acquaintances which characterizes some settled communities. It would seem to steer a middle way between the two extremes.[21]

With regard to the degree of chastity and fidelity of the English people, Gorer says:

I should like to emphasize once again that half the married population of England, men and women alike, state that they have had no relationship, either before or after marriage, with any other person than their spouse, and that the numbers are even greater in the working classes. My personal impression – and it is backed up by other material to be described subsequently – is that this is a very close approximation to the truth; and although there are no extensive figures available comparable to these I very much doubt whether the study of any other urban population would produce comparable figures of chastity and fidelity.[22]

Gorer found the same sort of thing in his investigation of the attitudes of the English towards the importance of sexual love in marriage, and towards pre-marital and extra-marital sexual experience. He writes in this section:

What seems to me most noteworthy is the high seriousness with which the great majority of English people approach and regard marriage. Whether pre-marital experience is advocated or reprobated, the effect on the future marriage is the preponderating consideration. Secondly, the high valuation put on virginity for both sexes is remarkable and I should suspect specifically English.[23]

Having inquired into the kinds of quality people look for in their prospective husband or wife, Gorer found that

Neither sex pays any appreciable heed to the aesthetic qualities of their spouse; beauty or strength, good looks or good figure, are very seldom mentioned, and then chiefly by the single . . . As a generalization it may be said that what English men most value in their wives is the possession of appropriate feminine skills, whereas what English women most value in their husbands is an agreeable character.[24]

Similarly, when asked to give their opinions on the factors making for happiness in marriage, most people mentioned qualities of character and certain material conditions, such as '. . . give-and-take (sharing 50–50), understanding, love, mutual trust, equanimity, sexual compatibility, comradeship, a decent income, mutual interests, happy home life, and no money difficulties . . .' Gorer says that 'one of the biggest surprises' he received from his investigation was the very small role accorded to infidelity as a cause of marital unhappiness. Having given many examples of attitudes to the effect that infidelity should not be considered a reason for terminating the marriage, and that divorce should be regarded only as a 'last resort' when all other attempts to preserve the marriage had failed, Gorer writes:

All the solutions so far discussed have the implicit or explicit assumption that adultery, real or supposed, should not terminate the marriage (if that can possibly be avoided) and does not justify the wronged spouse in adopting violent or aggressive behaviour . . . this can be described as the typical English response, covering as it does the views of more than half the men and nearly three-quarters of the women.

Furthermore, Gorer says,

... there is at least as much tendency to blame oneself for a spouse's dereliction as to blame or punish the offending spouse.[25]

There is nothing in these attitudes to suggest great instability in the modern British marriage, and this, indeed, is Gorer's conclusion.

'I would suggest', he says, 'that such attitudes imply a relatively low valuation of "love" and a very high valuation of the institution of marriage . . .' 'The spate of quotations – though only a fragment of those available,' he writes, in summarizing all his findings

... have I hope illustrated the great importance for English men and women of the institution of marriage and the seriousness with which they consider it. It is marriage itself which is important, not, I think, love or sexual gratification; and marriage is living together, making a home together, making a life together, and raising children. Perhaps even more for Englishmen than for English women, parenthood is the greatest joy and greatest responsibility of adult life.[26]

This book was published in the mid-fifties, but, bearing in mind all we have said about the increase in divorce during the sixties, the concern to which this has given rise, and the difficulties of interpreting the increase, it is of the greatest interest to note Gorer's findings in a second survey undertaken for the *Sunday Times* and published in 1970.[27] These not only bear out the earlier findings mentioned above, but give quite firm and substantial evidence of a growth of improved qualities of reciprocal consideration, mutual responsibility, and stability in marriage during the subsequent years. It is important to note, in looking briefly at some of these findings, that Gorer's sample of 1,987 English men and women was very carefully selected to be representative of the total population of the country.

One of the questions asked was: 'Now that the pill provides absolute safety, do you think faithfulness is or is not as important as ever in marriage?' Only 5 per cent thought that faithfulness was *not* now so important. Gorer comments: '. . . for the vast majority of the younger English population (over 90 per cent) faithfulness in marriage is still as important as ever.' Furthermore, the results made it clear that young people were thinking much more about marriage before they entered into it, though this, it seems, is more true of young women than young men.

All the young women in our survey of sex and marriage in contemporary England, no matter how innocent or how protected their lives, had thought enough about marriage by the age of sixteen to be completely articulate about what could make or mar a marriage and the qualities to be hoped for and the defects to be feared in a husband.

Gorer found that some of the traditional aspects of marriage (which he had noted almost twenty years earlier) still existed: for example, the fact that young husbands still regarded themselves as the 'guardians of their wives' well-being', and that young wives, far from objecting to this, seemed to accept it, want it, approve of it, and conceded the right of their husbands to feel like this. But what impressed him most was the emergence of a new 'ideal' of marriage:

... I think I discern quite a new pattern in the majority of the marriages of those under thirty-five; I am calling this the ideal of symmetrical marriage.

In symmetrical marriage the contrasts between the roles and characters of husband and wife are given little emphasis; what is emphasised is doing things together, going out together, helping one another and above all talking together ...

Comparing aspects of this 'ideal' with the views and attitudes of twenty years earlier, one of the things which most struck him was:

... the very much greater emphasis given today to discussing things, talking things out, articulateness, or to use a word much in vogue among younger respondents, communication; and, secondly, on comradeship, on doing things together, on going out together, as ingredients for a happy marriage, and of their absence as a major factor in wrecking a marriage ...

... articulateness and comradeship have displaced mutual trust, good temper, a sense of humour and love or affection in the order of ingredients for a happy marriage; and much less emphasis is placed today on the factors chosen twenty years ago as conducive to an unhappy marriage: lack of trust, poverty or extravagance, sexual incompatibility, no house of one's own, and bad temper and quarrels. One factor which bulks markedly higher today than it did twenty years ago as a cause for a wrecked marriage is infidelity and jealousy . . .

The new attitudes towards what makes a successful marriage and what breaks it were interestingly put together in the table shown on pp. 176–7.

Responsible attitudes were also shown in the responses towards marital difficulty of various kinds – such as infidelity. Only 7 per cent thought that automatic and immediate divorce was appropriate, and a further 5 per cent that divorce was a last resort. The vast majority wished responsibly to discuss the situation and to seek reconciliation.

Two other findings were conspicuous and impressive – especially in connection with the overall perspective and argument I am trying to press home in this book.

One was that *fathers* were shown to be extremely involved in family life, and to be much concerned for the welfare and happiness of their families, and, furthermore, that this was shown to be true of the 'lower classes' (so often pilloried for irresponsibility). 'It is the fathers,' writes Gorer,

. . . much more than the mothers, who mention the presence of children as an essential component of a happy marriage; and a very high proportion of these fathers come from the semi-skilled and unskilled working class . . .

For many fathers, the presence of a complete family unit is a source of deep satisfaction.

The other finding was that the material conditions of family, home, and environment were found to be so much improved over the twenty-year period as scarcely, now, to be taken into account at all as factors making for family stress or instability. Gorer was obviously very gratified and impressed by this, and drew special attention to it.

I think it should be a matter of national self-congratulation that the material causes of marital unhappiness which bulked so large twenty years ago are scarcely mentioned today. The misery of having no house of one's own, of having to live with the parents of one of the spouses, listed then by more than a fifth of the married couples as a major reason for a wrecked marriage, is today the lowest factor in the whole table; and having a home of one's own is so taken for granted that hardly any of today's respondents think it worth mentioning. And with the housing problem virtually solved, the problem of 'in-laws' interfering with their children's marriages has also shrunk to relative insignificance.

These findings (of a much more qualitative nature than the general statistical reviews, though still resting upon a careful, representative, quantitative basis) seem very encouraging indeed. Gorer concludes:

. . . the contemporary ideals of marriage . . . replace the traditional roles of husband and wife in favour of completely equal companionship, with all the emphasis on discussing things together and doing everything together, on being together all the time which is not demanded by work. As the 'unisex' fashion minimized the secondary sexual characteristics physically, so does the contemporary pattern of marriage do so metaphorically and psychologically. In a young household who can tell who has cooked the dinner or washed up after, or who gives the baby its night feed?

In many ways this marriage of good friends seems to me to augur hopefully for the future . . . and their children, hopefully, will grow up with far fewer problems of identity.

All in all, then, in spite of the problems brought about through change, the picture of marriage in modern Britain which emerges from statistics and from these qualitative studies alike is, surely, a picture of considerable health, considerable stability, and an enlarged degree of opportunity and happiness.

PARENTS AND CHILDREN

In view of the decrease in the size of the family, and the greater distance between the individual family and its wider kinship relationships (because of increased geographical and social mobility, and the increased economic indepen-

Present-day Attitudes to Marriage

WHAT DO YOU THINK TENDS TO MAKE FOR A HAPPY MARRIAGE? (Figures are percentages)		
Total percentage	Men	Women
Comradeship, doing things together	29	27	30
Give-and-take, consideration	28	24	31
Discussing things, understanding	28	26	30
Mutual trust, mutual help, no secrets	20	21	19
Love, affection	19	20	18
Children	14	17	11
Shared interests	13	13	14
Sexual compatibility	5	7	3

WHAT DO YOU THINK TENDS TO WRECK A MARRIAGE? (Figures are percentages)		
Total percentage	Men	Women
Neglect, bad communication, spouse going out	30	26	33
Selfishness, no give-and-take, intolerance	25	25	25
Infidelity, jealousy	25	29	22
Poverty, extravagance, money disagreements, wives working	17	15	19
Conflicting personalities, no common interests	12	13	12

...financial security, no debts	5	7	4
Happy home life	5	7	3
Good temper, humour	4	3	4
Home of one's own	1	1	0

Temper, arguing, quarreling, fighting	10	11	9
Sexual incompatibility, fear of more children, no children	10	11	9
Lack of affection, love, general irritation	7	7	8
Drunkenness	7	7	7
Lack of trust, untruthfulness	6	6	7
No house of one's own, bad management, in-laws	4	5	4
Don't know	2	2	1

Note: Totals in both tables exceed 100 per cent because more than one answer could be given.

dence of the family), it seems plausible to say that children
(and, indeed, parents) must now have a much narrower
range of shared social experience within the family, and
have far greater degrees of attention, effort, and expectation
concentrated upon them than hitherto. Some people feel
that dangers are involved here. Just as the love between a
man and woman can become tyrannical, so can the inor-
dinate and ill-governed love of parents for a child. An undue
concentration of high expectations upon the child may
create great burdens of anxiety. The anxiety attendant upon
the 11+ examination may be one example. But also some
people fear that this concentration on the child may en-
gender too self-conscious and too self-concerned an orientation of interest. We may be bringing into being a generation
of young people who are self-centred and uncooperative;
who are intensely aware of their rights and what they can
demand of society, but not so sensitively aware of their
duties.

How far these are matters of grave concern it is difficult to
decide. What is certain is that there is another side to this
picture. In the small modern family, aided by social provisions of all kinds, children have never before had such
opportunities for enjoying physical and mental health, and
for a full development of all their talents. Furthermore, the
evidence suggests that most parents are very concerned to
see that their children enjoy these benefits to the full. We
have already seen in the findings of Gorer and of Young and
Willmott that the duties of parenthood appear both to be
enjoyed and to be taken very seriously and responsibly by
the majority of the British people at the present time, and
many others share this view. Thus, Mr Gordon Bessey, in
his contribution to the conference on *The Family*, said:

I believed that all concerned with the education of children outside the home are more conscious than ever before of the deep
interest of an increasing number of parents in their children's
welfare and their education. The voluntary and statutory agencies,
the schools, are every day in every way being consulted by
interested and anxious parents.[28]

This widespread evidence of parental concern for the welfare and education of children is surely a good thing, even though, sometimes, it may be too intense. It should perhaps be borne in mind that many parents of the present day are people who themselves lacked these opportunities, but have come to realize the importance of them and are thus anxious to see that their children make the most of them.

A second aspect of the relationship between parents and children which causes concern is that there has been an increase in the number of wives and mothers who go out to work. The census figures of 1931 and 1951 show that between these years the number of married women at work was trebled. Now, approximately half the women at work in Britain are married – a total of about 4 millions. It is felt by many that this employment of married women with children entails some degree of unthinking, but none the less harmful, child neglect. A few things can be said about this supposed problem.

First, we have seen in our discussion of the conditions of the eighteenth and nineteenth centuries that it is no new thing for mothers to undertake productive work, and at least in the present day women work under much more humane conditions and hours of work. Second, the situation has not yet been adequately studied, so that no one yet knows what degree of child neglect may be involved. Third, there is no doubt that many women find themselves compelled to work because of the inadequacy of the wages of their husbands, and even if some neglect of children could be shown to exist here, this would have to be balanced against the gains for the welfare of the child which come with the additional income in the home. Fourth, it is certain that the full expansion of our economy now positively necessitates the employment of women, so that this problem cannot be solved by keeping women from work. Fifth, if women are to have *effective* and not only *nominal* social equality with men, their right to work if they wish to do so cannot be denied. If there is a grave problem here, its solution must lie in the direction of making available that kind of part-time work which will not infringe upon the mother's care for her children, and of making public provisions for child care itself (in nursery schools, for example*) in order to en-sure that the employment of women does not entail this kind of harm. Of course, the rights of a woman need not be acted upon. Some women are glad to escape the necessity of going to work and positively enjoy the life of the home. In any case, however, the extent to which a woman acts upon her rights must be balanced against her duties to her children and her home, but this must be the responsibility of each individual woman. Any *public* action seeking to prevent a woman from working, if she wishes to do so, militates against the equal status of woman, and reduces the extent to which it is really effective.

Although the question of the degree of child neglect attend-ant upon the employment of women has not yet been adequately investigated – in the sense that studies so far undertaken have not been sufficiently broad to provide knowledge of the over-all situation – it has, at least, been studied to some extent, and the results have not been such as to support the fears that mothers at work are guilty of any lack of responsibility towards their children. To give one example, the Social Science Department at the London

---

* It is sometimes forgotten that in the Education Act of 1944 it was stated that local education authorities should have regard 'to the need for securing that provision is made for pupils who have not attained the age of five years by the provision of nursery schools or, where the auth-ority consider the provision of such schools to be inexpedient, by the provision of nursery classes in other schools . . .' (Para. 8, (2)b, p. 5).

This provision has been implemented only to a negligible degree, largely because of the concentration upon secondary and primary educa-tion. But there is no doubt that children from the age of three and certainly from the age of four positively need the kind of stimulation, companionship with other children, constructive play, and elementary teaching which good nursery schools could provide, and especially in areas where spontaneous and informal play facilities are restricted. For children and parents alike the availability of nursery schools would be an excellent thing, and it is not too much to say that the provision of them, or of nursery classes, is a necessity of modern urban living.

School of Economics studied the daily life, at home and at work, of over 300 women workers at Peek Frean Ltd (the biscuit manufacturers), in Bermondsey. The investigation showed that women worked chiefly for financial reasons and secondly for the companionship they found at work. Their earnings were not 'essential' in the sense of strict economic necessity, but were desired in order to achieve a higher standard of life for their families.

What they meant by a higher standard varied, but much of their earnings went on refurnishing and redecorating their homes, a more varied diet and the durable 'consumer goods', furniture, bedding, grates, television sets, and, for some, the small second-hand car. It also went on better clothing for the whole family, and pocket money and toys for the children. The family holiday, often previously confined to hop-picking expeditions, became a major new pleasure.[29]

'Work', the report continues, 'was undertaken as a means of helping the family, not as an escape from it ...' and 'whenever possible, she [the working mother] fitted her hours of work to her family responsibilities.' Mothers made arrangements with, and received the willing help of, their husbands and their own mothers in order to make sure that their children were adequately cared for, and '... any breakdown in these domestic arrangements resulted in absence from work since the women put the interest of their families first in the event of a clash between the claims of work and of home ...'[30] There is no evidence here, then, of child neglect on the part of working mothers. On the contrary, the picture is one of family concern. Indeed, some of these women argued 'that the neglectful mother is not the one who works but the one who is too lazy or indifferent to take advantage of today's opportunities to raise her family's standards'.[31]

Here again, incidentally, evidence was provided of the new mutuality of consideration in marriage amongst working people. The report states:

The mothers with the youngest children tended to choose the

evening shift, which allowed them to be at home until their husbands could take over in the evening. Two out of three women on this shift had a child under five, and almost all the others had a child at school. This shift illustrates well the changing role of the husband. Not occasionally but every evening from Monday to Friday he had the job of putting the children to bed and clearing away the meal, to make it possible for his wife to work on the evening shift.[32]

Husbands and wives were thus shown to cooperate in the mutual effort to improve the standards of life for the family.

In this matter of the employment of women, the differences entailed by the class position of women are worthy of attention. For the girl who has the capacity to succeed in higher education and to secure some professional qualification – to become a qualified teacher, personnel manager, or almoner, for example – a fairly clear pattern of life seems to be emerging. The girl can complete her education and training, and perhaps have a few years of experience in her chosen occupation, before marriage. She can then marry, and in the few immediate years of marriage have the number of children she and her husband want. Thereafter, as the degree of dependence of her children diminishes, she can begin to re-enter the career for which she is qualified, and later can undertake it to the full. For a great number of women, however, this pattern does not apply. The vast majority of girls go to secondary modern schools, and, beyond this, have no kind of recognized training which will enable them to enter employment later, when, after marriage, they may wish to do so.[33] The work available to them will be factories, bus-services, shops, etc., where the hours of work may make convenient part-time employment difficult. If this problem is to be adequately dealt with, then, we need to give more attention to this position of the *majority* of women. They, too, have equality of status which should be made effective. They, too, are citizens who should have the opportunity of taking part in social activities – including wage-earning work – in addition to their life and duties in the home. Women should therefore be educated for some appropriate pattern of life so that they are able to enjoy their opportunities to the full, but, at the same time, so that some activities are not undertaken at the sacrifice of others, so that rights and duties are balanced as sensibly as possible. To take into account *both* the question of the effective status of women *and* that of the care of children, new hours of work should be contrived to take the home circumstances and duties of women into account – the sensible management policies of the Peek Frean factory show that this is possible – and social provisions for child care (nurseries, nursery-schools, and the like) should be extended as a normal part of our welfare provisions.

A third source of 'stress' in the modern family is the so-called 'problem of adolescence'. We are told that young people are maturing at an earlier age nowadays, but there is little evidence to suggest that the physiological and psychological characteristics of adolescence are any different now from what they have always been. It is the *social* situation of adolescents which has changed and this again can be said to have been the outcome of social improvements.

At school-leaving age a young person can now earn a reasonably good wage. Mark Abrams estimated that, in 1959, the average male teenager spent 71s. 6d. a week, and the average girl 54s. 'Britain's five million teenagers, after meeting their state and family obligations, and after putting aside approximately £70 millions as true savings, spent £830 millions, or slightly over 5 per cent of the national total consumer expenditure.'* Commercial enterprises, knowing that a sizeable proportion of the national income goes into the pockets of young people, obviously go out of

---

* *Teenage Consumer Spending in 1959* (Part II) by Mark Abrams (London Press Exchange Ltd), p. 3. The real earnings of teenagers have risen faster than those of adults during the past three decades, but, lest the reader should think that these figures constitute an enormous sum, we might note Mark Abrams's comment that '. . . this seems a very modest ratio for a group of people who constitute 10 per cent of the total population and 13 per cent of the population aged fifteen and over: it scarcely sustains a picture of an extremely prosperous body of young people. And yet this is the common view among most adults.'

their way to cater for 'teenagers', who have thus been made into a highly self-conscious stratum of society. 'By and large,' says Mark Abrams, 'one can generalize by saying that the quite large amount of money at the disposal of Britain's average teenager is spent mainly on dress and on goods which form the nexus of teenage gregariousness outside the home. In other words, this is distinctive teenage spending for distinctive teenage ends in a distinctive teenage world.'[34] This means that there are powerful influences in society pulling the young person towards early adulthood and away from his or her context of dependence in the family. This seems to be the chief ground for concern.

The pattern of teenage expenditure revealed by Mark Abrams, however, does not seem to give cause for much anxiety. It appears that the average working boy pays his parents roughly 35s., and the average working girl 25s., a week for board and lodging. Of the remainder (after National Insurance and tax has been taken into account), 31 per cent of the average boy's expenditure goes on drinks, cigarettes, and entertainment admissions, and nearly 40 per cent of the average girl's expenditure goes on clothes, shoes, and cosmetics. It must be noted, however, since the word 'drinks' has appeared, that only 6 per cent of the total of teenage expenditure is spent on alcoholic drink. 'The latest figures', says Mark Abrams, '. . . show that less than 40 per cent of male teenagers take any alcoholic drink as often as once a week. Among girls, the abstainers are even more numerous – less than 10 per cent have any alcohol as often as once a week.'[35] It must also be borne in mind, on considering these figures, that the definition of 'teenager' adopted by Mark Abrams for the purpose of his study is: 'those young people who have reached the age of fifteen but are not yet twenty-five years of age and are unmarried. Most of us, I think, would not include people between the ages of twenty-one and twenty-five in our conception of 'teenagers', but these young people are all included in these figures. It seems safe to assume that if only people literally in their teens – i.e. from fifteen to twenty, or, at the outside, twenty-one – had been considered, the size of the average expend-able income would have been much lower.

It might be argued, in any case, that this opportunity for early adulthood is a good thing. It may be that in modern society we are tending too much to extend artificially the period of supposed immaturity of children, to draw out the period of their dependence upon the family. Perhaps young people are mature before we choose to think they are, and perhaps many of the tensions experienced between parents and young people are a result of this delayed recognition of their maturity and their capability of independence.

Whether there is, in fact, a widespread and intense conflict between teenagers and their homes is open to doubt. In a pamphlet entitled *Club Members Today*, published in 1960 and giving the results of a questionnaire sent out to young people by the National Association of Youth Clubs, the author wrote: 'The most cheering fact that has emerged is that so many of them spend a good deal of time in their own homes.'[36] It was found in this study that for young people in the vast majority of homes there was no lack of affection from or towards their parents. Mr Harold Haywood, education officer of the association, commenting on the report in the *News Chronicle*, said: 'This is the young people's own view of themselves and one of the interesting things it shows is how much their homes mean to them.'

The tendency, of course, is to characterize all young people as being irresponsible, superficial, and without feelings of loyalty to their families, but this is an unwarranted exag-geration. For example, it is sometimes said that the availa-bility of easily earned wages at an unskilled level leads young people into an apathetic attitude with regard to training for skills. But recent studies of apprenticeship sug-gest that there is no lack of desire for such training amongst young people; the chief fault is that many industrial firms are failing to offer the facilities for training.[37] Similarly, young people are frequently said to be superficial and not seriously concerned with the problems of the modern world. Sometimes, however, to make a purely personal observation,

I am asked to address various groups and conferences of young people: for example, a sixth form conference in Southampton, where over three hundred young people from surrounding grammar schools voluntarily devoted their week-end to a discussion of 'Christianity and Humanism', and lunch-time meetings of young technicians in colleges of technology, who choose, incidentally, subjects such as 'Comparative Religion'. Such experiences leave me with no doubt that there are a great many young people who are eager for learning and discussion, and who wish to come to terms seriously and responsibly with the complex problems of the modern world. These more serious activities of 'youth', of course, do not 'hit the headlines', and the fact is that the press, in spite of many protestations to the contrary, seems to concentrate upon those young people who are prone to criminality or hooliganism, and who thus give rise to more 'sensational' news.

Actually, statistics suggest that Britain, in many ways, is becoming a more cultured country. The publication of serious books has increased, the number of concerts of classical music has increased, the number of exhibitions of sculpture and paintings has grown. Indeed, the only art which has shown any decline since the war has been that of the live theatre, and this decline is chiefly because of financial difficulties and, perhaps, the increasing competition of television. And it is plausible to suppose that much of this support of cultural activities comes from young people; certainly one's impressions of concert-going audiences and the people who visit art exhibitions are such as to suggest this. So that older people (and those not so old) who criticize the cultural deficiencies of the young might sometimes stop to compare the range of young people's cultural activity at the present time with that actually undertaken by themselves. It would, I think, in many cases lead to a modification of judgement.

The same tendency to 'blacken' the character of modern youth is found in much criticism of the sexual morals of young people; but here again such criticism seems to lack historical perspective and is not usually based upon a careful examination of evidence. Such statistical and 'qualitative' studies as exist* do not suggest, and are certainly far from demonstrating, that young people of today are any more licentious than young people of other periods or than people of other age-groups in our own society (indeed, almost any criticism of young people can be applied with equal validity to older people). In *Exploring English Character*, Gorer's findings led him to say:

... the younger generation – those under twenty-four – are just as strict in their views of desirable and undesirable sexual behaviour as their elders. There seems every reason to believe that the sexual morals of the English have changed very little in the present century.[38]

As we have seen earlier, Gorer's 1970 study was such as fully to support these findings, if not, indeed, to indicate that there was now a more sensitive and articulate approach to sexual morals and to marriage than was the case even twenty years ago.

And in his contribution to the pamphlet on *Teenage Morals* he writes: 'The evidence seems to me very slight that the present generation of teenagers is more licentious or more promiscuous than other generations in contemporary society, or earlier generations of adolescents.' The only difference Gorer dwells upon is with reference to 'the protected girls' of the middle classes:

Earlier generations considered that ladies needed help in guard-

* See particularly, *Teenage Morals* (1961), published by Councils and Education Press. A good example of the misuse of inadequate figures is given in this pamphlet by Stuart Maclure:
'One conference speaker has quoted a small piece of private investigation, not intended to be of universal significance. "In one class of fourteen-year-old boys and girls", she said, "in a secondary modern school serving a rural area, no less than 12 per cent of the boys and 25 per cent of the girls had already had sexual relations with more than one person before any scheduled sex instruction was given."
'These are staggering figures which have subsequently be enmisquoted freely. In fact, they mean what they say. The inquiry covered only one class, the numbers were far too small to generalize from' (p. 9).

ing their chastity; the last two generations have passed the responsibility to the young people themselves . . . We are putting a greater weight of responsibility on young girls today than they ever had to bear in the past for their own sexual conduct . . .'[39]

Here again, then, I have hoped to show that the 'stresses and strains' experienced between parents and children in the modern family do not by any means indicate moral retrogression, but are problems resulting from moral and social improvements.*

OLD PEOPLE AND THEIR YOUNGER FAMILIES

It is sometimes said that since much is now publicly provided for old people – pensions, old folks' bungalows and flats, meals-on-wheels, and the like – responsibility on the part of younger families for the care of the aged has fallen away. Consequently, though better provided for in a material sense, old people are more isolated from their younger families and feel more lonely and frustrated than before. Whilst not wishing to claim that there is *no* truth in this view, the evidence does seem to suggest that there is little ground to support it. In the conference on *The Family*, speaking on the topic of 'Old People', Mr Huws Jones said:[40]

Today the care of old people is far less a forced levy and much more a voluntary contribution . . . Comparative evidence bearing on the family relationships of old people is hard to come by and still harder to interpret. But it seems that in Bradford in 1949 only

* Some of the reports upon the behaviour of young people make quite amusing reading. Consider the following report in 'News in Brief' in the *Sunday Times* of 8 November 1959:
'A fact-finding quiz by a Roman Catholic organization to establish how teenagers of Wednesbury, Staffordshire, spend their leisure has disclosed that their chief hobby is courting. The mayor, Alderman George Stokes, said yesterday that the survey was a "nonsensical and untrue reflection" on the town's youth, who were hard-working and industrious. Courting was an international hobby not peculiar to Wednesbury, and to suggest that that was all the youngsters did in their leisure time was bunkum.'

in 1 per cent of the cases admitted to hospital had relations sought relief from responsibility without full justification. And, after inquiries in Birmingham, Professor Thompson wrote of the 'astonishing kindliness, charity, and devotion with which these poor people were tended by their neighbours, friends, and relatives'. In his opinion complaints about the decline of family cohesion and the sense of social and neighbourly responsibility were not justified.

Everyone here is concerned to help the family as an institution to contribute what it alone can contribute to the happiness and fulfilment of young and old. I suggest we do no good to our cause when we talk as if, more than ever before, we fail today in our family care of old people. The evidence does not warrant it.

In a paper read to the Manchester Statistical Society,[41] Brian Abel-Smith and Robert Pinker reported a very careful and painstaking attempt to compare the numbers of physically ill, mentally ill, welfare cases (cripples, blind, deaf and dumb, aged and infirm, etc.), and law-breakers who were housed and treated in institutions in 1911 with those in 1951. Some of their findings are very significant for our purposes here.

Their investigation shows that there seems to have been

... a large decrease in the proportion of men and women aged 65 and over in institutional care. The only exceptions are in the case of single and married women aged 75 and over. The figures for men are remarkable. In 1911, 8 per cent of single men aged 45–64 were in workhouses, as were about 25 per cent of single men over the age of 65. In 1951, the rates for single men rose from 2 per cent for the age-group 45–64 to 16 per cent for those aged 75 and over. In the case of widowed and divorced men, in 1911 5 per cent aged 45–64 were in workhouses and about 10 per cent over the age of 65. In 1951, the rates were only 1 per cent for men aged 45–64 rising to 6 per cent for men aged 75 or over. The proportion of the aged – particularly of aged men – in institutions has decreased between 1911 and 1951.

The authors conclude:

At the very least, our conclusions do not support theories of in-creasing family neglect or of a trend towards 'medicated survival'

– at least in an institutional setting. Despite much higher standards of social welfare, much smaller families, and above all a lengthening of life among the 'institutionally prone', society was not carrying a larger institutional 'burden' in 1951 than in 1911. It was carrying it in other ways.[42]

There is little evidence to suggest, then, that the 'isolation' of old people is due to any lack of responsibility on the part of their younger families. The problem may be explained and understood, however, in a completely different way.

It must be remembered, first, that the average expectation of life is higher than ever before, and, secondly, that conditions of health have improved considerably. This means that the period of retirement of old people is, on the average, longer than before, and during it they enjoy an improved state of health. It seems feasible to claim, then, that old people do not feel lonely and frustrated only because they are isolated from their younger families, but also, and perhaps chiefly, because they feel they have been discarded too soon. They have to retire when they still feel reasonably fit and active, when they could continue to provide independently for themselves, and when they feel that they have still much to contribute in terms of experience and productive work to the community. One's general impression is that, while old people do like to be within reach of their younger families, they do not clamour to live with them and to be cared for by them. This arrangement, often necessary in the past, can never have been an altogether happy one. It can never have been an easy matter on the part of old people to give up the homes they had built up during their lives, and the independence and privacy they had enjoyed in them. And it can never have been easy for young families to pursue their own lives and the upbringing of their children in the context of the attitudes of elderly parents and relatives, together with the additional burden of caring for them – though they may have done this in the most careful way possible. When introducing the National Assistance Bill, Aneurin Bevan, then Minister, said:

It is one of the distinguishing characteristics of the psychology of old people that they cling tenaciously to privacy. They do not want to be interfered with, they want to lead their own lives. They do not want to be dependent on other people and, as they grow older, they become jealous of their independence.[43]

Old people wish to maintain their independence as long as they are capable of doing so, so that their frustration may stem very largely from the feeling that they have been 'put upon the shelf' too soon.

This problem, then, may be incorrectly explained in terms of the moral decline of young families, and is not likely to be solved by trying to go back to the situation in which young people cared for their elder parents and relatives in their own homes. A few things can be said. First, while public provisions have been made for old people, they are certainly not enough to enable old people to view the period of retirement constructively, with security and pleasure. Much more needs to be done. Apart from the more obvious financial improvements in their situation which can be made, there are, of course, real difficulties in the way of providing suitable accommodation for old people in such a way as to allow them to live within easy reach of their relatives and friends and in the neighbourhood with which they are familiar, and this requires a good deal more effort in working out and implementing appropriate social policies. Interesting suggestions to this end are made by S. K. Ruck in an article on 'A Policy for Old Age'.[44]

Secondly, new attitudes are needed with regard to the employment of old people. It has been shown that old people can work well and effectively in a wide range of occupations; it is only in some things – for example, in the maintenance of high speeds of work – that difficulty and anxiety is encountered. With schemes of re-training during working experience, and with a careful allocation of jobs, there is no reason why old people should not go on working beyond the 'minimum retiring age' if they wish to do so.

Thirdly, new attitudes to the period of retirement itself should be engendered. It is very probably the case that many old people feel 'lost', and find it difficult to occupy them-selves in the sudden 'vacuum' of retirement, because of the perpetuation of attitudes (thoroughly understandable in the circumstances) to the effect that retirement is the 'stage before the end' – a negative period of rest from labour, a period of gradual decay. But if old people could be materially secure, there is no reason why the period of retirement should not be regarded in a positive and constructive way, as a time when many interests and activities, for which there has been neither time nor opportunity earlier, can now be undertaken. I believe that some colleges in America offer courses in various subjects – music, painting, philosophy – for old people, and that these courses are well-attended and keenly pursued. It is interesting to note that the City Literary Institute in London is beginning to experiment with such courses in preparation for retirement, a lead which ought to be followed elsewhere. The idea that retirement is just a period of decrepitude during which one waits for the last journey to the graveyard is an idea we should do away with.

With better provisions for the extended employment of old people, with material security, appropriate accom-modation, and provisions for leisure during the period of retirement, and with changed attitudes to retirement, it seems that the situation of old people and their relationships with their younger families could be considerably improved.

THE FAMILY AND WIDER KINSHIP RELATIONSHIPS

Earlier, I argued that there were various factors which could be supposed to have diminished the extent to which the individual family was dependent upon, and lived in close relationship with, its wider body of kindred. A little more must be said about this in the face of some recent quali-fications of this point. In their study of *Family and Kinship in East London*, Michael Young and Peter Willmott show that, in some areas at least, the 'extended family' is still of con-siderable importance, and that the generalization that the modern family has become 'isolated' from wider kindred is too sweeping. Their study shows that, in particular among working-class families, there is a considerable relationship of dependence and mutual aid between the wife of a family and her own mother (who has become well-known as the working-class 'Mum'). Social workers, too, frequently say that the rehousing of young working-class families in New Towns, at a distance from 'Mum', suddenly confronts young wives with a disquieting independence and a need for individual initiative and responsibility to which they are not accustomed. This clearly suggests that in their earlier neighbourhood experience the 'extended family' was of considerable importance to them. (It might be noted, however, that this self-same point demonstrates that the 'distance' between the family and wider kindred is in fact coming into being.) There are two things, however, that might be said about this.

The first is that, although such studies show that the extended family, in this very limited sense, is important in some areas, this evidence is not such as to warrant the assertion that the kind of generalization we have made earlier is untrue. In general, the kinds of geographical, occupational, and social mobility brought about by industrialization, transport, war, education, and so on, seem certain to have diminished the extent to which the family lives in a localized and long-abiding network of wider kinship relationships. Let anyone compare, for example, Flora Thompson's exquisite account – in *Lark Rise to Candleford* – of the quiet, settled tone of village life in the 1880s with the tone and complexity of his own experience in town and country alike at the present day. Let him compare any novel of Thomas Hardy with, let us say, *Room at the Top* by John Braine, or indeed with any contemporary British novel. And let him bear in mind the earlier situation when kinsfolk, all with the same family name, were so thickly represented in an area that they had to be distinguished by 'nicknames' of various kinds.

In the Forest of Dean in Gloucestershire, for example, even just before the last war when it still retained many characteristics rooted in customs and practices stemming from the Middle Ages, particular villages or groups of villages possessed a limited number of family names. Thus, in the Whitecroft and Yorkley district there were a great many families which went by the names Phipps, Jones, James, Morse, and a few others. But there were so many families of each name, all interrelated to varying degrees, that particular groups of families came to be designated by nicknames. There were the Tinker Phippses, the Tup Phippses, the Cuckoo Phippses, and, I believe, one group which went by the name of 'Bladders'. Places were named after the groups of families which lived there. Thus, a little hollow below a railway siding which contained perhaps ten cottages and a pub, was known as Phippses' Bottom. Similarly, there were the Jadder Joneses, the Broad'un Joneses, the Quick'un Joneses, the Cabbage Joneses, the Bogey Joneses, and the Noah Joneses. There were the Nip Jameses, the Councillor Jameses, and the Nubbin Jameses. And, bearing in mind the breadth of rural humour, there were the Wee-Wee Morses and the Poopshala Morses. In this sort of situation, there was an intimate degree of family interconnection, and individuals would be known not only by their family name, but also by their family nickname. So that if you were inquiring about a certain Mr Jones, your informant might say: 'Oh ah! He's a Bogey Jones,' or: 'He's one o' the Jadders.' And a man would often be known chiefly by his family nickname. Thus, a man would not be known as 'Georgie Phipps' but as 'Georgie Bladders'. And I remember that the woman who delivered our post was sometimes called Mrs Morse, but more frequently Mrs Wee-Wee.

The same sort of situation, in an earlier time, was well-known to Scott, who wrote in a note to *Guy Mannering*:

The distinction of individuals by nicknames when they possess no property is still common on the Border, and indeed necessary, from the number of people having the same name. In the small village of Lustruther, in Roxburghshire, there dwelt, in the memory of man, four inhabitants called Andrew, or Dandie, Oliver. They were distinguished as Dandie Eassil-gate, Dandie Wassil-gate,

Dandie Thumbie, and Dandie Dumbie. The two first had their names from being eastward and westward in the street of the village; the third from something peculiar in the conformation of his thumb; the fourth from his taciturn habits.[45]

In the passage to which this note refers, an old shepherd says:

'Ye see, sir, the folks hereabout are a' Armstrongs and Elliots, and sic like – twa or three given names – and so, for distinction's sake, the lairds and farmers have the names of their places that they live at – as, for example, "Tam o' Todshaw", "Will o' the Flat", "Habbie o' Sorbietrees", and our good master here, "o' the Charlieshope". Aweel, sir, and then the inferior sort o' people, ye'll observe, are kend by sorts o' by-names, some o' them, as Glaiket Christie, and the Deuke's Davie, or may be, like this lad Gabriel, by his employment – as, for example, Tod Gabbie, or Hunter Gabbie.'

This kind and degree of interdependence among kindred has surely been changed beyond recognition by our industrial and urban mode of life. It may be thought that my example of the Forest of Dean in very recent times serves to defeat my own argument, and shows how little disturbed such relationships have been until very recently. But my point is that this sort of situation must now be the exception rather than the rule. Actually, the Forest of Dean was very little affected by the wider aspects of industrialization, until the last war; it existed in a kind of cultural isolation and remained a closely knit community in itself. But new industry, extended transport services, were introduced during and after the war, and the character of the community is now much changed. The situation as I have described it is already being rapidly transformed, and within a generation or two I think that these earlier kin relationships, and even the memory of them, will be gone.

The fact is – with reference to the continued degree of importance of extended kinship relationships – that the situation must differ considerably from region to region,*

* Geoffrey Gorer, in Chap. 3 of *Exploring English Character*, has some evidence on this variation between regions and between different social

from locality to locality, and between social classes, throughout the country, and we clearly need many more detailed
and comparative studies before these differences can be
known. It seems plausible to suggest, for example, that in
localities (urban and rural alike) in which a strong community life and spirit has continued – as in Bethnal Green, in
the villages of the Forest of Dean, in small mining towns –
the interrelationships and the degree of mutual aid between
the family and wider kindred may still continue to be of importance. In the larger conurbations, in suburbs, in growing
dormitory areas, and in New Towns, however, the distance
between the individual family and its wider kindred is likely
to be much more marked. It is probable, too, that the actual
degree of desire for the perpetuation of extended kinship ties
may be different between, say, members of the professional
classes and members of the wage-earning classes. The kinds
and degrees of mutual aid, and the reasons for it, may differ
between social classes also. For example, young middle-class
parents may desire, and obtain, help from elder relatives in
order to send their children to public school; or they may
want their father's influence in prevailing upon a friendly
solicitor so that they can purchase their house with minimum
legal costs; and beyond such financial aid and influence
there may be little sentimental attachment and little desire
for closer interdependence. Young working-class parents, on
the other hand, will not and cannot expect or require these
degrees of financial aid of their elder relatives; their desires
and their problems will be different, and they may experience deeper sentimental feelings of attachment. The
truth is quite simply that more research is needed here
before we can know reliably what regional and social differences there are.

---

classes. By and large, he summarizes: 'People in the working class
outside the southern counties of England do tend to live near their
kinsfolk; it is the people of the south, especially the middle class . . . who
are most often separated from their kith and kin and therefore dependent
on friends and neighbours for help and companionship' (p. 46).

The second point, however, is that – whatever the truth in this matter, and whatever the worth of extended kinship ties – such social distance as may exist between the family and wider relationships can hardly be said to be an outcome of family 'decline' or of 'moral decline'; neither does it necessarily entail any worsening of human relationships. The problems encountered in this connection are, again, the outcome of factors which, on the whole, are decided improvements: the increased standard of living; the ability of the individual family to provide its own livelihood independently; the increased opportunities for geographical movement to undertake more promising occupations; the improvements in housing and the provision of new residential areas with better facilities; the increased opportunities for educated and individual advancement. All these have tended to loosen the ties which bound individuals and their own families to their earlier families and their wider relatives; and they are all factors of which we would approve. Also – though I do not wish, by any means, to imply that close relationships with kinsfolk are devoid of value – it is at least arguable that the relaxing of these close ties gives many people a degree of independence, privacy, and effective initiative which they find positively desirable. To put this in another way, the closeness of kinship ties in earlier times was largely a matter of necessity, and it entailed many elements of individual constraint. Indeed, it is certain that human relationships in these earlier, relatively closed, rural and traditional communities have been idealized well away from the truth. Some excellent recent studies – *The World We Have Lost* by Peter Laslett (a book of historical essays) and *Akenfield* by Ronald Blythe (the story of a Suffolk village, told more or less by its old people) – though written with the fullest sympathy for the conditions, problems, and experiences of those who lived in such communities, none the less show beyond any doubt what poverty, what a stark, harrowing, necessitous family dependence, what a rudeness of family relationships had to be endured. Closed, intimate communities; families tightly bound together by shared, inescapable constraints; these were far from the simple havens portrayed by backward-glancing sentiment. It is therefore arguable (a) that many people are happier with a new degree of freedom from these constraints, and (b) that their relationships with their earlier families and other relatives may be positively improved in that they can now be undertaken on the basis of choice. Since they are less an outcome of circumscribing demands, they can be entered into with discrimination and with a lesser degree of tension. Close kinship relationships have their value, but they can also be limiting, confining, frustrating, so that the loosening of these ties, for some people at any rate, may constitute a desirable improvement. It is true that the increase in freedom and independence of the family calls for the qualities of maturity and self-reliance in individuals. But is this a bad thing? And is there any real evidence that the majority of people do not want this situation, and are incapable of these qualities?

THE FAMILY AND THE WIDER SOCIAL ROLES OF ITS MEMBERS

The relationships between members of a family within their home, and the patterns of stress or harmony which they experience, are bound to be considerably affected by the characteristics of the wider social relationships in which they are involved. A final consideration, therefore, about which it is interesting to speculate is whether in modern society the wider and expanding roles which husbands, wives, and young people perform *beyond* the family are such as to bring about 'stresses and strains' *within* the family. There are at least some writers who are convinced that this is so.

The Work and Status of the Husband and Father

As a citizen, and as the head of a family, a man is looked upon as a responsible person. Reliability, initiative, the capacities for thoughtfulness and consideration, are required of him so that stability and security are achieved in his home, and the basis is provided for the satisfactory fulfilment of the lives of those who are largely dependent upon him. A certain dignity is expected of him, a certain authority, and much significance is attached to his performance of his family duties.

The detailed and highly specialized mechanization of work in large factories, however, has had important effects upon the nature of the work which a man performs, the status he enjoys in his work relationships, and the qualities which are required of him in his work. The work which many men perform has now become little more than a small, routine operation closely geared to the complicated and impersonal process of the 'production belt'. Men have become little more than 'accessories' to machines. They may therefore feel little or nothing of creative reward or of personal significance in the work they do. In a large factory, a man may have become an insignificant number on a clock-card; an item in the labour force; a factor in labour costs; one of the daily army which clocks in in the morning and clocks out at night. No independence of thought and action, no initiative, little responsibility may be required of him. His 'security of tenure' in his job, though perhaps improved with general economic stability, may be very limited and precarious indeed.

This means that, in many cases, there is a complete difference in the qualities required of a man in his work and in his family. There is a completely different estimation of him in the factory and in the home. But these features of a man's life cannot be held separate; they cannot be 'departmentalized' in his experience. As Professor Titmuss, who has stated this kind of problem best, puts it: 'People . . . do not "play" roles like actors. A role is something that a person *is*.' Consequently, this wide difference of roles and associated qualities will constitute a conflict in the inward experience of a man. Any frustration, dissatisfaction, diminution of self-respect, that a man experiences in his work is likely to be carried over into his feelings of his own worth within the family, and to affect the way in which he is regarded by members of his family.

Professor Titmuss puts this point very clearly:

If workers do not respect themselves and do not feel that they are being accorded respect by their fellows in the factory, may they not, therefore, tend to feel that they are not fulfilling satisfactorily, in the eyes of their wives and children, their roles as husbands and fathers? Society expects, for example, that children should admire and respect their fathers for qualities other than the size of their pay packets. In the eyes of the farm worker's child and the child in many middle-class and professional homes, father plays a comprehended and admired role in his work. But what of the child of the industrial worker on the assembly line who has little conception of his place in the scheme of things? ... In a culture that values efficiency, those who cannot achieve self-respect in their work may come to feel that there is something wrong with them not only as workers, but as husbands and fathers ...

In so far, then, as modern industrial techniques lead to feelings of personal dissatisfaction, to a dispossession of personality, the problem thus becomes a family and community problem. If the effects cannot be expressed at work, if relief and compensation cannot be found there, then the worker's home life is likely to be influenced and changed in many subtle ways.[46]

Improvements in modes of economic productivity do not, therefore, necessarily entail improvements in the estimation and treatment of men as individuals, and 'stresses and strains' in the family may result.

The Work and Social Relationships of the Wife and Mother

The possible difficulties of family relationships brought about in this way may be even further enhanced if the wife and mother of the family herself goes out to work (for whatever reason) and is therefore brought into relationship with a far wider circle of people. If a woman is herself employed on much the same basis as her husband, and similarly contributes a wage to the family, she may herself feel this same conflict between the qualities expected of her at work and at home, and may experience the same diminution of personal significance. But she may also come to have a more realistic appreciation of the small significance and low status of her husband beyond the family, and thus have a diminished respect for him. As she sees and perhaps comes into contact with people of higher status, with better and more secure standards of life, her tendencies towards social emulation may be intensified and she may become increasingly dissatisfied with her lot. The roles played by the woman beyond the home are therefore likely (but not, of course, necessarily) to have a considerable effect upon relationships within the home and the estimations which the members of the family have of each other.

The Wider Roles of Young People

Similarly, if young people enter early employment on a similar basis to their parents, they may be affected in precisely the same ways and their attitudes towards their parents may be changed; their respect for them may be diminished. In this context, any feelings of respect for the old on the part of the young may be undermined, and if young people, because of their incomes, find clubs and other avenues of entertainment easily available, they may encounter influences and enjoy activities which make the lives of their parents ('the older generation') seem insufferably dull and unexciting. Thus the usual conflict between the generations is likely to be accentuated. In this setting, any attempt on the part of parents to guide and govern the directions of activity of young people is likely to be of little avail: indeed it may only serve to aggravate the situation.

Also, if young people enjoy higher education and subsequent advancement in occupation and status, they are likely to develop tastes, views, and beliefs which are different from those of their parents and which may well clash with them. They may begin to mix in their work and in their social life with colleagues and friends whose family background and general social background is totally different from their own. In this way a distance, sometimes a distressing distance, can develop between parents and children. Conflicts of status which can involve agonies of sensitivity, of conflicting desires and loyalties, can be brought into being.

I need not elaborate upon this theme. It is sufficient to see that there are some stresses experienced in the modern family which are due, not only to changes in relationships within the family itself, but also to changes in the roles which members of the family fulfil in the wider society. This bears out our earlier view that the family cannot be considered only as a community in itself, but is integrally bound up with the wider network of social institutions. It can only be fully understood within the context of these wider institutions and is intimately affected by changes in them.

Again, however, it is clear that these problems in the modern family are not the outcome of any moral decline in the family itself, but are the unforeseen consequences of wider social improvements: improvements in productive techniques, the social participation of women, the standards of employment and education of the young people, and the like. Of course, the low status and relative insignificance of the worker in modern mass-production industry is far from being morally defensible, but even this is linked with the increase in productivity which, in terms of material welfare, is a good thing. What this means is that in social spheres other than the family (in this case, in industry) certain improvements have brought in their train new problems which need to be studied, understood, and resolved. It means, also, that if we are concerned to achieve and sustain good human qualities within the family, we must concern ourselves with the task of achieving and sustaining these same qualities in all other departments of social life. It means that we cannot expect to put matters right in *one* aspect of social life without considering, interdependently, *all* aspects of social life. No matter how difficult the task may be – and it is, indeed, difficult – we are faced with nothing short of the necessity of working out a full and comprehensive social philosophy, and an intricate application of these principles to every aspect of practical social policy. Nothing short of this can be enough.

*

We have now examined, though briefly, many of the problems characterizing relationships in the contemporary family. It is clear that problems do exist, and it is easy to understand why people have become anxious about them, and have been led to speak in terms of the 'deterioration' of family life. We have seen, however, that some of these problems are not so grave as they are often supposed to be, and that, in any case, they cannot by any means be explained in terms of 'family decline' – moral or otherwise. On the contrary, these problems are more correctly to be interpreted in terms of the consequences (sometimes unforeseen) of social changes which constitute positive moral improvements.

We are now in a position to draw a few clear conclusions from the analysis we have undertaken.

5 Some Conclusions

THE first conclusion which the foregoing analysis seems to warrant is that it is quite untrue to say that the family in contemporary Britain has been 'stripped of its functions' and has, as a consequence, become of diminished importance as a social institution. On the contrary, the modern family fulfils *more* functions, and in a far more detailed and sophisticated manner, than did the family before or during the nineteenth-century development of industrialization.

When sociologists speak of the 'functions' of an institution they have two things chiefly in mind: the human needs and purposes (whether intended or not) which the institution exists to satisfy, and the 'functional interconnections' which the institution has with the wider network of institutions in society – the ways in which it is interdependent in its operation with the other institutions in the whole social system. In both senses of the word 'function' our conclusion holds good. The family is now concerned with a more detailed and refined satisfaction of needs than hitherto, and it is also more intimately and responsibly bound up with the wider and more complicated network of social institutions in the modern state than it was prior to industrialization.

This conclusion can be demonstrated by taking the functions enumerated by MacIver and considering each of them in turn.

If we take, first all, the 'essential' functions of the family – the satisaction of the sexual needs of the married couple, the careful upbringing of children, and the provision of a satisfactory home for its members – it is perfectly clear that the modern family – entailing the equal status of wife and husband and their mutual consideration in marriage; the high status of children; and the improved standards of income, housing, household equipment – aims at, and achieves, a far more satisfactory and refined provision for these needs than did either the pre-industrial family or the family of early industrial Britain, in which women were inferior and subjected, women and children were frequently exploited within or outside the family, and conditions in the home were so deplorably inadequate.

What is not commonly stressed, however, in stating this qualitative improvement in the 'essential' functions of the family is that the demands upon the members of the family for the satisfactory performance of them have become increasingly heavy. Professor Titmuss has made this point admirably. In *Essays on the Welfare State*,[1] he writes:

That the children of the large working-class families of fifty years ago helped to bring each other up must have been true; no single-handed mother of seven could have hoped to give to each child the standard of care, the quantity of time, the diffusion and concentration of thought, that most children receive today. In this context, it is difficult to understand what is meant by those who generalize about the 'lost' functions of parents in the rearing of children.

And in his contribution to the conference on *The Family*:

Society is in process of making parenthood a highly self-conscious, self-regarding affair. In so doing, it is adding heavily to the sense of personal responsibility among parents. Their tasks are much harder and involve more risks of failure when children have to be brought up as individual successes in a supposedly mobile, individualistic society rather than in a traditional and repetitious society. Bringing up children becomes less a matter of rule-of-thumb custom and tradition; more a matter of acquired knowledge, of expert advice. More decisions have to be made because there is so much more to be decided; and as the margin of felt responsibility extends so does the scope for anxiety about one's children.[2]

As the expected standards of fulfilment of the 'essential' functions of the family have improved, therefore, so have the demands for responsibility on the part of members of the family increased.

I think that there would be little disagreement about this improved fulfilment of the 'essential' functions within the family. MacIver certainly agrees that such an improvement has taken place. Sometimes, however, this improvement is still insufficiently realized, and one still hears charges of 'declining sexual morality' among both adults and young people, and of 'declining standards' of parenthood. I do not want to repeat all that has already been said on this matter, but it may be worthwhile to point out some further differences between past and present.

Earlier, when considering the conditions of family life among the urban working classes during the nineteenth century, we mentioned the account of the Rev. Mearns, which indicated the extent of incest, prostitution, and other forms of immorality, and the correspondingly low standards of 'family morals', in poor, overcrowded districts. Similar conditions, however, have existed much more recently than this. Consider, for example, the following statements of Cyril Forster Garbett in his book *In the Heart of South London*, written when he was Bishop of Southwark.

On the ground floor of a house in South London there lived two families. In the front room were the father and mother with six boys and girls, the eldest was ten and the youngest one. Two of these slept in their parents' bed, the other four as best they could on mattresses on the ground. The rest of this floor was occupied by a family of ten; the parents and two children slept in one room, three in the kitchen, and the other three in a small boxroom most of which was occupied by furniture and perambulator. The whole house was in a bad state of repair and infested by rats. In the four rooms were four adults and fourteen children. Measles broke out among the children, one of them died from pneumonia following it; two were removed to the hospital suffering from the same complaint, and one of these also died. A crowning touch of horror was added to the tragedy when the undertaker entering the room with the coffin killed a rat which was trying to get at the dead body of the child . . . This is not a story of the Middle Ages or of some Asiatic village, but of South London in the year of Our Lord, 1930.[3]

Dr Garbett goes on to describe the immorality attendant upon these conditions of over-crowding.

Overcrowding, also, exposes quite young children to grave moral dangers. This is an evil difficult to write about plainly, but it is known to all social workers. Most parents take great care to protect their little children from corruption. Public opinion in the lowest of tenements is roused to indignation at any interference with children; in one of the worst streets in South London those who have attempted to assault a child have been mercilessly thrashed and driven out of the neighbourhood. Often, too, when only one room is possible, the elder boys and girls are separated from one another by a curtain or a screen. But from their earliest years children become familiar with the facts of sex. Premature familiarity blunts the sense of decency. In one room there were living the parents, two young boys and girls of eight and ten. The youngest girl was assaulted by an elderly man living on another floor, but was so unaccustomed to the decencies of life that she thought nothing of it. In another basement the parents (not married) and three children slept in the same bed, and the mother and the eldest girl (under sixteen) were found both pregnant by the same man. In a basement room was a family of eight; it included a boy and girl of twelve and fourteen respectively. They began to behave indecently together until separated and sent to training homes. A certain crowded tenement has stairways badly lighted; complaints have been made and nothing done. The children are terrified of these stairs at night; at least twice on them men have behaved improperly to young girls. It would be possible to lengthen almost indefinitely this horrible list. But these things will happen as long as both sexes of all ages are crowded into one room . . .[4]

This is a story of the family conditions of working-class people in London not long before the last war. Surely it must be the case that the improvements in housing and material conditions made since that time have done much to improve the nature of family morals. At least children and parents in modern council houses, housing estates, and the much-criticized New Towns are not exposed to the same probabilities of incest and corruption. The family no longer has to share the same mattress among the rats, mice, and black-beetles.[5] Of course, some areas of squalor still remain in our large towns and cities, and the sooner they are removed the better. But at least considerable improvements have been made since the war, and the general level of family relationships must have been raised. At least, in these new living conditions, people now *know* what is an incestuous relationship and are *aware* of the indecency of an assault upon a child, whereas in these earlier conditions many people evidently neither knew nor cared.

There is little doubt, then, that the 'essential' functions of the family, centred upon sexual relationships, parenthood, and home-making, are fulfilled far more satisfactorily in the modern family than they were in the family of the distant or the recent past. It is more interesting, however, to consider the so-called 'non-essential' functions of the family, which, the generalization states, have been increasingly fulfilled outside the family by the specialized agencies of the modern state.

Government

If we begin with MacIver's function of 'government' in the family, and take this to mean the family's government of its own affairs and the activities of its members, it would seem that the modern family is just as much concerned with this function as was the family in Britain before industrialization. But if we interpret this function more widely it can be seen that a great and important change has taken place. In the modern family, both husband and wife are recognized citizens of the state. Both have a voice and a vote in deciding upon the acceptance or rejection of those policies of the state which affect the conditions of the family. The adult members of the modern family are now, in a democratic community, largely responsible for determining those provisions of public health, public education, economic security, which, taken together, determine the conditions and the destinies of the family. In the pre-industrial family, husband and wife had no such voice. The members of the modern family are now, therefore, drawn far more closely into the tasks of government than ever before. They enjoy far greater degrees of responsibility for government, and, correspondingly, far greater demands are made upon their capacities for responsibility.

This function has considerably increased in effectiveness and in importance in the modern family.

Economic Functions

Secondly, let us consider the 'economic functions' of the family, and the generalization that the modern family is no longer an 'economic unit'. Certainly the modern family is not a productive unit as was the case with labouring-class families in agriculture and domestic industry; but to leap to the conclusion that the modern family is in *no* important sense an economic unit is unwarranted.

Much is sometimes made by some writers of the fact that many domestic (economic) tasks of the housewife have disappeared. Women no longer bake their own bread, make the clothes for the family, preserve their own jams, etc. But the importance of such changes can be over-estimated. Although many of these tasks are now, to a degree, superseded by factory modes of production, it is still the case that cooking, sewing, washing, and the general work involved in the maintenance of the home, are the tasks of the housewife (perhaps, to some extent, now shared by men). Indeed, one sometimes suspects that with the accumulation of domestic gadgets (refrigerators, washing machines, vacuum cleaners, coffee grinders, electric toasters, and the like) the complex chores of the household might have become even more preoccupying. Certainly, it would seem probable that – with increased knowledge of food-values – a more sophisticated amount of care goes into the balancing of the family diet. And these all remain 'economic tasks' in the household, though they are not wage-earning.

The family also remains an important economic unit from the viewpoint of the patterning of consumption, or, as the economist would put it, of the 'consumer's outlay'. This expenditure of family income – whether this is contributed by one or more members, and whether it is to any great extent 'pooled' or not – is still patterned not solely on 'individual preferences' but also on the needs of the family as a whole and the preferences of the family as a group. Advertisers are clearly aware of this, and sometimes play upon it to a rather nauseating extent, as may be seen by watching television advertisements for some foodstuffs, soap powders, holiday arrangements, and the like. Furthermore, although the degree and extent of this throughout the country cannot be said to be known, it is probable that there is still, to some extent, a 'pooling' of proportions of family incomes for the upkeep of the family as a whole, and for the improvement of the home. Indeed, if one is to judge from the present concentration upon schemes of furnishing, schemes of interior decoration, 'do-it-yourself' techniques with appropriate tool-kits, and from the extent to which families devote themselves to improving their 'homes and gardens' along these lines, the present-day concern for the improvement of the family's household must be held to be very considerable indeed.

Interesting confirmation of this is to be found in a radio talk given by Mark Abrams in November 1959, entitled 'The Home-Centred Society'.[6] Reviewing patterns of consumption over the past ten years, he states that much more money is now being spent on household goods. 'The proportion of families with a vacuum cleaner has doubled, ownership of a refrigerator has trebled, owners of a washing machine have increased tenfold; we have stocked our homes with vastly more furniture, radiograms, carpets, space-heaters, water heaters, arm-chairs, light fittings, lawn mowers . . .' All this, he says, has resulted in the fact that 'for the first time in modern British history the working-class home, as well as the middle-class home, has become a place that is warm, comfortable, and able to provide its own fireside entertainment – in fact, pleasant to live in.' And the modern husband 'spends his evenings and his week-ends not with his workmates but at home with his family, enjoying common fireside relaxations with them, or else "pottering" round the house maintaining or improving its comfort and appearance.'

It must be borne in mind, too, that present-day parents

have considerably more leisure-time to devote to these various aspects of home-making than had the majority of parents during the eighteenth and nineteenth centuries. We have seen in the work of Dr Pinchbeck and others that the parents and children of labouring families in the past were scarcely ever free from exhausting toil, and that the standards of domestic life were therefore extremely low. The increase in leisure has increased the time which can be spent upon these 'economic' tasks within the home.

When, further, one considers the whole array of social services provided by the 'specialized agencies' of the state (national insurance, public health, education, etc.) together with the structure of taxation which accompanies them, it becomes increasingly evident that the family in modern society is, in fact, considered and treated as an economic unit. Professor Graveson, writing of this supposed decline of the family as an economic unit, claims:

Where, however, the economic ties *within* the family have loosened,[7] *outside* it they have increased with every new form of social welfare provision.[8]

Professor Kahn Freund writes similarly:

The law of social security, like the law of maintenance, is more realistic than the law of property; account is being taken in these branches of the law of the existence of the household as an economic unit and of the natural inequalities in the economic functions of husband and wife.[9]

The economic and other provisions of the state which aid the family do not, therefore, 'strip' the family of economic functions; on the contrary, they recognize and treat the family as an economic unit, and acknowledge the different economic functions of husband and wife in the family.

It is worthwhile to recall again Geoffrey Gorer's recent (1970) findings that the possession of a 'home of your own' with good material and neighbourhood facilities had become so accepted and assumed a fact among the vast majority of families as not even to be raised as a problem at all; and, furthermore, that there was scarcely any differentiation of functions within it. Husband and wife were actively involved in doing things in their home together. All the debate and legislation throughout the 1960s on matrimonial property, on the matrimonial home, on the financial provisions on divorce, and similar matters, are substantial evidence that government, law, and social services alike are more than ever concerned to shape their provisions to come as close as possible to the social and economic actuality of the family as a unit.[10]

A further point might be considered, which may not, perhaps, be so weighty, but about which it would be interesting to know more. Writing in 1906, Helen Bosanquet, disturbed by changes in landed property and by the decline in the *productive* aspect of the family as an economic unit, inquired whether there might not be, even so, some other continued community of interest of an economic nature which might bind families and generations together. Her conclusion was that such a bond probably did exist, and this was the continuity of occupation, or kind of occupation, between fathers and sons.

She suggested, first, that there was a well-marked continuity of occupation between the generations among members of the professional classes – clergymen, politicians, literary people, actors, and lawyers. And secondly, on the basis of information from the secretaries of trade unions, she found some continuity of occupational tradition from fathers to sons among hand-frame knitters, French polishers, typefounders, papermakers, coopers, printing machine managers, iron founders, bricklayers, pattern-makers, tinplate workers, miners, and some agricultural workers – for example, shepherds. She concluded:

I think, then, it is no exaggeration to say that wherever we find an industry of any degree of specialization, as distinct from unskilled and unspecialized labour, there we may find to a greater or less extent a continuity of work binding the generations together, and affording a basis for continuous family life as real and firm, if not as tangible, as landed property itself.[11]

Of course, specialization has grown increasingly since 1906, and educational and occupational opportunities have been considerably extended, so that it is probable that this kind and degree of continuity of occupation is nowadays less frequently found. But it would be interesting and worthwhile to have more knowledge of this. Just before the last war this continuity clearly existed in some regions – in some rural areas and in small colliery towns, for example – and it is interesting to note in Professor Glass's recent study of *Social Mobility in Britain* (1954) that the several social strata in Britain, resting upon occupational gradings as the central criterion, were found to be self-recruiting to a very high degree. That is, recruits to the various occupational groupings were very largely children of parents who were themselves already members of these groupings. Professionals, for example, were to a very large extent the children of professionals (still very much as Helen Bosanquet suggested). Although, therefore, we would expect, at the present time, to find a somewhat diminished continuity of traditional trades between parents and children, it may still be the case (a) that this continuity exists in some regions and in some occupations,* and (b) that, if not sharing precisely the same occupation, parents and children may still belong to the

---

* I have seen an unpublished survey of working-class families in London which gives evidence of a strong continuity of occupation between the generations. Also, to give a specific example, the *News Chronicle* of 27 September 1960 contained an article by Margaret Stewart pointing out this traditional continuity among ocean ship tally clerks (known in dockland as OST). The author writes: 'The strong family traditions of the dockers are never more in evidence than when it comes to filling the OST register.

'A father will name his son, an uncle his nephew, and one can find clerks who are proud that their father, grandfather and great-grandfather had worked in this job.'

Similarly in a radio talk (*Listener*, 27 July 1961) on glove-making in Worcester, where the industry dates back to at least the thirteenth century, Nick Young said that in spite of some mechanization 'gloving has not changed a bit . . . leather gloving is still essentially a craft, and, moreover, a *family* craft', and he gives examples of families with 'generations of gloving behind them'.

same broad occupational categories and may thus share the same economic conditions and social attitudes. There may be, then, a firmer economic basis making for a continued community of experience in families, and between the generations, than we are usually inclined to suppose.

Without attaching a great deal of weight to this last point, however, since we cannot be sure about it, it is still clear that although the modern family is not a productive unit of the pre-industrial kind, it continues to be an economic unit in very important ways: performing economic functions within itself, being closely bound up with the other economic institutions of society, and being considered and treated as an economic unit with regard to taxation, public provisions, and social services. It is also worthwhile to note, again, that just as the general political responsibility of parents has increased and has a new degree of efficacy, so has the trade union activity and responsibility of parents increased; so that parents in the specifically economic sphere, as well as in the wider political sphere, have much more voice in the determination of their economic and social circumstances.

Education

Thirdly, let us consider the 'educative' functions of the family.

In the more limited sense of providing the basis for the 'socialization' of the child during its earliest years of complete dependence, the modern family is just as much an educative unit as was the pre-industrial family, with the difference that in these earlier times children did not possess the status they now have and were introduced, in their upbringing, to harsh and impoverished conditions in which they were often exploited, whereas the child now enjoys a high status and is increasingly treated as an end in himself. With increased public regulation and public aid, and possibly with an increased sensitivity to new psychological knowledge and opinion, the upbringing of the child is undertaken in a far more considerate and careful, perhaps even fastidious, manner.

But in the less limited sense of providing the child with a wide education as a basis for his own subsequent fulfilment, and for the fulfilment of his duties as a responsible citizen, the situation is completely transformed. The pre-industrial family did not possess this basis of education at all, whereas this is extensively provided by the state at the present time. When we say, however, that education is now 'provided by the state', let us not fall into the error of thinking *either* that the state is some specialized agency completely independent of families and citizens, which grants its beneficence without pressure and without financial contributions from them, *or* that the public provision of education *removes* the education of children altogether from the sphere of the family, or *relieves* the family of responsibility for the education of its children. 'The state' is simply the organ of government which effects those policies approved by the electorate, and the extension of public education has been the outcome of long pressure and struggle on the part of the representatives of parents who have desired it for their children. Similarly, the state does not *give* education to children. The parents of families throughout the country *pay* for this education in the taxes which they contribute to the collective fund. It is the parents of families, among others, who responsibly maintain such public education as is, at any time, provided.

Furthermore, the idea that when education is provided in schools, colleges, and universities, the 'educative functions' of the family are stripped away is clearly nonsense. These provisions constitute an *increase* in the family's responsibility for the education of the children, a responsibility which did not exist in the absence of such provisions. We now expect parents of the modern family to have an informed awareness of these educational provisions, and of the alternative educational avenues and opportunities open to their children. Parents are expected to do their best to guide, encourage, and support their children in their educational and occupational choices and careers. Throughout the entire period of the child's educational experience, the attitudes of the family, and the facilities offered by the family, are of vital importance with regard to the extent to which the child really benefits from and makes full use of his formal education. And since the continuity of education to an advanced age entails different degrees of stress in different families, requiring different degrees of financial support from parents in accordance with family circumstances, the extent of the child's education still depends centrally upon family considerations.

Surely, too, 'education' is not something provided *either* by schools *or* by the family. It is a continuing cultivation of the child's experience in which *both* schools *and* families jointly take part. As parents become more influenced by the agencies of formal education and more conscious of the importance of education, their concern for the education of their child within the family increases in refinement rather than diminishes. They become more fully aware of the importance of the child's family experience in relation to the wider opportunities of formal education that he or she can enjoy.

Here again, therefore, it is clear that the provision of public education by 'specialized agencies' has not by any means 'stripped' the family of its educative functions; it has in fact increased the nature and the extent of these functions. The family is drawn more intimately into the network of educational institutions than ever before, and has to meet new demands and new responsibilities in this sphere.

Health

Precisely the same considerations apply to the functions of the family in caring for the health of its members in the context of the provisions of public health services.

It can hardly be maintained in any serious sense that the family in pre-industrial Britain provided for the health of its members, beyond doing its best (by employing a bizarre equipment of semi-magic and old wives' tales) to prevent and endure the sufferings of ill-health and early death. Now, however, from the very conception of the child onwards, provisions for the maintenance and furtherance of both bodily and mental health are made. There are family allowances for the child, pre-natal and post-natal provisions for mother and child; medical, dental, and other services are easily and cheaply available for all members of the population, together with economic benefits during periods of ill-health, and an extended hospital service. These services and benefits are certainly provided by 'specialized agencies' going beyond the family; but, here again, they have not been simply 'given by the state'. These public provisions are the outcome of political policies which stemmed from the desires of parents and which had to meet with their support and approval, and they continue to be financially maintained by the public at large. The effective provision of them has not, by any means, stripped the family of the function of caring for the health of its members. As is the case with publicly provided education, these wider health services have not superseded features which previously existed within the family unit. The family is still centrally concerned with maintaining the health of its members, but it is now aided by wider provisions which have been *added* to the family's situation since pre-industrial times. And again, as standards of health and hygiene have improved with knowledge, parents are faced with more exacting demands in caring for the health of their families. In addition to meeting the demands of these more sophisticated conceptions of health, they are now expected to have an informed knowledge of the wider network of provisions and agencies which have come into being.

The family's functions in the sphere of health must also, then, be said to have *increased* rather than diminished. It is worth noting, also, that in all of these wider provisions of public health, the importance of the family as a central consideration for the health of the individual has been increasingly recognized, emphasized, and taken into account. Thus the hospital almoner tries to achieve a liaison between the patient in hospital and his family problems and circumstances, since these have to be taken into account in his treatment. The entire development of concern for 'mental health' has strongly emphasized the central importance of the family for the mental stability and well-being of the individual. And, similarly, the growing 'psychosomatic' approach to the study of illness is finding that it is necessary to take the family and other social groupings into account. These wider health services, therefore, do not so much diminish the role of the family as recognize more fully and stress more emphatically its central importance in matters of health.

Indeed, with the insistence of modern psychology upon the fact that the earliest years of the child's experience in the family are of supreme importance for the subsequent development of his or her adult personality, it might be said that an almost completely new dimension has been added to the concern for health in the modern family. Parents are now thought to be responsible not only for the physical health of their children but also for the secure and healthy development of the child's whole personality.

Religious Functions

Not so much can be said about the 'religious' functions of the family.

In what sense the pre-industrial family could be said to perform 'religious' functions is, to my mind, very far from being clear. Increasingly, the view seems to be emerging that the working classes were never extensively represented in, concerned about, or catered for by the religious denominations during the eighteenth and nineteenth centuries. One suspects that the attitude towards religion of the mass of the working classes has always been similar to the view of a Devon fisherman reported in *A Poor Man's House* by Stephen Reynolds:

Tony the fisherman pronounces religion to be the business of the clergy, who are paid for it, and of those who take it up as a hobby, including the impertinent persons who thrust hell-fire tracts upon the fisher-folk.

'Us can't spect to know nort about it,' says Tony, 'Tain't no business o' ours. May be as they says; may be not. It don't matter, that I sees. Twill be all the same in a hundred years' time, when we're a-grinning up at the daisy-roots.'

However, there is no doubt that religious beliefs and sanctions have been considerably challenged during the past hundred years or so. All one can do here is to state a personal view. It seems to me:

(a) that, whatever the constellations of beliefs and practices held by parents (Roman Catholic, Jewish, agnostic, or whatever they may be), it is still in the context of the family that these beliefs and practices are first encountered by the child, so that the family continues to be extremely influential in this respect, and

(b) that the general growth of a more liberal attitude in these matters – i.e., that children should come to their views on such important questions by way of their own careful deliberation, and not by means of dogmatic family indoctrination – is all to the good. And this is probably particularly the case when religious doctrines are as confused and problematical as they now are, and as they are now bound to be with the growing influence of scientific and philosophical modes of thought. Those who wish to go back to dogmatic certainty are crying for the moon – and the moon is, as we know, behind the romantic symbol, a dead planet.

My essential point is that if we conceive the 'religious' functions of the family as being the provision of a basis for the development of well-considered views and convictions and of a satisfactory outlook upon life, then the family is still as important in this sphere as ever it was, though easy dogmatic certainty is no longer available. Why, however, easy dogmatic certainty should ever be thought well of, I do not know. Difficult undogmatic uncertainty is, to my mind, far more to be valued in terms of the desired qualities of human character.

Recreation

Similarly with regard to recreation, it is dubious to what extent we can say that the recreative activities of people in pre-industrial Britain, such as they were, were provided by the family itself. Recreative activities, even in pre-industrial Britain, seem to have involved groups going beyond the family. The picture of the large, contented family practising its manifold recreations in the cosy fire-lit homestead is itself something of a caricature. Indeed, it would be interesting if someone would tell us precisely what *were* the recreations carried on by the pre-industrial family within the home and how much leisure time people were able to devote to them.

Certainly, however, the provision of public entertainment has increased and now exists extensively outside the home. Cricket matches, football matches, tennis matches, boxing matches, athletics matches, pubs, clubs, cinemas, concerts of music, exhibitions of paintings and sculpture, horse-racing meetings, 'stock-car' destructions, angling societies (the list would obviously take up several pages) have all proliferated, and have all taken people outside the home. But how these developments can be said to have disturbed recreation in the family, or to have stripped the family of its recreative functions, is not easy to see.

Obviously many of these sports, games, and entertainments are a matter of individual choice and practice. But do fathers and sons never go together to see cricket and football matches? Do they never uproariously support the same team, or violently disagree because they support different teams? Do fathers and sons, brothers and cousins, in Yorkshire never travel miles to watch Yorkshire win their way to their former and rightful cricketing glory? Do not whole families, including the womenfolk, have warm feelings of affection for players and ex-players such as Len Hutton and Freddie Trueman, just as, in the cricket-benighted south, they remember the glamour of Denis Compton, and try to persuade themselves, hopefully, that Colin Cowdrey is still alive? And amongst football supporters, are there not many families, women included, who almost live and die during the winter according to the results of the local club? – who scream for Liverpool, or Spurs, and plaster their bedroom walls with pin-ups of Georgie Best? Certainly, they almost live and die (mostly die) in accordance with the results of their Pools on a Saturday evening. Do mothers and daughters never go to Wimbledon together? Do families never go to the cinema or the circus together? Do brothers never ride in the same cycling clubs together? Do brothers and sisters never join the same social clubs, church clubs, scout troops, guide troops? Do families never scramble round the floor manipulating electric train sets? Do they never play canasta, monopoly, cards, chess, draughts, and the like; and if not – who buys these playthings and why? Do husbands and wives not visit pubs together more than they used to? Do families never gather at the end of the day around the fateful face of television? Do they not argue over the respective merits of 'High Chaparral', 'The Black and White Minstrel Show', 'Panorama', 'Top of the Pops', 'The Wives of Henry VIII', or even 'The News'? Are they not irritated by Robin Day and charmed by Robert Dougall? Do families never go touring together in their motor-cars on Sunday afternoons, or are we mistaken in thinking that they stuff our roads to bursting point? Do families never go for holidays together, or is the poor Englishman, in his braces, a lonely and isolated individual on the Continent? Is there, or is there not, a kind of modern cult of family 'entertaining' spreading like a rash through the glossy magazines? Is it not unfortunately the case that even angling – that sport of solitude and contemplation among the willows and beneath the quiet of the evening sky – has nowadays become an occasion for a family outing? Watch the groups of fathers and children on the trains leaving London for the pleasant river stretches not far away. See them scattering their family litter on the green banks twenty miles from the city. Visit these quiet waters and see the families encamped among the reeds: the women knitting, giggling, and trying to ward off the flies by smoking; the men and boys seriously, grimly, and often irritably preoccupied.

I do not know the answers to all these questions with correct sociological and statistical precision. But in view of the probable answers, can anyone seriously maintain that the family in Britain has been stripped of its recreative functions? that it can no longer be considered a recreative unit? I, at any rate, think not.

Indeed, we must bear in mind the considerable increase in leisure time available to the majority of families. Leisure time has made possible the proliferation of recreative activities. These family recreations have not superseded something already existing in earlier days, they have been *added* to the experience of most families. Michael Young and Peter Willmott give a pointed illustration of this:

> The reduction of working hours after 1918, and again after 1945, has made a difference to every family. The spread of the five-day week has created the 'week-end', a new term and a new experience for the working man. With it has come the sight of young fathers wheeling prams up Bethnal Green Road on a Saturday morning, taking their little daughters for a row on the lake or playing with their sons on the putting green . . .[12]

This is not a picture of family life disrupted by individual recreation; the 'week-end' seems rather to have provided the opportunity for an extension of family recreation. The same picture is given in the previously mentioned talk by Mark Abrams.[13] 'Once,' he says, 'the working-class husband sought to escape from the crowded shabbiness of his home to the warmth and conviviality of "pubs" or the club rooms of voluntary associations . . . But now, as far as shabbiness and smartness are concerned, the boot is on the other foot; so the new man stays at home . . .' Moreover, quite apart from the enjoyment of 'common fire-side relaxations', including television, 'it is primarily in the home that the worker now has his greatest opportunities for exercising and enjoying his craftsmanship'.

I conclude, then, that the idea that the family in Britain has been 'stripped of its functions' during the process of industrialization is false. Both in the sense of being concerned with a more detailed and refined satisfaction of the needs of its members, and in the sense of being more intricately and responsibly bound up with the wider institutions of society, the functions of the family have increased in detail and in importance. As the provisions of wider agencies have been increased, the functions of the family have not been diminished, but have themselves been correspondingly extended. These wider provisions are *additional* to the conditions of the family in pre-industrial Britain; they have not super-seded functions which the family at that time fulfilled within itself; and they have positively added to the expectations which society has of the family. These more detailed and extended functions have been, as we have seen, the outcome of substantial moral improvements. To say, then, that the family has 'declined in importance as a social institution' and that it has suffered a 'moral decline' is quite false. The family has simply *changed* in such ways as to become adjusted to the demands of a highly complex industrial and urban society, and in such ways as substantially to reform the miserable conditions of the pre-industrial and early industrial family alike. The wider public provisions which have been made have not denuded the family of its importance. On the contrary, they have been the manifestation of a *continually increasing recognition of its importance*. They have been effected in order to aid the family in fulfilling functions whose importance has been gradually acknowledged.

This conclusion is stated in rather a different way by Professor Titmuss, who claims that the family of today must be considered *more* of a social institution than hitherto:

No longer is the family taken for granted as it was, like progress, in Victorian England. Again, like economic progress, it was in those Victorian days essentially a private affair; a closed area for the cultivation or neglect of private affections and private ambitions; a parking place for the exploitation of patriarchal authority. Private ambitions are now matters of public interest, not least to the Commissioners of Inland Revenue, while, in discovering the family, we have simultaneously discovered that the quality of its internal life is also a matter of public concern. In this sense, *the family of today is a social institution*. The health and stability of the community is now seen to rest on the health and stability of its families; the social health of the individual personality is now judged to depend in great measure upon the quality of parent-child relationships. These are accepted generalities today; fifty years ago they were not.[14]*

* It is of interest to note, too, that in her study of the family in Banbury, Margaret Stacey also concludes that the family continues to fulfil what

ATTITUDES TOWARDS SOCIAL POLICY

This first conclusion has important implications for the attitudes we should adopt when considering social policies with regard to marriage and the family. If our assumption is that the family has declined as a social institution, morally or otherwise, then we shall tend to adopt a backward-looking approach to social policy, indeed a reactionary approach. And there seems to be, at the present time, an all too powerful tendency to adopt a backward-looking point of view which is both false and dangerous. There are many who appear to believe that, in attempted reforms, we have gone 'too far, too fast', and that in our efforts to create a Welfare State we have given rise to irresponsibility and moral decay.

If, however, our conclusion is that, as an outcome of many social improvements, we are, as a society, expecting of the family that it should possess a knowledge of, and should utilize responsibly, the wider network of agencies and provisions of which it is a central element, and also that the family should perform many functions of a more fastidious standard of excellence, then our attitude will be one of helping to clarify this situation for the members of society, of helping them to see clearly and act effectively in relation to

have been called 'non-essential' functions. Commenting on MacIver's view that these had been 'stripped' from the family, she writes: 'Yet, observations in Banbury indicate that a number of important social functions remain to the family' (p. 136ff.). She claims that in some cases the family still functions as 'an economic unit (not merely a consuming unit)'; that the family still performs important educative functions. She also shows that the attachment to religious and political institutions is almost always shared by husband and wife, and that 'These attachments are shared, at least at first, by the children.' 'Children "inherit" their parents' religious denomination . . .' 'Similarly, political attachment is frequently looked upon as a family loyalty.' The author also finds that the family plays an important social role in relation to social status. Her account is extremely interesting, providing a useful empirical illustration of the continuity of the wider social functions of the family. *Tradition and Change: A Study of Banbury*, Margaret Stacey (Oxford University Press, 1960).

these extended responsibilities. Similarly, if we decide that the stresses and strains experienced in family relationships are not the outcome of moral decay, but the unforeseen consequences of improved social policies, we shall adopt the forward-looking view of seeking to reconsider and renew our study of the nature of these problems, to understand those apparent entailments of previous policies which we had not fully anticipated, and to formulate further and effective policies to deal with them. We shall recognize that great improvements have been made, that we need to consolidate them, and then make efforts to move beyond them – to resolve the new problems which have arisen. But it is wise always to bear in mind that social reforms never solve human problems once for all; they only solve particular problems to some degree, and are always likely to bring into being new problems which were not foreseen. When these new problems arise, we should not think of going back upon the reforms which have been made, but should realistically appraise them in a reliable historical perspective and then deal with them in such a way as to improve the conditions and relationships of human life still further.

The conclusion of our analysis is, clearly, that this latter, forward-looking attitude to social policy is the only one which can be justified. As part of this attitude to policy, however, it should also be recognized that many problems stemming from the apparent inadequacies and shortcomings of some families are not only due to the fact that reforms have been effected, but are a direct consequence of the fact that even the reforms we have mentioned *have not yet gone far enough*. Thus, any child neglect resulting from the increased employment of women is in some measure due to the fact that the provisions for child care envisaged in earlier acts – for example, the provision of nursery schools envisaged in the 1944 Education Act – have not in fact been implemented. The provision of any kind of nursery service has thus tended to be regarded as a provision for the unfortunate, rather than a normal and desirable service for the ordinary family. But there are more striking and perhaps more important examples.

We have said that housing conditions and general sanitary and urban conditions have been considerably improved, and this is true. But let us not think that these reforms have been carried as far as they should be. For example, giving figures for 1951, Sir Alexander Carr-Saunders and his colleagues showed that, taking into consideration all households in England and Wales, 6 per cent were without piped water, 2 per cent were without a cooking stove, 6 per cent were without a kitchen sink, 8 per cent were without a water closet, and as many as 37 per cent were without a fixed bath. These are over-all figures, and when specific kinds of household are considered, the figures for some categories are even worse. For example, among men aged seventy-five or over who were living alone, 13 per cent had no piped water, 10 per cent were without a cooking stove, 16 per cent had no kitchen sink, 15 per cent had no water closet, and 67 per cent were without a fixed bath. Similarly, many areas of our large towns are still in deplorable 'slum' conditions, and it is in these areas especially that inadequate family conditions and relationships are found; they are termed, by social pathologists, our 'delinquency-producing' areas.[15] It would seem, then, that any substantial reduction in the incidence of delinquency would be most likely to follow *not* from a condemnation of the moral stature of the families in these areas, but from the extended improvement of their home and environmental conditions.

We have tended, so far, to speak of deplorable housing and town conditions as though they were things of the past (since we have been concerned to show the improvements which have been made on the early nineteenth-century situation), but, as anyone will know who remembers the conditions of working-class areas in our towns before the war, and who sees the continuance of these conditions in some areas even now, these conditions are, as it were, *on our doorstep* in time. Indeed, it is worth bearing in mind that all the changes we have been considering in terms of the transformation of our society by industrialization have taken place in the last two or three human life-times, an extremely short period of time.

A reading of Masterman's *The Condition of England*, written in 1909, will serve to show how rapid and recent many of the improvements we have mentioned have been.

As Professor Titmuss puts it:

. . . the violent upheavals of the nineteenth century, the poverty, the unemployment, the social indiscipline, the authoritarianism of men and the cruelties to children, are by no means so remote today in their consequences as some economists and historians would have us believe. The reform of housing conditions, to cite one example of a material kind, was both remarkably slow and late in its development . . . One inheritance, several generations later, is that social workers spend much of their time coping with the problems of families disabled and deformed by bad housing conditions.[16]

Furthermore, although we have justifiably spoken of the considerable improvements brought about by public provisions and social services, it is becoming increasingly clear that a constant vigilance is required to see that the real benefits of such social welfare do not deteriorate. Again, Professor Titmuss, who is one of the few scholars who, with detailed knowledge and continuing human concern, practises such a diligent and up-to-date surveillance of the situation, writes:

All one can say with assurance is that, in terms of the relationship of national insurance benefits and allowances to average industrial earnings, most beneficiaries are relatively worse off today than they would have been in 1948. The fall in standards for them is a greater fall into poverty. The objective of social policy during the 1950s, it has been said repeatedly, is to concentrate resources on those who most need help. But what are the facts ? The new National Insurance Scheme of graded pensions, which adds a few shillings to 50s. in ten years' time, omits everyone earning less than £9 a week, yet the Minister has stated quite emphatically in the House 'We do not want to encourage more people to rely on Assistance'. This policy has been made effective substantially through the operation of 'disregards' in the means test (capital assets, war savings, sick pay, voluntary gifts from relatives and friends, and charitable payments). In important respects these tests are relatively harsher today than in the middle of the war when the Determination of Needs Act was insisted on by Ernest Bevin; harsher in some respects than at the height of the slump in 1932; and even harsher in allowing relatively smaller payments for sick pay than in 1904 under the poor law. Yet they were attacked in 1951 by the *Economist* as 'too generous for a nation which, in one way or another, is going to be forced to curtail its social services'.

The improvements which were hurriedly made before the election to the scales of national assistance are of no help to those who are discouraged or deterred from applying. In any case, an administrative agency – like the Assistance Board – which finds it necessary to be severe in its handling of the feckless, the 'work-shy', and the coloured immigrant is not likely to be attractive to the 'respectable poor'. And for those who are on assistance – nearly 2,500,000 people – these belated improvements have to be weighed against a host of incalculables: the removal of food and general housing subsidies, the loss of tobacco coupons, higher prescription charges, a more expensive and poorer transport system, and the fact that many old people, relative to the standards of the rest of the population, are probably worse off today than they were in 1951 in terms of housing conditions and domestic equipment.

'No one whom I marry,' said the Vicar of St George's, Camberwell, 'now has a chance of getting their own place through the housing list for at least four and a half years.' If this is the situation for young married couples today in such areas, it is likely to be far worse for the elderly and those on national assistance.[17]

In his *Essays on the Welfare State*, Professor Titmuss gives many other examples of the need for continual vigilance in examining the detailed changes – and, frequently, lapses – of social welfare which are taking place almost unknown to the general public. He claims that these lapses in the efficacy of earlier reforms particularly characterized the 1950s, and that we are in danger of becoming an 'irresponsible society' in so far as responsible public effort is not directed to a continuing calculation and supervision of these problems.

In so far as a society fails to identify, by fact and not by inference, its contemporary and changing social problems it must expect its social conscience and its democratic values to languish . . .

We are only just beginning to see [he concludes] that the problems of raising the level of living, the quality of education, housing, and medical care of the poorest third of the nation call for an immense amount of social inventiveness; for new institutional devices, new forms of cooperation, social control, ownership, and administration, and new ways of relating the citizen and consumer to services that intimately concern him. Social ideas may well be as important in Britain in the next half century as technological innovation.

These claims and concerns emphasized by Titmuss throughout the 1960s, are still as important now. Many investigators point to the growth, rather than the diminution, of this area of the unfortunate, and, as I write (at the beginning of 1972), economists and politicians are grappling again with the threat – very close now – of a million unemployed; some even beginning to assume that a high level of unemployment must be accepted as a long-term expectation.

In spite of many improvements, then, our social problems are far from being over, and the improvements that have been made are far from being secure. Our attitude must therefore be forward-looking, basing itself upon a realistic assessment of the new problems which face us, but it must also include the realization that, not only have we *not* gone too far, too fast, but that, in many cases, reforms initiated in the past – and recognized in the past as being just and necessary – have not yet gone far enough, and, indeed, are in constant danger of losing even their present degree of efficacy.

RESEARCH

A final and obvious conclusion is that we are greatly in need of more research on the family to clarify further the historical changes to which it has been subjected, and to achieve a reliable knowledge of its variable nature and conditions at the present time in different parts of the country and among different social groups and classes. Little has been said in this analysis of the aristocratic family, but sufficient perhaps to indicate that a history, up to the present time, of what has happened and is happening to the family of the aristocracy would be of very great interest indeed. But apart from matters of interest only, we positively need to know more about the contemporary family before the problems we have all too briefly reviewed can be thoroughly assessed and appropriately dealt with.

What precisely are the effects upon family relationships of the wider social roles of its members? If problems arise within the family as a result of these wider social roles, how far is reform in groups beyond the family – for example, in industrial organization – necessary for their resolution? How much and what kinds of child neglect are actually entailed in the increasing employment of married women, and how can this be obviated whilst still making effective the improvement in the status of women? Although the characteristics of the family are now more similar than hitherto among social classes, how far and in what ways are there still subtle but important differences between the families of different classes? That there still are significant differences of conditions and attitudes is borne out, for example, by the different lengths of education of children from different classes and their different levels of attainment, but what precisely are these differences? How far can the modern family still be considered an economic unit? Is there still any significant continuity of occupation between fathers and children in various trades and in various parts of the country, and thus a continuing style of family life between the generations? How far are there significant regional and local differences in the continuation of the 'extended family', in the degree of 'social distance' between the family and its wider kindred; and how important are these considerations? How far is the family still a 'recreative unit'? How far are old people 'isolated' from their younger families, and what housing and community policies can most happily and effectively deal with the situation? How extensive have been the effects of war on family relationships and how are they being dealt with? How far are adolescents irresponsible and without loyalty to or concern for their families? What are the conditions of families broken by separation as distinct from those broken by divorce?

These are but a few of the interesting questions which arise, and our discussion has indicated many others. The essential point is that, although we all have very deeply-rooted assumptions about these matters, not one of us knows with full reliability what the answers to these questions are; and until we have fuller knowledge, we cannot possibly know whether the policies we propose and support are reliably based. More detailed sociological research on the nature of the family in Britain is now beginning, but it has not gone far, and our conclusion is that it must clearly go much further.

It may be thought that, in arguing against many current and somewhat pessimistic opinions, this analysis has tended to be too optimistic. Of course, the anxieties of many people for the retention of moral and cultural values in an age which seems to devote all its aspirations towards greater material possessions can be understood. We all share these anxieties. And such anxiety, such perpetual vigilance, for the perpetuation of important values is a necessary and a laudable thing. My argument is only that, though this continuing anxiety is right and understandable, it should not be misplaced and lead us into false perspectives and backward-looking points of view which may serve to undermine even those improvements which have been achieved. Moral denunciation and undue pessimism, especially if they are based on faulty perspectives, will get us nowhere.

Masterman, writing round about 1909 – when the works of Anatole France and H. G. Wells were symptomatic of this anxiety over the possible decline of moral values in the face of materialism, as the *Brave New World* of Huxley and the *1984* of Orwell are symptomatic of the same anxiety in our own time – said:

I am not pessimistic as to the future of this 'Sceptred Isle'. Who could be pessimistic who had traced the history of a hundred years, and compared the England of 1811 with the England of today! I believe there are possibilities as yet undreamt of, for the enrichment of the common life of our people, and that in another century men and women – and children – may be rejoicing in an experience better than all our dreams.

I am not *pessimistic*, but I am *anxious*, as I believe all the thinking men of today are anxious when they realize the forces which are making for decay.[18]

And he concluded:

. . . amid a people of such vast prosperity and comfort, the voice of anxiety should never be entirely stifled.

Anxiety, then, is to be understood and commended, but it should not be allowed to distort our perspectives and so falsify our judgements.

Trying, himself, to apply some sort of perspective over a century of social change, Masterman also wrote of the British people:

The Multitude is the People of England; that eighty per cent (say) of the present inhabitants of these islands who never express their own grievances, who rarely become articulate, who can only be observed from outside and very far away. It is a people which, all unnoticed and without clamour or protest, has passed through the largest secular change of a thousand years: from the life of the fields to the life of the city. Nine out of ten families have migrated within three generations: they are still only, as it were, commencing to settle down in their new quarters, with the paint scarcely dry on them, and the little garden still untilled. How has the migration affected them? How will they expand or degenerate in the new town existence, each in the perpetual presence of all? That is a question of as profound interest in answering as it is difficult to answer. The nineteenth century – in the life of the wage-earning multitudes – was a century of disturbance. The twentieth promises to be a century of consolidation. What complete product will emerge from its city aggregation, the children of the crowd?

About three-quarters of the way through the twentieth century, we ourselves are now responsible for the answer to that question.

All in all, however, I would like to reiterate my conclusion that our analysis does clearly point out that the family in contemporary Britain has not declined in nature or importance as a social institution; that its characteristics do not warrant at all the charge of 'moral decline'; and that no good end will be served by any falsely conceived and backward-looking judgements and policies. Though all is not well with the modern British family and its conditions, we can at least take heart from the considerable improvements that have been made, after generations of struggle, to overcome and efface an abysmally wretched situation. On this basis we can attempt a realistic appreciation of the problems which now confront us, and so shape our policies as to make even greater improvements in future.

As Professor Graveson writes, after having reviewed a century of family law:

> If we have cause for shame over the past, we may take pride in the present for the efforts that have been made in our time, inadequate as they may be, to ensure a better future for succeeding generations.

6 The Future of the Family

So much for the correctness of forward-looking attitudes with regard to the future of the family.

But can we say what this future is likely to be? Some directions of effort arise very clearly from our assessment of what has happened so far. But are there any future developments concerning the family and marriage which can now be discerned? Can anything be said about the consequences of such trends and the problems to which they will give rise?

It is not for the sociologist to try to predict the future. Indeed, the future will depend a good deal upon our own efforts (acting on the basis of such knowledge as we can secure) to make it what we want it to be. But, though they cannot be exhaustive, it is tempting to make a few final comments. Some trends do seem reasonably clear and some of them are suggestive with regard to the developments of societies in the modern world which I mentioned briefly at the beginning of this book. It may be of some use, at least, to try to see clearly some of the tasks that may lie before us.

Earlier, I described the British family of today as being:

1. of long duration, since it is founded at an early age,
2. small in size, as a consequence of birth control,
3. separately housed in an improved material environment,
4. economically self-providing, and therefore independent of aid from wider kindred,
5. founded and maintained by partners of equal status, enjoying a marital relationship based increasingly upon mutuality of consideration,
6. democratically managed, in that husband, wife, and children are all taken into account in arriving at family decisions,

7. centrally and very responsibly concerned with the care and upbringing of children, and, finally,
8. aided in achieving health and stability by a wide range of public provisions both statutory and voluntary.

These characteristics and all that they entail clearly represent a considerable improvement upon family types of the past, but there are a few points which are worth giving a good deal of emphasis in a summary way.

Firstly, these improvements are really three-fold. They embody a more considerate relationship between husband and wife, a more sensitive and sympathetic relationship between parents and children, and a better relationship between families and the wider society, or between families and government – which increasingly recognizes the importance of stable, happy family life.

Secondly, the grounds of these improvements are not isolated in, or peculiar to, the family; they are attendant upon wider improvements in society at large. They are, in short, the outcome of securing the rights and improving the status of women and children (and improving those of men), together with the more effective movement towards economic security and equality of opportunity. They constitute a general moral improvement in the status of the citizen in our community – irrespective of age or sex.

Thirdly, these improvements have been made possible by, and in relation to, the rapidly changing circumstances, problems, and demands of an industrial and urban society. The modern family is the type of family appropriate to the conditions of a complex industrial society.

We might consider the future of this type of family by meeting, first of all, one possible criticism.

It may be said in all this that I have described, really, the *formal* characteristics of the modern British family, and that this is in danger of being a rather ideal picture – of a *type* of family, rather than of the thousands of actual, problematical families that exist. It may be said that, in spite of the formal improvements to which I have pointed, many families are still in trouble, and cannot cope with the demands made upon them. There is still much about which we should be anxious, and it is not yet time to be unduly optimistic.

It should be clear from what I have said that I agree with this – with some qualification.

I do not believe that the picture I have drawn is only a formal one. I believe that the great majority of British families are of the kind I have described, and that they do in fact cope successfully with all the internal and external demands made upon them; successfully in the way in which families do – with much conflict, difficulty, irritation; with much that is not only trying but positively exasperating; but with firm loyalties, with ties which go deeper than is often known and acknowledged, with abiding attachments, with much happiness, and engendering a core of character which is a strength in all their members.

Some families, however, do not. This is distressing – but is it a matter for surprise, for blame, or for talk of moral retrogression? Is it really difficult to understand why some marriages break down, and why some families are problematical and badly managed? Surely one reason is that marriage is tough! – the most exacting, demanding, difficult – though, if it succeeds, the most richly rewarding – of all the relationships we have to work out. Another reason is that some people do not possess the personal qualities required. Some people are ignorant and shiftless, dirty and undisciplined, insensitive and sluttish, small-minded and selfish, just to mention a few things. And before we settle down with a vision of the east end of London or the black proletarian north, let us hastily remind ourselves that such people are not confined to the working classes. There are middle-class slums too, if you go through the door. In any society, and especially in a society as complicated as our own, there are bound to be personal insufficiencies and marital and family casualties. And it is worth noting that the more we improve our standards and increase our demands, the more difficult we make matters for some people. Good relationships are harder to maintain than bad ones. Although

I do not want to dwell upon the figures of divorce again, it may be noted that a relatively high divorce rate may be indicative not of *lower*, but of *higher*, standards of marriage in society.

My point is that it is certainly true, in terms of the formal characteristics of the modern family, that the family of today is a great improvement on anything we have known in the past, and the majority of families live up to these new expectations. But this is far from saying that we have no difficulties, or that this is the end of the matter. The higher our standards the greater some of our difficulties. We are really at the beginning, not the end – for we now have to see by the good upbringing and education of our children that generations of the future will be adequately equipped to realize what is involved in family relationships and to live fully and happily within the improved formal structure which has been to some extent secured.

What future trends seem likely?

There is every reason to suppose, firstly, that the trend towards this kind of family – in Britain and in all industrial societies – will continue. Every movement of thought and policy seems to be moving towards an increasing awareness of what, in terms of human relationships (both conflictful and otherwise), is involved in this kind of family, and an increasing tendency to support it and to improve it still further. The economic and social conditions of our modern industrial and urban society seem to make for it, and every moral persuasion seems to desire it. The freedom and mobility required in our society – geographical movement, and the extended degree of educational opportunity and movement between social class and status groups; the desire on the part of families for economic independence, security, and the personal freedom of their members; the growing sense of the moral rightness of limiting the size of a family to the number who can be adequately cared for, and with regard, too, to the happiness and fulfilment of the parents; all these factors seem to make it clear that the small, planned, democratic family is here to stay. Increasing standards of welfare and greater security may well lead to a slight increase in the average size of the family, but, given the ordinary population problems of a large industrial society, and the enormous population problems of the world at large, it does not seem likely that this will be considerable. In any case, any such increase would be a matter of choice in accordance with family means, and there seems no likelihood of a return to the completely unplanned large family and the situation of the annual pregnancy. Indeed, there are some signs to suggest that those large families which, through ignorance, still suffer annual pregnancies may well be relieved by the extension of family planning advice through domiciliary services in addition to clinics. And this is a development to be welcomed.

It seems, too, that the degree of dependence of each family upon its wider kinship relationships will continue to diminish. Independence seems to be desired by every family. This does not mean at all that every relationship beyond the immediate group of parents and children will be cut off, or will cease to be desired. Nor does it mean that, for example, the aged, in particular, will suffer from a lack of continued relationships with their children and grand-children. This could certainly happen. But the benefits of industrial security and prosperity which, in a way, give rise to the problem, may also lead to its solution. Old people themselves – whether still married, alone, or remarried – are increasingly likely to desire their own independence, just as much as their children do. And in the days of telephone and car, there is no reason why the degree of contact desired by everyone should not be maintained. But such wider relationships will be *chosen*, not – any longer – imposed by *necessity*. There is every reason to suppose that new conditions of security and independence will make for happier – not more miserable – relationships between kindred. But in the broadest sense of the term, the 'extended family' – the large interdependent network of extended kindred – is outmoded in a modern industrial society. The days of the clan, and of the village network of aunts, uncles, and forty-second cousins, is over. The functional roots of the extended family have gone.

All the other characteristics of this 'modern' family are also likely to continue. The improved status of women is here to stay, and will be carried even further. The economic necessities of employing women; the desire of women to lead a more active personal life in a situation in which they are relieved of child-bearing and child-rearing to the extent that they and their husbands want to be relieved of it; and the moral persuasions concerning the rightness of the equal status of women, will all ensure this. The same is true of the improved status of the child in modern society. There may be problems attendant upon the new degrees of freedom and self-sufficiency young people have with early employment and relative affluence, but it seems inconceivable that these problems will be resolved by going back to the restrictions upon young people of an earlier age. The problems will be solved by improved education related to the new situation in which young people are placed.

The tendency towards earlier marriage seems also likely to continue, and reflects the widespread well-being of our society and the increased ability of young people to earn adequate incomes and establish secure homes at an early age. The number of both men and women who marry under the age of 21 continues to increase. In 1961 there were 42,769 marriages in which the bridegroom was under 21 (the figure in 1960 was 40,160). By 1967 this had become 65,956, though the number slightly decreased in 1968, and was 60,562 in 1969. There were, in 1961, 130,400 marriages in which the bride was under 21 (the figure in 1960 being 125,096), and this, by 1967, had become 162, 145, though, again, the number decreased to 149,196 in 1969. Of the brides, a very large proportion are 18 years old or younger (in 1961, 21,176 were 16–17, and 28,712 were 18). But it is interesting to notice that the *proportions* of bridegrooms and brides under the age of 21 is changing. In 1938, for example, there were 5 brides to 1 groom under the age of 21. In 1954 this had become 4 to 1, and in 1961, 3 to 1. In 1967 (the peak year so far) the proportion had dropped to 2·45 to 1, and the interesting fact is that though the numbers of marriages of both men and women under 21 had fallen by 1969, the proportion of brides to grooms had slightly fallen again, so that in 1969 it was 2·41 to 1.

But the tendency towards an earlier age of marriage is not only to be seen among the under 21 age-group. It is clear, too, in other age-groups. Since the period before the Second World War, the proportion of bachelor bride-grooms aged 20–24 has risen from just over a third to over a half of the total, whilst the proportion aged 25–29 has fallen from just over 40 per cent to just over a quarter. There has been a striking increase in the marriage rates of bachelors under 25 (and especially under 20) whilst the rates for the ages 30–54 have tended to fall. The lower age of marriage for spinsters is even more marked, and marriage rates for spinsters have risen for all ages.[1] The continued popularity of marriage is beyond all doubt.

The rates of remarriage are also considerable. Of the 346,678 marriages contracted during 1961, there were 10 per cent in which one partner was remarrying, and a remaining 6 per cent in which both partners were remarrying. 37,835 men remarried – slightly more than half being widowers and slightly less than half being divorced. 34,421 women re-married – slightly less than half being widows and slightly more than half being divorced. One particularly interesting fact is the changing age of remarriage. The average age at remarriage of widowers has consistently increased from about 50 years of age in 1931 to 58 in 1961. Similarly, the average age at remarriage of widows has increased from 45 in 1931 to about 52 in 1961. In 1961, 44 per cent of the widowers, and 27 per cent of the widows, who remarried were 60 years of age and over. Among divorced people too there has been an increase in the average age at remarriage, though this is relatively slight. But the most significant change is that during the period 1941–5, the largest concentration of divorced men remarrying was between the ages of 25–49, whereas in 1961, this concentration had much diminished, and there was a considerable increase in the proportion of men over 49 years of age who were remarrying. Similarly, during 1941–5, the largest concentration of divorced women remarrying was in the 30–44 age-group, whereas in 1961 this had diminished, and a far larger number of women over the age of 45 were remarrying. These trends can be clearly seen in the table on p. 242.[2] It is worth noting, too, that during 1967–9, whilst the total number of marriages of young men and women under the age of 21 went down (by about 5,500 and 13,000 respectively) – the number of marriages of both men and women of 45–54 years of age remained more or less constant, and that of both men and women over 55 years of age actually increased – though more for men than for women.

It is to be noted, too, that the rates of remarriage for divorced men and women at all ages continues to be higher than those for widowed men and women, and there seems to be a relatively short average interval between divorce and remarriage. It is decidedly not marriage itself which divorced people are seeking to avoid.

The central point that I wish to emphasize in all this is that marriage seems to be becoming, and is likely to become increasingly in future, a relationship of affection and companionship quite apart from the having and rearing of children. It remains true, of course, that for the vast majority of married couples, the founding of a family and the enjoyment of parenthood is a central feature of their happiness. But it is clear first, that if, in the future, a larger number of marriages are going to be founded at an early age, and if the present limitation of births continues, this must mean that many couples will have completed the child-rearing period of their family life at a relatively young age, still having a long period of life before them, from their middle years onwards, for whatever activities – whether undertaken jointly, or independently of each other – they wish to pursue. Both during the child-rearing period of their family life, and especially afterwards, marriage has become and will become increasingly a matter of personal companionship. But also, there seems little doubt that those people beyond their middle years who are widowed or divorced will increasingly

Proportional age distribution per 1,000 at all ages and average age at remarriage of divorced persons, 1941–64, England and Wales

Period	Age at remarriage											Average age at remarriage
	Under 25	25–	30–	35–	40–	45–	50–	55–	60–	65 and over	Not stated	
DIVORCED MEN												
1941–5	11	78	196	247	202	135	73	35	15	7	1	40·34
1946–50	12	150	242	236	168	102	51	23	10	5	1	38·16
1951–5	11	117	223	206	181	129	75	34	15	9	0	39·70
1956–60	15	118	194	199	161	140	92	49	20	12	0	40·58
1959	14	114	192	206	154	137	96	51	23	12	1	40·79
1960	16	119	187	198	151	139	98	54	23	14	1	40·84
1961	18	126	195	193	156	128	94	52	24	14	0	40·52
1962	17	132	197	184	161	122	96	52	25	14	0	40·50
1963	20	145	203	180	159	116	89	50	25	13	–	40·08
1964	21	160	205	178	159	104	82	51	24	15	–	39·76
DIVORCED WOMEN												
1941–5	30	169	262	229	161	87	37	16	6	1	2	36·79
1946–50	66	285	251	188	109	60	26	9	4	1	1	34·25
1951–5	49	213	260	187	137	85	42	17	6	3	1	36·09
1956–60	57	191	215	196	140	105	57	24	10	4	1	37·13
1959	57	185	208	200	136	109	62	26	11	5	1	37·42
1960	62	191	201	193	139	108	60	28	11	6	1	37·33
1961	69	193	204	180	137	107	61	30	11	7	1	37·23
1962	72	207	194	174	145	100	60	29	13	5	1	37·09
1963	77	216	201	161	141	92	62	29	14	6	–	36·85
1964	82	229	200	155	141	88	58	29	13	7	–	36·55

be able to contemplate remarriage as a new companionable relationship – and a relationship of long duration – without any reference to children.

Though it remains true, as I have maintained in earlier chapters, that marriage is centrally rooted in the founding of the family and in shared parenthood, and that, as such, it can be enjoyed with more freedom and security now than before – it now seems clear that there is a sense in which marriage as a relationship in its own right is being liberated, as it were, from any necessary connection with parenthood. It can now increasingly, and at all ages, be entered into as a relationship of enjoyed intimacy for its own sake. And this tendency is likely to continue. Also, if attitudes towards marriage and divorce continue to change as they are now changing – that is, away from the sacramental conception of marriage, and from the conception of divorce as necessarily resting upon a matrimonial offence – then there will be a far greater opportunity of achieving happy marriages than ever before.

This leads to a consideration of another important area of changing ideas and values which must have a marked effect upon the future nature of marriage – that is, the area of sexual morality. The issues raised here are so many, complex, and controversial that it would be absurd to attempt an exhaustive discussion of them in a final chapter. But some facts and their implications seem clear.

Firstly, sexual impulses and sexual experience are now being released from the dark clutches of 'sinfulness' with which the Christian tradition has long strangled them. In future, sex will be regarded as a natural desire and a fulfilment of certain aspects of our nature. There will be nothing improper in claiming that sexual experience is enjoyable, and that it is an important aspect of a marital relationship, quite apart from procreation.

Secondly, techniques of birth control will reach new levels of efficiency, so that sexual intimacy may be enjoyed without any likelihood of conception.

Now these two developments alone must have very far-reaching consequences for sexual ethics. Sexual intimacy and marriage will no longer necessarily be thought synonymous. And, if sexual intimacy is entered into with responsibility and mutual consideration, there is no evident reason why this should not be so. The whole question of whether pre-marital sexual experience is permissible, desirable, right or wrong, will have to be examined again. It is true that sex is one of the important bases of a happy marriage, and, consequently, of a happy family life – but, it might be argued, *this is just why* people should be as clear in mind and experience about it as possible before they commit themselves to the serious status and duties of marriage, entailing, centrally, the having and rearing of children. Also, though important, sex is far from being the only important thing in marriage. Married love includes sex, but it is certainly not to be equated with sex; it is much more than romanticized sex; and it is of the very greatest importance that young people should not enter into marriage on the grounds of the sudden or mounting pressure of the desire to sleep with each other.

When people totally reject the propriety of any experience of sexual intimacy before marriage, it is usually on the grounds (a) that marriage is a sacrament and that sexual intimacy should not precede it, (b) that people may make a disastrous mistake in involving themselves so deeply before marriage, and it is therefore better to avoid sex until the partners are actually committed in marriage, and (c) that sex before marriage entails the possibility of deception and the exploitation of one partner by the other for his or her own gratification. But these points are not very firm.

If, because of a belief that marriage is a sacrament in its own right, men and women are forbidden to know each other before marriage, and are then to be bound together throughout their lives no matter what mistakes they may have made, no matter what misery they may be suffering through whatever maladjustment (that is, unless they have committed a matrimonial offence), this is clearly to treat human individuals not as ends in themselves but as a means only – in this case a means to the correct observance of religious law, or even the divine law. But if God exists, and is a moral being, he could not possibly want it so. He could not treat a person as a means only, even if it were as a means to the maintenance of his own law, or even to his own greater glory. Such a religious law falls very far short, therefore, of our ordinary human standards. Indeed, one sad feature of social policy during the early 1960s was the vision of the Church standing in the way of the humane reform of the divorce law on unethical grounds. If the Church maintains with such rigour that true marriage can be founded only on mutual love, how can it possibly maintain with equal rigour that marriage should be perpetuated when that same love has ceased – and perhaps for reasons for which no one is to blame? Is this not a curious inconsistency? – a religious insistence upon an immoral situation?

As a matter of fact, however, the Church has conceded much, and the successful drafting and passing of the Divorce Reform Act (1969) was in large part a result of a considered compromise on its part; the acceptance of the 'irretrievable breakdown' of marriage as the basic ground for divorce making much more ethical sense than any rigid sticking to the doctrine of the matrimonial offence.

Secondly, though it is true that people may make mistakes and suffer deception and exploitation in sexual relations before marriage, it is equally true that the same things can happen *within* marriage. The truth is that, in general, people never think about the ethics of sex *within* marriage, only outside it. And their attitude seems to carry the rather appalling implication that, once marriage has occurred, less concern need be felt about these matters. Sex is all right now – it is safely confined, firmly controlled, hedged round with social and legal safeguards. This, too, is surely a treatment of individuals not as ends in themselves but as a means to what is thought to be a socially necessitous regulation of sex.

It is difficult not to conclude that the conception of marriage which these objections imply – a kind of social or religious impounding of the sexual impulse, only to be allowed expression on the presentation of a licence – is itself immoral. In the future conception of marriage, the sanctioning of sexual intimacy seems likely to be a diminishing factor, though this does not mean at all that sexual fidelity may not continue to be a desired characteristic of marriage.

In this, as in all human relationships, individual discrimination and responsibility will come to be emphasized as the basis of morality. What people actually do in their own sexual behaviour – whether pre-marital, marital, or extra-marital – must be their own responsibility. Our public duty can only be to make available all relevant knowledge – of sex itself and reproduction, of venereal disease, of contraceptive techniques – so that everyone has an adequate basis of knowledge on which to take their decisions, and so that – whatever they decide to do – a minimum of unhappiness will be caused either to themselves or to others.

It is worthwhile to repeat here – with reference to almost all the points mentioned above: the acceptance of sex as an enjoyable part of marriage (without sole reference to procreation); the acceptance of sexual experience as something to be enjoyed equally by both women and men; the acceptance of contraceptive practice and voluntary family limitation; the acceptance of a thorough-going egalitarianism in marriage, with a minimal differentiation of roles, and the desire for a personally worked-out companionship – that Gorer's most recent findings are that the vast majority of young people have come to approach and develop their relationship responsibly, and still with fidelity and family concern at the heart of it. Despite what seems to many like a revolution in attitudes towards sexual relationships, the responsible companionate marriage seems to be becoming a reality.

There seems no doubt that these changed attitudes towards the nature of sex, the use of contraceptive techniques in marriage, etcetera, will spread and become commonplace. The present-day deliberations of the Roman Catholic Church, in particular, constitute clear evidence of how even the most strict religious doctrines must bend and give way before new knowledge, modern techniques, and fundamental changes of behaviour. And these changing conceptions of sex and marriage must lead to changes in the law.

It seems certain that, in future – and it is already beginning – there will be a considerable increase in the social and legal investigation of all aspects of the family and marriage which will lead to extensive changes in the law, and in the attitudes underlying the law, to remove remaining sources of conflict, hardship, and unhappiness. Even since the first edition of this book, for example, Mr Leo Abse's attempt to reform the Divorce Law has successfully passed its troubled and much hindered way through Parliament. His insistence (a) that serious attempts at reconciliation should not be prevented by the requirements of the law; and (b) that a period of separation indicating that a marriage has, in fact, ceased to exist should be recognized as grounds for divorce, have forced themselves upon the law and the public as being rationally and morally undeniable. Similarly, the ideas that divorce should rest not only upon a matrimonial offence (frequently leading to the committing of the required offence in order to gain the divorce desired), and that divorce by mutual consent should be possible – at least in marriages where there are no children; these have been substantially recognized in the new 1969 Act. And with the continuing work of the Law Commission, other changes in the law are bound to come.

We may remind ourselves, too, that the chief reason why there is now a larger quantity of divorce than earlier, is that in the past it was available only to the well-to-do. The poor had to lie on the marriage bed they had made. Now divorce is, justly, available to all. It is odd, in this connection, that all of us remember with repugnance the gross poverty of the nineteenth century and other social evils, but not the gross marital misery attendant upon the lack of divorce facilities. We all remember Charles Dickens's picture of Oliver Twist, but not his equally telling picture of the misery of Stephen Blackpool in *Hard Times*.[3] More and more, too, the comparative evidence is demonstrating that such changes in the law can make for a happier state of affairs, rather than bring about the disastrous disintegration of marriage that many people fear.

It is interesting to note, for example, that, following the new Uniform Divorce Act in Australia – which made divorce available on grounds such as separation for five years, failure to pay maintenance for two years, and by mutual consent, and which was bitterly opposed by the Anglican and Roman Catholic Churches – the number of divorces has fallen. 'The falling divorce figures,' says one Australian divorce lawyer, 'are proving that the people who had said the new act would flood the courts with divorce petitions were wrong', and Mr Justice Dovey, divorce judge in Sydney, has described the act as 'the greatest advance in social legislation since

Australia's federation'. Others have described some of the social benefits of the Act as the regularizing of many unions which would have remained illicit; removing the stigma of illegitimacy from offspring; and removing incentives to perjury. One Sydney lawyer points out – what we all know quite well – that it is not the law which makes or breaks marriages. 'What it can do,' he says, 'and now does, is to make it easier for people to live respectable lives in the community.'

Those who oppose the changing of the divorce law do not see that other things have already changed, and will change with it. All this was clearly foreseen by a much neglected nineteenth-century sociologist – Mr Herbert Spencer.[4]

'Already,' he wrote, towards the end of the nineteenth century, 'increased facilities for divorce point to the probability that whereas, hitherto, the union by law was regarded as the essential part of marriage and the union by affection as non-essential; and whereas at present the union by law is thought the more important and the union by affection the less important; there will come a time when the union by affection will be held of primary moment: whence reprobation of marital relations in which the union by affection has dissolved.'

Spencer knew quite well that his prediction, which is now being fulfilled, would be unacceptable to many, but, he said, those who rejected his arguments:

... nearly all err by considering what would result from the supposed change, other things remaining unchanged. But other things also must be assumed to have changed. With higher sentiments accompanying union of the sexes, with an increase in altruism, must go a decrease in domestic dissension. Whence, simultaneously, a strengthening of the moral bond and a weakening of the forces tending to destroy it. So that the changes which may further facilitate divorce under certain conditions, are changes which will make those conditions more and more rare.

The bonds of love, affection, and mutually accepted duties, are the bonds on which marriage should rest, not the bonds of legal compulsion. Individuals should not be sacrificed to some supposed verity of religion and law. Marriage should not be constrained to fit the existing law. The law should be so shaped that marriage is not hindered from becoming a thing of love and happiness.

But other aspects of the law, and of legal and social procedures regarding marital and familial situations, are also likely to be more closely investigated and changed. Procedures of adoption, for example, especially the provision of some supervision of adoptions arranged by third parties, are already under scrutiny, as are the detailed facts concerning the members of families which have been effectively broken by separation and dealt with by the magistrates courts. Research is now being pursued in these fields, and both social scientists and lawyers are seeking and developing closer collaboration with each other in investigating the facts of these matters, and in order to secure the firmest possible ground for deliberating upon the most just and advisable changes.

Are there, however, any dangers in all these developments?

One, perhaps. In our concern to remedy unhappiness, we may be in danger of focusing our attention too narrowly upon the family. Both in terms of personal life and in terms of social reform and administration, we may be in danger of expecting that too much can be done by concentrating upon the family alone. In all the diagnoses of the ills of society, in all the suggestions for improvement, the family tends to be considered far too much in isolation. Just as one can become sick of all the talk about sex in isolation from other aspects of feeling and experience, so one can become sick of all the talk about the family. It is true that the family is a group of basic importance in society, but it is also true that *there is much more besides*. I would like to comment briefly on a few aspects of this point.

First, the family, as we have seen, is *blamed* for too much; indeed, for every ill of society which we do not understand – crime, delinquency, and the like. And this is all much too one-sided. If a young boy is promiscuous, for example, there are those who think immediately that it must be due to his family background and some disturbance he suffered during the early years of life. But during the scandal of some years ago which centred upon the figure of Mr Profumo, Dr A. J. P. Taylor in a light-hearted article mentioned a string of sparkling names of people in high places in the past who had committed similar actions.[5] And – to take some names from this list – does anyone ever ask what it was that the Duke of Wellington, Earl Grey, Lord Melbourne, Palmerston, Disraeli, Dilke, Lloyd George, or Edward VII saw in the shed at the bottom of the garden when they were three years old, and whether their family background was such as to give rise to insecure personality development? And the people who continue to manufacture and advertise cigarettes, knowing that they are maintaining and furthering a high rate of deaths from lung cancer (now something over 23,000 a year); or those advertising firms who, without a qualm, will sell chewing gum, fruit-juice, tobacco, the Conservative Party, ladies' underwear, the Labour Party, even the Church of England, if they are given a paying contract for the job; have all these people suffered from poor family backgrounds? Maybe. It is a possibility. But the significant thing is that we never ask. The family has become a scapegoat on which we lay the blame for all those anti-social acts which we happen not to like, and for which we have no other explanation.

Secondly, it sometimes seems to be thought that if we put the family right, if we live happily within our family groups, concentrating upon being healthy and stable personalities within the home, then the state will no longer totter. And in order to secure this firm family life we hear much about the ethics of sex education and education for family life.

Also, it may be that the family is in danger of becoming too enclosed a group; there may be a tendency in the more comfortable conditions of our society for people to become content with the garden, the warm fireside, the do-it-yourself kits, and, of course, the television screen. I think it was Mr Jimmy Edwards who once said that we were becoming a race of troglodytes. And – with not such a cosy atmosphere – many families in dense urban areas are driven inwards upon themselves in their small two-roomed flats, not through choice, but simply because they have no social contacts in the hard brick-and-concrete neighbourhood. And this raises another point we should not forget – the necessity of providing good housing and good neighbourhood facilities in our rapidly spreading conurbations. Whether by compulsion or choice, the family may be becoming very inward-looking; too much, perhaps, immersed in itself.

Now, no one with any sense will criticize the enjoyment of the comforts, pleasures, and privacy of home life, and no one can deny that if family life is secure and happy we shall have the best prospects for an adult population of good citizens. But there is one central point which it does seem to be of the very greatest importance to realize.

The family is not self-contained. Though a group within which our deepest satisfactions are found, the family is also, for the child, an introduction to life in the wider society, and, for the adult, a basis for life in the wider society. If this is forgotten, the relationships and personalities within the family may be both impoverished and spoiled, and may well suffer from a kind of intractable and self-consuming intensity. What I mean is that people, if they are impoverished in other and wider aspects of human life, impoverished in certain dimensions of their nature, may look intensely for some kind of satisfaction in marital and family relationships which is simply not there to be found at all. They may come to expect too much. Family relationships may positively suffer from too inward-looking, too self-contained, too enclosed an attitude to the family, and in this context I believe that there is a positive danger in emphasizing sex, love, and romanticism in general, to the exclusion of other qualities and activities. There are other things in life. Sex and love are very enjoyable – but we cannot forever be folded in one another's arms. And a tight perpetual embrace is in danger of becoming a stranglehold.

There is another aspect of this which is important. If we

examine the matter fully, it becomes clear that there is no such thing as the 'ethics of sex' or 'family ethics' – separate from ethics in general. The ethical principles in the light of which we should regulate our sexual and family relationships are the same as those on which we should base *all* our conduct in *all* human relationships. They are – to glean a few examples from the moral philosophers – that we should always:

1. try to increase happiness and diminish pain,
2. treat other individuals as persons, as ends in themselves, and never only as a means to some end of our own,
3. behave towards others as we think it right that they should behave towards us,
4. seek to attain the highest level of excellence of which we are capable in any task to which we commit ourselves, and
5. seek to secure, in society, those human rights which these principles entail, and which *require* to be secured for their operation and fulfilment.[6]

And it is this mention of society which matters. If we are concerned to improve the family and marriage, we cannot do this by concentrating on the family alone, but only by concerning ourselves with the attainment of social justice and the improvement of human relationships throughout the whole of our society; in factories, schools, government, and all other institutions. Consequently, it is not education in the ethics of sexual and family relationships which we want; it is education in the widest sense for responsible citizenship, within which sexual and family relationships will have their proper, but not an all-embracing, place.

One other point which, I believe, deserves great emphasis is this: *how new this type of society, and how new this type of family is in the history of man.* Never before have men, women, and children both within and beyond the family enjoyed such personal freedom, equality of status, and mutuality of consideration within the context of the helpful provisions of sympathetic government. In our own society, this is little more than forty years old. Only in 1928 did women become political citizens, equal to men. Only since the last war has educational opportunity been extended to all our children, and, of course, *much* more has still to be done in this direction. But all this is so new that even our own parents did not enjoy it, and even we ourselves are not acclimatized to it. *This is a new situation in the entire history of mankind.*

And this leads to my final consideration. Earlier, I have tried to show that the family in modern Britain was shaped in coming to terms with the characteristics of an industrial society, and as a result of securing, within the whole structure of society, the wider principles of social justice. It requires little imagination to see that what has happened in Britain is now rapidly spreading throughout the world. Industrialization is spreading everywhere. Everywhere, people are clamouring for the rights of man to be institutionally secured in their own independent societies. As one small example, consider the following law of marriage:

The new democratic marriage is based on free choice of partners, on equal rights for both sexes, and on protection of the lawful interests of women and children . . .

Marriage shall be based upon the complete willingness of the two parties. Neither party shall use compulsion and no third party shall be allowed to interfere.

Husband and wife are companions living together and shall enjoy equal status in the home.

Husband and wife are in duty bound to love, respect, assist and look after each other, to live in harmony, to care for the children, and to strive jointly for the welfare of the family.

Both husband and wife shall have the right to free choice of occupation and free participation in work or social activities.

Both husband and wife shall have equal rights in the possession and management of family property.

Both husband and wife shall have the right to inherit each other's property.

Parents have the duty to rear and to educate their children; children have the duty to support and to assist their parents.

Children born out of wedlock shall enjoy the same rights as children born in lawful wedlock. No person shall be allowed to harm or discriminate against children born out of wedlock.[7]

Are these rules not remarkably like our own? If the

Archbishop of Canterbury were to insert them into a sermon on family relationships, would they not sound Christian in the fullest sense? And yet they are taken from the new Marriage Law of Communist China. This is a good example of how similar moral improvements can be brought about by widely differing political régimes. The improvement in the status of women, for example, embodied in this new Chinese Law is a tremendous achievement. 'They were not Negroes or Jews or refugees,' as Marghanita Laski once put it, 'they were simply women – the other part of the human race.'[8] Everywhere, in modern conditions, women are both desiring and beginning to achieve this improved status.

This is the note on which I would like to end this book.

Throughout the world in the twentieth century, the new type of family we know in Britain is becoming universal – it is becoming the universal family of mankind. And this rests everywhere upon the spread of industrialization, improvements in material and moral welfare, and the securing in every society of human rights and the principles of social justice. Nations are being drawn ever more closely together to resolve common problems and to pursue common purposes. In short, in a difficult, extremely painstaking way, through the United Nations Organization and through many other channels of negotiation, a new family of man is coming into being. After millenia of separating differences and widely different levels of social development, the unity of mankind is within our grasp; is within sight of achievement. The ideals of mankind are now – with our effort, patience, and understanding – within the bounds of realization.

In this situation who can speak of looking back? Who can waste his breath and his time in speaking of moral decline? Who can say that we suffer from a lack of purpose in Britain? – or in the contemporary world? Who can speak of decline and fall? Surely our task and the solution of many of our dilemmas are perfectly clear?

The stature of an individual, a family, a nation, is made great not by a process of inward-looking, but by a devotion to purposes which lie beyond, and are greater than, themselves.

We shall not find stable, fulfilled, satisfying family lives sitting round our fires, inwardly examining our own personalities. But if, in our time, we devote ourselves, in cooperation with others, to the achievement of the new family of man whose ethical outlines are now so clear before us, then – as nations we shall be invigorated; as individuals our lives can have clear and worthwhile purpose and meaning; and we need then have no fear for the stability, health, happiness, and character of the families we ourselves rear – for these foundations are firm.

Appendix
Introduction to the First Edition (1962)*

THOSE who love traditional continuity may rest assured that, in one respect at least, Britain has not changed. Our society still produces its crop of moralists who, 'despondent about their own times', continue to deplore and to denounce their contemporaries, and whose testimony would richly supplement Mrs Knowles's proposed game of tracing our process of supposed retrogression since the time of the Norman Conquest. According to them we are still going to the dogs, and fast.

Dr Leslie Weatherhead (somewhat after the manner of an Old Testament prophet – except that he was armed with badly considered statistics rather than exquisite poetic utterance) recently delivered his judgement that we are a nation in 'dire moral peril' owing to the spread of 'sexual depravity': a danger to modern youth which, in his view, is 'a greater danger than nuclear war'; giving the testimony of an unnamed headmistress of a large unnamed girls' school in London who by unnamed methods had discovered that not one girl in her sixth form was a virgin, and the sale of over a million copies of *Lady Chatterley's Lover* 'to readers who certainly did not suddenly develop a taste for the alleged literary ability of D. H. Lawrence', amongst other 'facts' (all of which were challenged in the spate of correspondence which followed) as evidence. Some of his colleagues, Presidents of the Methodist Conference, have shared this propensity to

---

* This original Introduction was left out of the second edition, and some reviewers had clearly not seen the first, and did not understand the kinds of judgement I was attacking. The Introduction to the first edition is therefore reprinted here as a matter of interest and information.

purvey gloom and wholesale condemnation. In 1956, the Reverend Crawford Walter told his delegates in Leeds that 'in the last half-century we have seen a moral landslide . . . Moral positions which our fathers thought were indisputable and impregnable have been swept away.' The slogan of popular opinion, he said, has become 'It doesn't matter what you do so long as you can get away with it'. Much more recently, in a delightful New Year Message (which he, too, chose to associate with the case concerning the publication of *Lady Chatterley's Lover*), the Reverend Edward Rogers, declaring that the present moral climate of Britain was 'poisonous', went on to speak of 'the seedy, dingy moral apathy of our time'.

During the post-war years a definite direction in this denunciation of the British public has become clear. The main targets for attack have increasingly become the family and the Welfare State. To unfortunate sociological generalizations to the effect that the family has been stripped of its functions and is diminishing in importance as a social institution has come to be attached what can only be called a moral wailing and gnashing of teeth. All the ills from which our 'sick' modern society is suffering – crime, delinquency, the disreputable behaviour of some teenagers – are laid at the door of the 'growing instability of marriage', the 'continual increase of divorce', and the 'decline' of the family; and this 'deterioration' of family life is held to be closely connected with the easy-going irresponsibility, the moral laxity, engendered in the Welfare State. We have gone too far, too fast, and it is time we looked back to the moral stability and integrity of the past, before people 'had things too easy', and when the family and our society at large possessed a stability, dignity, and nobility which it has now lost.

Towards the end of the last war and shortly after it, the Reverend E. C. Urwin declared '*the stability of the family is in real peril*', and maintained that it was '*the moral failure of the home*' which was responsible for some of our worst social problems. A few years later, Dr David Mace informed the public that marriage counselling was necessary because, amongst other reasons, '*the decay of the close-knit family associations of the past* has made people unwilling to make confidants of parents or relatives'. Young people of today, he said, 'love and honour their senior relatives, but are reluctant to go to them in trouble'. Later, at a British National Conference on Social Work in 1957, Professor Richard Ellis raised the question '*whether the Welfare State was in any way responsible for a weakening of parental responsibility*' and the writer of the front page article in *The Times Educational Supplement*, commenting with approval on Sir John Wolfenden's contribution to the same conference, said: 'Many parents are now happy to let the state and the schools do things for their children that they would not have dreamt of allowing before the war. There have always been slack parents, but many people feel that *the Welfare State merely gives equality of opportunity for parents to be irresponsible. They fear that we shall soon begin to wonder what parents are for*. Parents themselves have been a little passive in the matter perhaps, and have not thought much about their own position, as a benevolent state has taken more and more of their functions.' In 1960, a secondary modern headmaster, writing on 'Social Burdens' in connection with basic training in modern schools, commented on the new material prosperity enjoyed by the British people in the following way. There is, he said, 'a complete and all-out worship of money and what it can buy', and the saddest effect of this is '*in the time taken from the home and its life* in pursuing the aim. *Many parents are now too engrossed to live with or for their children*, and the individual child is becoming more and more isolated, often even from his brothers and sisters as well as his parents.' When the consequent lack of values in children leads to trouble '*it is often repaid by blows from the parent who has been too indifferent or too busy to help or advise*'.

These opinions have become so widespread and taken for granted that a film reviewer, for example, can preface his remarks with the statement: 'Now, more than ever before, home influence or the lack of it, *the breakdown of family life as we used to know it* and the problems of the teenager are occupying the serious attention of all thinking people.' Similarly, an influential editorial can say: 'If adolescents are half as criminal and as vicious as the publicity given to them suggests, the root cause, *as is generally agreed*, must lie in *the breakdown of family life and social standards generally.*'

In decrying this decline of the family, some critics clearly regret the diminished authoritarianism of the father. Mr George Mack, a grammar school headmaster, speaking to representatives of the British Medical Association in July 1961, said: 'It seems to me that the father figure *has lost much of his awe and all of his majesty.* In the kind of security state we are creating, the state does for the child many of the things that in my youth were the hallmark of good parenthood.' Families are losing 'some of the close personal relationship' and there is a 'reluctance to accept the father as a mentor and guide'. It is interesting to note, however, that Mr Mack was compelled to admit that 'Unfortunately, the number of naughty boys who come from good homes is most disturbing.' Other critics appear to regret equally the improved status of our wives and mothers. One of the correspondents in the 'Dr Weatherhead correspondence' wrote: 'The decline in moral standards during the past fifty years has been coincident with the gradual emancipation of our women. Is it not time we asked ourselves how far it is consequent upon it?'

The moralists still raise their voices amongst us, and in very prominent and influential quarters. Sir David Eccles, in a memorandum to principals of training colleges, maintains that perhaps it is true that '*today an exceptional number of parents* are without those firm convictions which had to be the basis of the protection from evil which every child needed'. The Archbishop of York, Dr Coggan, said recently in his address to the National Union of Teachers' Conference: 'It is part of the *sickness* of modern society that *many parents have abdicated from their share of their responsibilities*' in the upbringing of children, and, consequently, 'The school teacher today finds himself necessarily concerned with *the total health and with the character formation of the child in his care.*' Lord Shawcross, too, in a recent speech to the Royal Society of St

George in London, asked whether *the Welfare State was making the British people too soft*. We must see, he said, that the changes taking place 'did not destroy *the great permanencies, hitherto deeply ingrained through all the generations of our people*', and, having set aside any particular worry about young people, he said '*It is the parents who frighten me most.*'

It seems clear that this band of moralizing brothers all march under the same banner, the wording of which must surely be:

> *Backward!* Christian soldiers,
> Marching as to war,
> Yearning to recapture
> The 'Good Old Days' of yore.

When all these charges are summarized is it not evident that we, the present parents of Britain – you and I – are a poor, dastardly lot? Compare us with the earlier generations of parents, and we are seen to be a very shabby crowd. We are in a state of moral decay, lacking firm convictions to protect our children from evil, losing those permanencies which were ingrained in all earlier generations. We are so concerned with our selfish pursuit of wealth that we ignore and ill-treat our children; we have taken advantage of our new equality of opportunity to be irresponsible; the emancipated women amongst us have contributed to our moral deterioration; the kinder and more tolerant fathers amongst us have lost our awe and all of our majesty; indifferently, uncaringly, without affection and concern, we hand our children over to the care of expert school masters. A black generation indeed!

Even as I write this introduction, *The Times Educational Supplement*, under the heading 'Family in Eclipse?' comments upon the most recent pronouncement from a sociologist, Dr Bryan Wilson, that the family is 'associationally in decline'. 'The most striking feature of his sociological analysis', the writer says, 'is the way Dr Wilson *assumes the eclipse of the family.*' This commentary, however, has the good sense to declare that 'The layman, however, may wonder if it is all so cut and dried.'

Now, not only is the matter not so cut and dried, but all these pessimistic generalizations and denunciations are sheer, unfounded nonsense. And I, for one, am becoming increasingly irritated by these collective insults of the generality of present-day British parents, who cannot, of course, answer back. For this, surely, is what these high-handed and pompous condemnations amount to? But it is not only irritation which moves me. This moral denigration will do no good whatever if only because it is based upon a completely false diagnosis. The family has *not* declined. The family is *not* less stable than hitherto. The standards of parenthood and parental responsibility have *not* deteriorated. If earlier generations were all ingrained with great permanencies, then – to judge by a comparison of their social life and their family life with that of our own – we are better off without them. These charges are not only false, however, they are also positively harmful. If there are problems which confront the modern family, and with which we should concern ourselves, they will not be solved by looking back to a glorified past which never existed, but only by a well-informed understanding of social change, and constructive, forward-looking social policies.

This book, then, is an attempt to argue strongly against the prevailing current of gloom and moral denigration; to prove that these charges are false; and to provide a more realistic and a more encouraging assessment of the family in modern Britain. I have tried, in the context of a reasonably systematic framework of analysis, to demonstrate that the changes that have occurred in the family during the past two hundred years of industrialization, urbanization, and rapid social change have all been substantial improvements – both material *and* moral. In doing this I have tried also to bring together a wide body of literature, both historical and contemporary, in order to show that the argument is firmly substantiated by the evidence. In addition, I have considered some of the problems of present-day family relationships in order to show that they cannot properly be accounted for in terms of 'moral decline' but require a different interpretation. In short, this book supports, and extends even further than they do, the conclusion of a committee of the Church of England Moral Welfare Council in their report, 'The Family in Contemporary Society' (a document to which our moralists appear to have paid scant attention), that *'the modern family is in some ways in a stronger position than it has been at any period in our history of which we have knowledge'*.

Here, then, is a defence of the modern family and, implicitly, of modern parents. Since, however, new generations of parents are continually coming into being, and since, if sociological generalization is anything to go by, they will continue to be maligned, the dedication at the beginning of this book will be readily understood.

Notes

Chapter 1   The Family as a Social Group

1. *The History of Human Marriage*, p. 72.
2. *Casti Connubii* (1930, 2nd ed.). See also: *Marriage and Canon Law*, A. H. Van Vliet and C. G. Breed (Burns Oates, 1964).
3. *Law in a Changing Society*, p. 211.
4. ibid., p. 210.
5. *Twentieth Century*, November 1955, p. 407.
6. i.e., sometimes, as we have said, men and women do not marry from choice, but on the basis of other, imposed, considerations. In addition, though people may choose to marry, the *form* of the family existing in their society is *not* a matter of personal choice. In Britain, for example, one cannot establish a polygamous or polyandrous family depending upon one's personal tastes and convictions. Monogamy is *enforced*.
7. *The Future of Marriage*, p. 170.
8. *Mother Russia* (Collins, 1943).
9. Putnam, 1940; Penguin Books, 1970. Published in the Soviet Union in 1939.

Chapter 2   The Family and Industrialization: Sociological Generalizations

1. *Essays on the Welfare State*, Chap. 6, 'Industrialization and the Family' (Allen & Unwin, 1958).
2. For a more detailed account of Le Play, see R. Fletcher, *The Making of Sociology*, Vol. 1, Appendix 3, p. 655.
3. *The Science of Society*, p. 123.
4. *Sociology*, p. 145.
5. *Problems of the Family*, p. 121.
6. *Family and Civilization*, pp. 805–8.
7. *Marriage and Morals*, p. 142.
8. ibid., p. 162.
9. 'The Teacher's Role – A Sociological Analysis', *British Journal of Sociology*, Vol. XIII, No. 1, March 1962, pp. 26–7.
10. *Sertum Laetitiae* (1 November 1939).
11. pp. 97–8.

Chapter 3   The Family and Industrialization in Britain

1. 'The Idea of the Industrial Revolution', pp. 28–9.

2. *The Industrial Revolution*, pp. 27–9. Mr Beales's quotation is from G. Unwin, *Studies in Economic History* (ed. R. H. Tawney, 1927), p. 15.

3. *Revolution in France*, p. 60.

4. *The Black Book*, pp. 258–9 (1st ed., 1820). These, and following quotations, are taken from the 1835 edition.

5. *England in the Eighteenth Century*, p. 84.

6. *Divorce in England*, p. 68.

7. ibid., p. 69. The facts taken from *The Prince Consort*, Roger Fulford, 1949.

8. *The Black Book*, pp. 26–7.

9. ibid., p. 260.

10. 'The Law and Custom of Primogeniture', *Systems of Land Tenure in Various Countries*, ed. J. W. Probyn (Cassell Petter & Galpin, London, 3rd ed., 1876).

Brodrick quotes the following analysis published in *The Times* of 7 April 1876, showing the small number of proprietors of estates of over 20,000 acres.

Acres	Number of Proprietors
Over 100,000	3
80–100,000	2
70–80,000	2
60–70,000	3
50–60,000	9
40–50,000	8
30–40,000	28
20–30,000	45

In the Financial Reform Almanack for 1879, figures were given of holdings of 10,000 acres and upwards. The claim was made that '977 individuals are shown to hold amongst them 30,064,534 acres, i.e. 3,927,361 acres more than one-third of the whole area of the United Kingdom, including the Channel Islands.'

11. *Free Land* (Kegan Paul, London, 1880).

12. *The Family*, pp. 186–7.

13. *The Land Laws*, Essay IV, 'Questions for a Reformed Parliament' (1867).

14. I. Pinchbeck, *Women Workers and the Industrial Revolution, 1750–1850* (Routledge & Kegan Paul, 1930), p. 19.

15. ibid., p. 24.

16. *England in Transition* (Penguin Books, 1953).

17. ibid., pp. 89–90.

18. *A People's History of England*, p. 320.

19. *Women Workers and the Industrial Revolution, 1750–1850*, p. 47.

20. *The Case of Labourers in Husbandry*. Davies, a Berkshire parson, assembled detailed family budgets for his own parish and collected similar information from parishes in Britain.

21. *The State of the Poor.*

22. *Women Workers and the Industrial Revolution, 1750–1850*, pp. 48–51.

23. ibid., p. 105.

24. An excellent and extremely detailed account is given in Dr Pinchbeck's book.

25. ibid., p. 106.

26. ibid., p. 108.

27. *England in Transition*, p. 139.

28. *Industrial and Commercial Revolutions*, pp. 99–100.

29. *The Subjection of Women* (1869).

30. *Divorce in England*, pp. 77–8.

31. *England in the Eighteenth Century*, pp. 150–51.

32. Quoted by Dr Pinchbeck, *Women Workers and the Industrial Revolution, 1750–1850*, Chap. 11, from Wesley's *Journal*, and from R. Ayton, *Voyage Round Great Britain*.

33. 'Alfred' (Samuel Kydd), *The History of the Factory Movement.*

34. H. de B. Gibbins, *The Industrial History of England* (1890).

35. Rev. A. Mearns, *The Bitter Cry of Outcast London* (1883).

36. I have given a brief account of this opposition in a pamphlet, *Issues in Education*, pp. 62–71.

37. Part III, Commentary, p. 8.

38. Table and graph: Registrar General's Statistical Review 1964, Part III, Commentary, pp. 21–2.

39. See also Professor R. M. Titmuss, *Essays on the Welfare State*, Chap. 5, p. 99.

The continuity of the high marriage rates and the earlier age of marriage may be seen in the table (p. 268) and the graph (top of p. 269) showing women's marriage rates, from the Registrar General's Statistical Review of England and Wales (Part III, Commentary) for 1961 and 1964. Detailed comments are given on pp. 20–24 of the 1961 volume, and pp. 17–26 of the 1964 volume.

40. Registrar General's Statistical Review 1961, Part III, Commentary, Table XLII, p. 70, amended for 1943–64 by selections from Table C.57 of Statistical Review 1964, p. 72.

The graph accompanying the full 1961 table was as shown at foot of p. 269.

41. Papers of the Royal Commission on Population, Vol. VI, Table 2. The full analysis of the 1946 Family Census is to be found in this volume, 'The Trend and Pattern of Fertility in Great Britain', D. V. Glass and E. Grebenik, 1954.

42. Taken from Papers of the Royal Commission on Population, Vol. I, Table 37. 'Family Limitation and its Influence on Human Fertility during the past Fifty Years', E. Lewis-Faning, 1949. These

Numbers of marriages and marriage rates, 1931 and 1938–64, and to 1970 (in part), England and Wales

Period	Marriages	Per 1,000 total population	Marriage rates Per 1,000 unmarried population			
			Men aged 15 and over	Women aged 15 and over	Men aged 20–44	Women aged 15–39
1931	311,847	15·6	53·4	41·6	106·4	68·6
1938	361,768	17·6	61·2	47·8	124·5	85·5
1939–50*	381,910	17·9	68·2	53·0	139·7	106·2
1951–5*	350,916	15·8	68·4	51·4	129·9	110·6
1956	352,944	15·7	70·9	53·0	138·9	120·7
1957	346,903	15·4	70·3	52·4	138·9	121·5
1958	339,913	15·0	69·0	51·5	137·7	120·2
1959	340,126	14·9	68·7	51·3	138·9	119·2
1960	343,614	15·0	68·9	51·6	141·5	119·9
1961	346,678	15·0	67·1	50·8	137·0	116·4
1962	347,732	14·9	65·3	50·2	135·8	112·7
1963	351,329	14·9	64·9	50·2	135·1	111·4
1964	359,307	15·1	65·5	51·1	136·2	113·3
1965	371,127	15·5				
1966	384,497	16·0				
1967	386,052	16·0	from the Annual Abstract of Statistics 1971			
1968	407,822	16·8				
1969	396,746	16·2				
1970	414,689	16·9				

* Annual averages.

differences in contraceptive practice are reflected in the fact that the average size of the family varies with occupational status, or between social classes.

43. *The Sanitary Condition of the Labouring Population of Great Britain*, by Edwin Chadwick.

44. Public Health Act, 1848.

45. R. Mackenzie, *The Nineteenth Century: A History*, pp. 147–8.

46. It might be said that the modern British family is recognized and regulated by laws which specifically enforce the equality of man and wife. The attitude of mind of the law, for example, towards property mutually

Marriage rates of women by age, 1911 to 1961, England and Wales

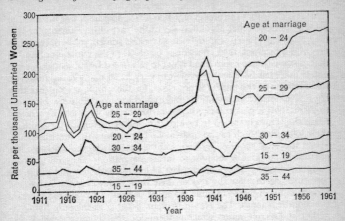

Mean ultimate family size of marriage cohorts since 1861, all marriage ages under 45, England and Wales

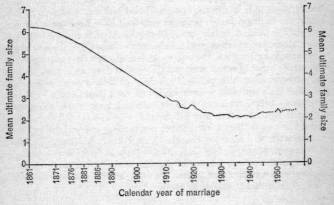

——— Marriages of 1871, 1876, 1881, 1886 and the averages of 1861-9, 1890-9 and 1900-9

——— Marriages of single years 1910-48

- - - Marriages of single years 1949-51 (projected part of ultimate family size between 10 and 20 per cent)

·········· Marriages of single years 1952 and after (projected part of ultimate family size 20 per cent or more) provided for, and used by, the family – what Lord Denning terms 'the family assets' – may be seen in his judgement in a particular case:

'If it is clear that the property, when it was acquired, was intended to belong to one or other absolutely, as in the case of investments, or that they intended to hold it in definite shares, as sometimes happens when they run a business, then effect must be given to their intention; and in that case the title so ascertained is not to be altered by subsequent events unless there has been an agreement to vary it. In many cases, however, the intention of the parties is not clear, for the simple reason that they have never formed an intention: so the court has to attribute an intention to them. This is particularly the case with the family assets, by which I mean the things intended to be a continuing provision for them during their joint lives, such as the matrimonial home and the furniture in it. When these are acquired by their joint efforts during the marriage, the parties do not give a thought to future separation. They do not contemplate divorce. They contemplate living in the house and using the furniture together for the rest of their lives. They buy the house and furniture out of their available resources without worrying too much as to whom it belongs. The reason is plain. So long as they are living together, it does not matter which of them does the saving and which does the paying, or which of them goes out to work or which looks after the home, so long as the things they buy are used for their joint benefit. In the present case it so happened that the wife went out to work and used her earnings to help run the household and buy the children's clothes, whilst the husband saved. It might very well have been the other way round. The husband might have allotted to the wife enough money to cover all the housekeeping and the children's clothes, and the wife might have saved her earnings. The title to the family assets does not depend on the mere chance of which way round it was. It does not depend on how they happened to allocate their earnings and their expenditure. The whole of their resources were expended for their joint benefit – either in food and clothes and living expenses for which there was nothing to see or in the house and furniture which are family assets – and the product should belong to them jointly. It belongs to them in equal shares.'

Fribrance v. Fribrance (1957). Quoted by P. M. Bromley: *Family Law* (1957), p. 391, and by O. R. McGregor and G. Rowntree who give a brief and excellent account of changes in the law relating to family property in Chap. 21 of Glass, Welford, Morris and Argyle (eds.), *Society: Problems and Methods of Study*.

Chapter 4   Relationships in the Contemporary Family

1. See Professor R. M. Titmuss, *Essays on the Welfare State*, Chap. 5, p. 92. Comparing the family of fifty years ago with the family of today, Professor Titmuss writes:

'... by the time the full cycle of child care had run its course the mother (i.e., of fifty years ago) had only a few more years to live – an analogous situation to the biological sequence for many species in the animal world. The typical working-class mother in the industrial towns in 1900 could expect, if she survived to fifty-five, to live not much more than another twelve years by the time she reached the comparative ease, the reproductive grazing field, of the middle fifties.

The situation today is remarkably different. Even though we have extended the number of years that a child spends at school and added to the psychological and social responsibilities of motherhood by raising the cultural norms of child upbringing, most mothers have largely concluded their maternal role by the age of forty. At this age, a woman can now expect to live thirty-six years . . . What these changes mean is that by the time the typical mother of today has virtually completed the cycle to motherhood she still has practically half her total life expectancy to live.'

See, also, the contribution of Professor Titmuss to *The Family* published by the National Council of Social Service, 1954.

2. R. S. Peters, *Authority, Responsibility and Education* (1959), p. 49.

3. See, for example, 'The Stability of the Family in the Welfare State', *Political Quarterly*, Vol. 31, No. 2, April–June 1960.

4. Well over 90 per cent of all petitions are undefended and hence by the 'consent' of the spouses.

5. For a full analysis of the statistics, see O. R. McGregor, *Divorce in England*, Chap. 2; Barbara Wootton, 'Holiness or Happiness' (*Twentieth Century*, November 1955); and Griselda Rowntree and Norman H. Carrier, 'The Resort to Divorce in England and Wales, 1858–1957' (*Population Studies*, March 1958, Vol. XI, No. 3).

6. The Registrar General's Statistical Review 1946–50, Text, Civil, p. 56, Diagram C.

7. Statistical Review 1961, p. 46.

8. Taken from Table XXV, p. 45, Statistical Review 1961, Part III, Commentary.

9. Statistical Review 1964, p. 38.

10. Statistical Review 1967, pp. 20–21.

11. Annual Abstract of Statistics, No. 108, 1971, p. 91.

12. Registrar General's Statistical Review of England and Wales 1957, Part II, Tables, Civil. Extracted from Table 84, p. 84: 'Dissolutions and annulments of marriages made absolute in 1957, by wife's marriage age and duration.'

13. Statistical Review 1967, p. 24.

14. Statistical Review 1957, p. 54, Table 34.

15. ibid.

16. Statistical Review 1946–50, Text, Civil, p. 67, Table 39.

17. Statistical Review 1964, p. 49.

18. 'The Resort to Divorce in England and Wales', pp. 217–18.

19. Extracted from Table 38, p. 64. Statistical Review, Part III, Commentary, for 1956.

20. Michael Young and Peter Willmott, *Family and Kinship in East London* (Routledge & Kegan Paul, 1957; Penguin Books, 1962). These findings are presented pp. 5–15.

21. *Exploring English Character* (Cresset Press, 1955), p. 85.

22. ibid., p. 87.

23. ibid., p. 97.

24. ibid., p. 125.

25. ibid., pp. 154–5.

26. ibid., p. 161.

27. *Sunday Times*, March 1970, and *Sex and Marriage in England Today* (Nelson, 1970).

28. *The Family*, National Council of Social Service, p. 36.

29. *Woman, Wife and Worker* (Department of Scientific and Industrial Research, 1960), p. 11.

30. ibid., p. 30.

31. ibid., p. 23.

32. ibid., p. 27.

33. In a radio talk, James Hemming criticized the inadequacies of education for girls. See 'Is there a Flight of Girls from School?', *Listener*, 31 August 1961, pp. 312–13.

34. *Teenage Consumer Spending in 1959*, p. 5.

35. ibid., pp. 5–6.

36. *Club Members Today*, February 1960. Questionnaires analysed by Dr Kathleen M. Evans of Cardiff University College.

37. See Gertrude Williams, *Recruitment to Skilled Trades* (Routledge, 1957).

38. *Exporting English Character*, p. 82.

39. *Teenage Morals*, p. 13.

40. *The Family*, National Council of Social Service, p. 42.

41. *Changes in the Use of Institutions in England and Wales between 1911 and 1951* (10 February 1960).

42. ibid., pp. 32–3.

43. House of Commons Debates, 24 November 1947.

44. *Political Quarterly*, Vol. 31, No. 2, April–June 1960.

45. Quoted by Helen Bosanquet, *The Family*, p. 320.

46. *Essays on the Welfare State*, pp. 115–16.

Chapter 5   Some Conclusions

1. Chap. 5, p. 92.

2. *The Family*, National Council of Social Service, p. 9.

3. *In the Heart of South London* (Longmans Green, 1931), p. 8.

4. ibid., p. 13.

5. ibid., p. 81.

6. *Listener*, 26 November 1959.

7. i.e., in so far as the family is no longer a *productive* unit within itself.

8. *A Century of Family Law*, Chap. 16, p. 412.

9. *Matrimonial Property Law* (ed. Friedmann, 1955), p. 314.

10. See Olive Stone, 'The Family and the Law in 1970' (*The Family and its Future*, Chap. 7, Churchill, 1970).

11. *The Family*, p. 217.

12. *Family and Kinship in East London*, p. 10.

13. 'The Home-centred Society.'

14. *The Family*, National Council of Social Service, p. 8.

15. See, for example, John Barron Mays, *On the Threshold of Delinquency* (Liverpool University Press, 1959).

16. *Essays on the Welfare State*, p. 108.

17. *The Irresponsible Society* (Fabian Society, 1960), pp. 8–9.

18. *The Condition of England*. These quotations are taken from the 1911 edition.

Chapter 6   The Future of the Family

1. See Note 39, Chapter 3, pp. 267–9.

2. Registrar General's Statistical Review 1964, Part III, Commentary, Table C 18, p. 27.

3. See Charles Dickens, *Hard Times*, Chapter 11.

4. Herbert Spencer, *Principles of Sociology*, Vol. 1, pp. 753–4.

5. A. J. P. Taylor, 'Are We So Bad?', *TV Times*, 13 September 1963.

6. See Ronald Fletcher, 'A Humanist's Decalogue', *New Society*, October 1963, and reprinted in pamphlet form by the Pioneer Press and in *Youth in New Society*, Rupert Hart-Davis, 1966.

7. *The Marriage Law of the People's Republic of China*, Peking, 1950, pp. 1–6.

8. Marghanita Laski, 'It was a bitter fight for the vote', *News Chronicle*, 1 April 1957.

Suggestions for Further Reading

Abel-Smith, B., and Pinker, R., *Changes in the Use of Institutions in England and Wales between 1911 and 1951*, Paper to the Manchester Statistical Society, 10 February 1960.

Abrams, M., *Teenage Consumer Spending in 1959* (Part II), London Press Exchange Ltd, 1961.

'The Home-centred Society', *Listener*, 26 November 1959.

Anderson, Michael (ed.), *Sociology of the Family*, Penguin Books, 1971.

Andry, R. G., *et al.*, *Deprivation of Maternal Care: A Reassessment of its Effects*, World Health Organization, 1962.

Anshen, R. N., *The Family: Its Functions and Destiny*, Harper Bros., 1949.

Banks, J. A., *Prosperity and Parenthood*, Routledge & Kegan Paul, 1954.

Bell, Colin, *Middle Class Families*, Routledge & Kegan Paul, 1969.

Bosanquet, H., *The Family*, Macmillan, 1906.

Bott, E., *Family and Social Network: Roles, Norms, and External Relationships in Ordinary Urban Families*, Tavistock Publications, 2nd edn, 1971.

British National Conference on Social Work, *The Family*, National Council of Social Service, 1954.

Bromley, P. M., *Family Law*, Butterworth, 1957.

Carr-Saunders, A. M., Caradog Jones, D., and Moser, C. A., *A Survey of Social Conditions in England and Wales*, Oxford, 1958.

Chester, R., and Streather, Jane, 'Taking Stock of Divorce', *New Society*, 22 July 1971.

Church of England Moral Welfare Council, *The Family in Contemporary Society*, S.P.C.K., 1958.

Group appointed by the Archbishop of Canterbury, *Putting Asunder: A Divorce Law for Contemporary Society*, S.P.C.K., 1966.

Douglas, J. W. B., *The Home and the School*, MacGibbon & Kee, 1964.

Elliott, Katherine, *The Family and its Future*, C.I.B.A. Foundation Conference, Churchill, 1970.

Eppel, E. M., 'Adolescent Values', *New Society*, 28 March 1963.

Eppel, E. M. and M., 'Teenage Values', *New Society*, 14 November 1963.

'Teenage Idols', *New Society*, 21 November 1963.

Farmer, Mary, *The Family*, Longmans, 1970.

Firth, Raymond, 'Family and Kinship in Industrial Society' in *The Development of Industrial Society* (*Sociological Review*, Monograph No. 8, October 1964).

Two Studies of Kinship in London, Athlone Press, 1966.

Firth, Raymond, *et al.*, *Families and their Relatives*, Routledge & Kegan Paul, 1970.

Friedmann, W., *Law in a Changing Society* (Chap. 7), Stevens, 1959.

Garbett, C. F., *In the Heart of South London*, Longmans Green, 1931.

George, D., *England in Transition*, Penguin Books, 1953.

Glass, D. V., and Grebenik, E., *The Trend and Pattern of Fertility in Great Britain*, Papers of the Royal Commission on Population, Vol. VI, 1954.

Goode, W. J., *World Revolution and Family Patterns*, Free Press, 1963.
    The Family, Prentice-Hall Inc. (Foundations of Modern Sociology Series), 1964.

Gorer, G., *Exploring English Character*, Cresset Press, 1955.
    Sex and Marriage in England Today, Thomas Nelson, 1970.

Gorer, G., Maclure, Stuart, and others, *Teenage Morals*, Councils and Education Press, 1961.

Graveson, R. H., and Crane, F. R. (eds.), *A Century of Family Law, 1857–1957*, Sweet & Maxwell, 1957.

Hall, M. P., *The Social Services of Modern England*, Routledge & Kegan Paul, 1960.

Hemming, J., *Problems of Adolescent Girls*, Heinemann, 1960.

Hubback, J., *Wives Who Went to College*, Heinemann, 1957.

Jephcott, P., Seear, N., and Smith, J., *Married Women Working*, Allen & Unwin, 1962.

Kerr, M., *The People of Ship Street*, Routledge & Kegan Paul, 1958.

Klein, Josephine, *Samples from English Cultures*, Routledge & Kegan Paul, 1965.

Klein, V., *Working Wives*, Institute of Personnel Management, 1960.
    Employing Married Women (Occasional Papers No. 17), Institute of Personnel Management, 1961.

Lewis-Faning, E., *Family Limitation and its Influence on Human Fertility during the past Fifty Years*, Papers on the Royal Commission on Population, Vol. I, 1949.

Linton, R., *The Study of Man* (Chap. 10–11), Appleton Century Co., New York, 1936.

Litwak, E., 'Geographic Mobility and Extended Family Cohesion', *American Sociological Review*, Vol. 25, 1960, pp. 385–94.
    'Occupational Mobility and Extended Family Cohesion', *American Sociological Review*, Vol. 25, 1960, pp. 9–21.

Litwak, E., and Szelenyi, I., 'Primary Group Structures and their Functions: Kin, Neighbours and Friends', *American Sociological Review*, Vol. 34, 1969, pp. 465–81.

MacIver, R. M., and Page, C. N., *Society* (Chap. 11), Macmillan, 1957.

Marris, P., *Widows and their Families*, Routledge & Kegan Paul, 1958.

Masterman, C. F. G., *The Condition of England*, Methuen, 1911.

McGregor, O. R., *Divorce in England*, Heinemann, 1957.

'The Stability of the Family in the Welfare State', *Political Quarterly*, Vol. 31, No. 2, April–June 1960.

'The Social Position of Women in England, 1850–1914', *British Journal of Sociology*, Vol. VI, No. 1, March 1955.

'Some Research Possibilities and Historical Materials for Family and Kinship Study', *British Journal of Sociology*, Vol. XII, No. 4, December 1960.

'Maintenance, Separation and Divorce', *Twentieth Century*, Vol. 172, No. 1020, Winter 1963/4. The whole of this issue of *Twentieth Century* is worth reading.

McGregor, O. R., Louis Blom-Cooper, and Colin Gibson, *Separated Spouses* (Legal Research Unit, Bedford College, University of London), 1971.

Mill, J. S., *The Subjection of Women*, 1869.

Mitchell, G. D., *Sociology* (Chap. 10), University Tutorial Press Ltd, 1959.

Mogey, J. M., *Family and Neighbourhood*, Oxford, 1956.

Myrdal, A., and Klein, V., *Women's Two Roles: Home and Work*, Routledge & Kegan Paul, 1956.

Newson, J., and Newson, E., *Four Years Old in an Urban Community*, Allen & Unwin, 1968; Penguin Books, 1970.

  Patterns of Infant Care in an Urban Community, Allen & Unwin, 1963; Penguin Books, 1965.

Noble, Trevor, *Family Breakdown and Social Networks*, British Journal of Sociology, Vol. XXI, No. 2, June 1971, pp. 135–50.

Peters, R. S., *Authority, Responsibility and Education*, Allen & Unwin, 1959.

Phillips, M., and Tomkinson, W. S., *English Women in Life and Letters* (Chap. 10), Oxford, 1927.

Pierce, Rachel M., 'Marriage in the Fifties', *Sociological Review*, 11, 2, July 1963.

Pinchbeck, I., *Women Workers and the Industrial Revolution, 1750–1850*, Routledge, 1930.

Plant, M., *The Domestic Life of Scotland in the Eighteenth Century*, Edinburgh University Press, 1952.

Plumb, J. H., *England in the Eighteenth Century* (Part II, Chap. 2, and Part III, Chap. 1), Penguin Books, 1950.

Rapoport, R., and Rapoport, R., 'Work and Family in Contemporary Society', *American Sociological Review*, Vol. 30, 1965, pp. 381–94.

  Dual Families, Penguin Books, 1971.

Rosser, C., and Harris, C. C., *The Family and Social Change*, Routledge & Kegan Paul, 1965.

Rowntree, G., 'New Facts on Teenage Marriage', *New Society*, 4 October 1962.

Rowntree, G., and Carrier, N., 'The Resort to Divorce in England and Wales, 1858–1957', *Population Studies*, Vol. XI, No. 3, March 1958.

Rowntree, G., and McGregor, O. R., 'The Family', *Society – Problems and Methods of Study* (edited by A. T. Welford and others), Routledge & Kegan Paul, 1962.

Rowntree, G., and Pierce, R. M., 'Birth Control in Britain', *Population Studies*, Vol. xv, Nos. 1 and 2, July and November 1961.

Royal Commission on Population: *Report* (Cmd 7695), 1949.

Royal Commission on Marriage and Divorce: *Report* (Cmd 9678), 1956.

Russell, B., *Marriage and Morals*, Allen & Unwin, 1932.

Smelser, N. J., *Social Change in the Industrial Revolution: an application of theory to the Lancashire cotton industry, 1770–1840* (Chap. 9–11), Routledge & Kegan Paul, 1959.

Social Science Dept of the London School of Economics, *Woman, Wife and Worker* (D.S.I.R., *Problems of Progress in Industry*, 10), H.M.S.O., 1960.

Stacey, M., *Tradition and Change: A Study of Banbury*, Oxford, 1960.

Stone, Olive, 'The Family and the Law in 1970', in *The Family and its Future*, Churchill, 1970.

Titmuss, R. M., *Essays on the Welfare State*, Allen & Unwin, 1958.
 The Irresponsible Society, Fabian Tract 323, 1960.

Townsend, P., *The Family Life of Old People*, Routledge & Kegan Paul, 1958.

Vliet, A. H. Van, and C. G. Breed, *Marriage and Canon Law*, Burns Oates, 1964.

Westermarck, E., *The History of Human Marriage*, Macmillan, 1921.
 The Future of Marriage, Macmillan, 1938.

Wootton, B., 'Holiness or Happiness', *The Twentieth Century*, November 1955.

Young, M., and Willmott, P., *Family and Kinship in East London*, Routledge & Kegan Paul, 1957; Penguin Books, 1962.
 Family and Class in a London Suburb, Routledge & Kegan Paul, 1960.

Zimmerman, C. C., *Family and Civilization*, Harper, New York and London, 1947.

Index

Penguinews

AND

Penguins in Print

Every month we issue an illustrated magazine
Penguinews. It's a lively guide to all the latest
Penguins, Pelicans and Puffins, and always
contains an article on a major Penguin author,
plus other features of contemporary interest.

Penguinews is supplemented by *Penguins in Print*,
a complete list of all the available Penguin titles –
there are now over four thousand!

The cost is no more than the postage; so why not
write for a free copy of this month's *Penguinews*?
And if you'd like both publications sent for a year,
just send us a cheque or postal order for 30p
(if you live in the United Kingdom) or 60p
(if you live elsewhere), and we'll put you on our
mailing list.

Dept EP, Penguin Books Ltd,
Harmondsworth, Middlesex

Note: *Penguinews* and *Penguins in Print*
are not available in the U.S.A. or Canada.

Communities in Britain

Social Life in Town and Country

Ronald Frankenberg

Communities in Britain brings together the findings of some of the most important field studies recently made in the British Isles. The village, the market town, the urban housing estate, and sections of great cities are examined successively, revealing the power structures, the degree of communality or isolation, and the relationship patterns prevailing in different environments.

From the results of these detailed studies the author, Professor of Sociology at the University of Keele, develops in his final chapters a theory of social development in Britain which can hardly fail to intrigue the educated natives of a modern society.

Patterns of Infant Care in an Urban Community

John and Elizabeth Newson

Mother, doctor, health visitor, midwife – Spock, Gibbens, de Kok, Truby King . . . the amount of theory and advice, both professional and amateur, that showers on the young mother is equalled only by its astonishing contradictions. And indeed, as the authors quietly point out, 'very few theories of child rearing have been subjected to the inconvenience of being reconciled with the empirical evidence'.

What then is that evidence? Armed with common sense and a tape recorder, the authors interviewed in their Nottingham homes over 700 mothers of one-year-old children to find out, quite simply, how babies are brought up in England today. The result is a landmark in our knowledge of childhood. The answers parents gave on subjects ranging from breast- and bottle-feeding, sleeping, eating, and punishment, to father's place in the home and class differences in infant rearing make a fascinating and, on occasions, hilarious kaleidoscope of life with young children.

'Wonderfully human piece of sociological research' – *Yorkshire Post*

Also available
Four Years Old in an Urban Community

Family and Kinship in East London

Peter Willmott and Michael Young

The two authors of this most human of surveys are sociologists.

They spent three years on 'field work' in Bethnal Green and on a new housing estate in Essex. The result is a fascinating study, made during a period of extensive rehousing, of family and community ties and the pull of the 'wider family' on working-class people.

'Probably not only the fullest, but virtually the only account of working-class family relationships in any country. The general reader will find it full of meat and free of jargon' – *New Statesman*

'This shrewd – and in places extremely amusing – book combines warmth of feeling with careful sociological method' – *Financial Times*

'Observant, tactful, sympathetic, humorous . . . I really feel that nobody who wants to know how our society is changing can afford not to read Young and Willmott' – Kingsley Amis in the *Spectator*

'No short account can do justice to this book, charmingly written, engaging, absorbing' – *British Medical Journal*

Obviously there have been changes in the two districts under survey during the last few years. This edition in Pelicans, with its fresh introduction and simplified appendix, is justified by the standing the report has achieved as a modern classic of sociology.

Because They're Black

Derek Humphrey and Gus John

Because They're Black, first published as a Penguin
Special, is the winner of the 1972 Martin Luther King
Memorial Prize. Its two authors (one of them is a black
social worker and the author of the Handsworth report)
have managed to get black people in England to 'tell
it like it is'. The major part of their book, which the
Tribune called 'admirable', describes in detail, through
individual case histories, what it feels like to be on the
receiving end of discrimination in our society.

The authors then examine the way out. Integration
is discussed and shown for what it is: the desire to
convert black men into white men. Black power,
different in kind from its U.S. counterpart but equally
strong, is seen as a humanizing necessity for black and
white alike; and political conflict and struggle are
essential if we are to change ourselves and our society.
As the *Guardian* wrote: 'It is an exhilarating development
and this pugnacious little book will speed it along.'